BRONX DA

BRONX DA

TRUE STORIES FROM THE
SEX CRIMES AND DOMESTIC VIOLENCE UNIT

SARENA STRAUS

BARRICADE BOOKS

Published by Barricade Books Inc.
185 Bridge Plaza North
Suite 308-A
Fort Lee, NJ 07024

www.barricadebooks.com

BRONX DA
Copyright © 2006 by Sarena Straus
All Rights Reserved.

Library of Congress Cataloging-in-Publication Data
A copy of this title's Library of Congress Cataloging-in-Publication Data
is available on request from the Library of Congress.

ISBN 1-56980-305-6

10 9 8 7 6 5 4 3 2 1

Manufactured in the United States of America

To my Grandma Dora and in memory of my Grandma Ethel—
family, mentors, role models, friends,
and the spectrum of possibilities . . .

And to S.P. (Chapter 14): The bravest girl I've ever known.
I tried for you. I tried so hard. . . .

CONTENTS

ACKNOWLEDGEMENTS

THERE ARE MANY people that I would like to thank for their input and their help with this book. I thank everyone whose real name I used even if they did not give me permission. Your real name is in here because you inspired me in some way and I thank you. I thank Breeanne Clowdus, Jeffrey Horblit, and Michael Stoer for their comments early on. I especially thank ADA Alexandra Militano for her comments on the final draft and for keeping me up to date on all of the office gossip and changes in the law. I thank my parents for their input and support and for letting me share their stories. I thank my brother, Ari, for being there for me from the day I was born and my sister-in-law, Molly, for trying to help with this book, but for not being able to because she puts my two nieces and my nephew first, always. Thanks to my agent, Agnes Birnbaum, for believing in this book and in me. To Professor Deborah Denno, one of the most amazing, entertaining and gifted teachers that I ever had, thank you for supporting and encouraging my love of criminal law and for continuing to be my friend long past law school. Thanks to The Honorable Patricia Anne Williams for allowing me to work with and learn from her, for being my friend and mentor, and for being fair and impartial when I tried my first felony in front of her. To Hal Kennedy, Esq. for giving me my first legal job and for introducing me to Judge Williams. To Bill Flack for giving me an amazing opportunity to work with him and to learn from him during the Michael Vernon case. And to the 25 brave, honest, and talented people that I started with at The Bronx District Attorney's Office on September 11, 1995. It was a pleasure to work with you.

Finally, I thank my husband, Jamil. For supporting me, loving me, listening to me, and scotch-taping inspirational quotes by Marcus Aurelius to my phone. You make my colors brighter. Because you believe in me, my dreams come true.

"Thou must be like a promontory of the sea, against which, though the waves beat continually, yet it both itself stands, and about it are those swelling waves stilled and quieted."
—MARCUS AURELIUS

■

"Dig within. Within is the wellspring of good; and it is always ready to bubble up, if you just dig."
—MARCUS AURELIUS

■

"The pursuit of truth shall set you free— even if you never catch up with it."
—CLARENCE DARROW

PROLOGUE

SOMETIMES YOU KNOW when you've reached your breaking point. Mine came on September 5, 2000, at approximately seven in the evening. I was a felony prosecutor in the Domestic Violence and Sex Crimes Unit of The Bronx District Attorney's office.

A few hours earlier, I had been sitting at my desk, daydreaming. I was facing away from the door and looking out my window into a parking lot below. I had just come back from a biking trip with my father—a week in the vineyards of Burgundy. I was thinking that the South Bronx was the furthest place in the world from where I had just been with my father when my supervisor opened the door — he never knocked. I spun my chair around to face Alvin Yearwood, now Judge Yearwood, a man with a booming voice and an even larger presence. He told me of an autistic six-year-old who had witnessed his sister's murder that morning. "Go to the four-six to interview the boy," he ordered, using cop-speak to direct me to the Forty-Sixth Precinct. "Get as much as you can from him. Without this kid, we have nothing." Indeed, the furthest place in the world from the vineyards of France.

I crossed 161st Street to The Bronx County Criminal Court Building and picked up a police placard that gave me temporary license to park illegally. I also picked up the keys for the "homicide car," a glamorous name for a stripped-down burgundy Chevy Lumina with sticky vinyl seats, plastic floor coverings, and the distinctive smell of rot, which was interesting given that there was nothing organic whatsoever in the vehicle. I got behind the wheel, gagging over the smell of a balled-up bag of days-old, half-eaten "US Fried Chicken" that was shoved behind the passenger's seat. I put the key into the ignition, rolled down the windows, and backed out. Riding shotgun was David Staton, a fellow assistant DA, who briefed me on the way to the precinct house.

At all times, day or night, even on holidays, a member of The Bronx DA's office is on homicide duty. This so-called "homicide assistant" is given a pager, and for 24 hours — 9 AM to 9 AM — is on call in case anything needs to be done about a killing. This includes interviewing witnesses and suspects, drafting search and arrest warrants, writing up cases, and going to crime scenes.

I'd heard all kinds of horror stories about what people saw on homicide duty: Bodies melting from the heat. Brains splattered on walls and across concrete. A retarded child suffocated after his siblings duct-taped his entire head and then tied him to a chair in the closet because he was ruining their drug orgy. They hid him there for days until neighbors called the police about the stench. Nine years later, the ADA who was at the scene still can't forget the sight of the boy's eyeballs coming out with the tape as his face was unwrapped by the medical examiner.

Homicide Duty meant long, wakeful nights, whether you were called out to a crime scene or simply waiting to be and, today, the dubious honor had fallen into David Staton's lap. Dave and I worked together many times over my five years in the office. During my first year at the office, he was one of the people who helped train me: The first case that I ever took to trial, I inherited from him. He was a tall, thin black man with a sweet, dimpled smile and a gentle disposition. I never detected in him any of the grit or sarcasm so common among ADAs. I liked and trusted him. Like so many people born and raised in New York City, Dave couldn't drive. For him, this may have meant sometimes sleeping at the office when he was on call so that a detective could drive him to a crime scene. Having been raised in the suburbs, I had been driving since I was fifteen, so the honor fell on me and Dave began to debrief me as I drove.

David told me that he'd arrived at this day's crime scene about 1:00 PM and saw "a young Hispanic female with multiple stab wounds about her face and chest, one of her eyes gouged out, and her head practically hacked right off her neck." The murder weapon, a 12-inch kitchen knife, lay on her chest. He described it all precisely and using clinical, detached terminology. It was the way we learned to talk in the DA's office. It was the way we distanced ourselves from what we were looking at. David elaborated on what Alvin had already told me. The only witnesses to the murder were the victim's newborn infant and her six-year-old autistic brother, whom she was watching that day. The suspect was the father of the baby and he had fled after committing the murder.

Within 10 minutes, we arrived at the precinct with our telltale briefcases. The D.A.'s office is not like the law firms of today where business casual is the norm. We were in court almost daily and wore suits as a matter of course. They were a uniform recognizable in The Bronx no less than the uniforms of the police department. The desk sergeant barely glanced at our black suits and shiny shoes before shooting his thumb over his shoulder, directing us up the staircase to the detective squad. Detectives Kevin Leonard and Daniel Withers, handling the case, were standing by the door.

The squad office, like in most precinct houses I'd seen, was a large room crammed full of gray metal desks. The cinderblock walls were a similar dingy shade and in bad need of a repaint. About half the lights were out and large-size Dunkin Donuts coffee cups were poking out of every available nook and cranny. Snapshots of the gapped-toothed children of cops were taped to blotters and nearby filing cabinets, incongruous in the company of mug shuts, lineup photos, and wanted posters. Since none of these detectives had the luxury of having his own desk, faces from different families sat side by side on the tabletops so you never knew who belonged to whom. One kid taped to the side of a push-button phone with no cord was giving me the thumbs-up.

I had worked with both detectives Leonard and Withers in the past. Leonard used to tell me he'd been with the police department "since your boss Elisa Koenderman was still little Elisa Spittola." Withers and I went back to some of my first cases in the office. We had started off on the wrong foot after an argument about what crimes to charge against someone. The debate ended with my saying, "Don't tell me how to be a lawyer and I won't tell you how to be a cop." But we soon called it a truce and I came to consider him a friend. Withers, a very handsome, muscular guy with a sandy crew-cut and a goatee, was the constant brunt of jokes by his co-workers who seemed obsessed with his ass. It was always entertaining to be around him. I was relieved that both these men were on the case. They were smart, easygoing, funny, and devoted to their work.

Leonard showed me to a free desk where I could spread out my papers and then briefed me. The victim was a young stripper named Esmeralda DeJesus. She got into an argument with her son's father, Dennis Lopez, or baby-fatha' as they called such relationships in The Bronx. They had broken up a week earlier and were fighting because Dennis didn't want Esmeralda stripping anymore. He had also just discovered that she had a new boyfriend and was working as a call girl on the side. I guess he didn't take the news so well.

He took a kitchen knife from the cutlery drawer and showed her exactly how he felt about her new career move. First he stabbed her under the chin where the knife came up through her jaw and out of her mouth. Next he stabbed her in the cheek, the eye, and the forehead, four times in the chest and, finally, he slit her throat. "Great set-up for an EED [extreme emotional disturbance] defense," Leonard said. After the stabbing, Dennis ran out of the apartment, leaving his infant child and Andy, the victim's mentally impaired six-year-old brother—my sole eyewitness—alone with the body.

I put down my briefcase and took out the grape Blow Pop I had brought from the office for six-year-old Andy. Three years of working with children had taught me to arm myself with all kinds of bribes and entertainment. I went into the interview room where Andy waited with his appropriately hysterical mother and a neighbor. Andy, a thin child with unruly dark hair and wide eyes, sat in his mother's lap, placidly watching the tears leak out of her eyes. The walls of this office were blank except for the reflective side of a two-way mirror.

I explained to Andy's mother who I was, that I would be handling her daughter's case, and that I needed to speak to her son. She stared numbly at me. Her neighbor touched my arm to get my attention. I looked down and saw that she had two thumbs on her left hand and had manicured the nails of both with an iridescent pink polish. She saw me stare and hid her hand, as if out of habit, as I quickly looked away. She quietly told me that it was okay to take Andy.

I knelt down, showed the boy the lollipop, and told him he could have it if his mother said it was okay. The mother nodded and I gave Andy the pop, taking his hand and pulling him out the door. He tripped along behind me, looking back toward his mother. We went into the next room where the two-way mirror was papered over with newspaper so that you could not see into the room where Andy's mother was sitting. Each precinct was required to have a room dedicated to interviewing juveniles. In the Forty-Sixth Precinct detective squad, for some inexplicable reason, this was the room. It was dark and damp, the paint peeling off the walls. There were no pictures, books, drawings, or toys: nothing that would lead you to believe that this room was dedicated to children. All the lights were out except for one, a flickering halogen bulb. It was an interrogation room.

WHEN I STARTED in the Domestic Violence and Sex Crimes Bureau after two years at the DA's office, I had never interviewed a child before. At the time, I had no nieces or nephews or children. I had no idea how to talk to children or how to deal with them. I had no knowledge of what age meant in relation to maturity level. I spent my first year as an ADA working on misdemeanors, small-time drug cases, larcenies, fare-beats (or turnstile jumpers), and the like. My second year was spent only indicting cases. I knew nothing about the laws relating to sex crimes and/or children. Frankly, I was uneasy around kids. I liked them, but like an unfamiliar animal, I did not know how to approach them. Now, I was finding myself in situations where I had a few short hours to get a child to like and to trust me, and to be willing to speak to me about the unspeakable.

The law in New York presumed that a child under 12 (it was lowered to 9 after I left the office) cannot be sworn. This presumption can only be rebutted by proving that the child understands the difference between the truth and a lie, understands the importance of the truth and can articulate it. I had children under 5 who could be sworn and children as old as 10 who could not. But Andy not only did not know the difference between the truth and a lie, he didn't know what grade he was in. He did not know his own birthday or his address or telephone number. He did not know all of his colors or how to spell his name. Andy only knew the very simplest of things, like his name and his mother's name. And he knew his sister's name and that she was dead.

As I did with most children, I began by speaking to the boy about school. We talked about his teachers and his friends. He told me that he liked school and that he had lots of friends, but beyond that he was unable to tell me much of anything. His speech was slurred and difficult to follow, his vocabulary extremely limited.

If a child who is the only witness to a crime cannot be sworn, the case has to be thrown out unless what he says is corroborated by another person or by some other compelling evidence. All of us who handled cases involving children came across situations where a child was clearly abused and totally credible, but the case had to be dismissed because there was no one or nothing to back up the story. I understood the importance of Andy being swearable, but I also understood that it was not going to happen. We would have no viable witness to the homicide except for the defendant—and supposing that we could find him, the odds that he was going to talk were slim.

About 10 minutes into the interview, Andy's mother started wailing. The boy got up from the bench and pulled aside a torn piece of the paper on the two-way mirror. He looked toward me as he held the paper back. I could just see his mother through the small opening. "She crying because she love her and she dead. She dead and there was blood and her neck was like this," Andy said, drawing his finger across the side of his neck. "You see, she love her. And she dead now and baby has no mommy." Andy's hand was shaking. He dropped his lollipop.

I picked up the candy, taking Andy's hand. "Let's go wash this off," I said quietly. I wanted to hold him. Of all things for him to be able to understand, I wished that he could not understand this. The boy returned to the room where his mother sat, climbing into her lap and resuming his placid stare. When you are six years old and your mother is crying, does anything else matter? I went to Detective Leonard's desk and put the lollipop down. "The interview is over," I told him.

As I walked away, I skidded on a pickle chip that someone had dropped off a Quarter Pounder. It left a streak on the dirty floor. There were gum-wrappers all over the place. A group of detectives was standing around ribbing each other about beer guts and girlfriends. A tall, thin detective with military cropped hair and glasses pointed to the candy I'd just put down. Turning red, he yelled: "What the hell is this?"

"That, sir," I said, "is the lollipop that I gave to a six-year-old boy. He just watched his sister get stabbed to death this morning. Her head was barely attached to her neck and her right eye was gouged out and he was alone in the apartment with her for about a half hour. He dropped it on the floor. I told him I would wash it but this place is too fucking filthy to get anything clean. I just slipped on a pickle chip on your god-damned floor, so calm the fuck down."

And with that, I picked up my briefcase and left. I got into the car and backed away from the precinct. Crossing the Grand Concourse on the way back to work, I ran over the median. I hadn't even seen it. I went back to the office. It was 7:00 PM. Everyone was gone. I sat in my office and cried.

I SPENT THREE years as a felony assistant in the Domestic Violence and Sex Crimes Bureau of The Bronx District Attorney's office, one of approximately 400 Assistant District Attorneys working in the midst of an area of America with the highest crime and poverty rates. I began at the office at the age 25, straight out of Fordham Law School and life in an affluent New York suburb with my father the doctor and my mother the professor.

I interviewed for DVS when I was first hired, but wasn't accepted into the elite unit until my third year at the office. This book is essentially about my experiences in combating crimes against women and children during my three-year stint with DVS. Most DVS attorneys don't last much longer. The literal and emotional battles, both won and lost, eventually destroy you. I was far from the first person to tell my chief that I just couldn't handle it anymore. I will not be the last. I began with a burning desire to be part of the safety net, to prosecute criminals who terrorize the most defenseless among us. How and why I finally had to stop is the unusual psychological tale of this book.

There are ways to try to survive this job and I used them all during my work at DVS. I compartmentalized. I kept all personal feelings under wraps. I retreated into writing poetry. Once as a child I heard my father, an oncologist, make a joke about a sick person. I was horrified. "How could you say that?" I said.

"Because sometimes, Sarena, if you don't laugh, you'll cry."

My father's personal struggle with years of treating so many cancer patients wasn't totally clear to me until he published his own book of poetry a few years ago. Likewise, I kept my own turmoil buried deep within while I forced myself to get through each day. You can imagine what the jokes were like in the Domestic Violence and Sex Crimes Bureau: "What do you call a woman with two black-eyes? Nothing, you already told her twice." I'm not proud of it, but I will admit that I laughed at some things that weren't funny. My father was right. You have to. But, quite frankly, most of it wasn't funny at all. And I did not understand the full depths of my own trauma until years after I left the DA's office. I am still learning.

As an attorney dealing with these cases, I had to separate myself as much as I could. People dealt in different ways: therapy, drinking, sports. For me, it was poetry along with a bit of the others thrown in. You talk to victims and you tell them that your job is to "assess the strength or weakness of the case." Your decision about what to offer has to be based upon an objective view. You leave the emotional support to someone else by sending these people to the crime victim advocates for counseling.

My breaking point came when I could no longer separate myself from my work, when I began to hug my victims, when I lost the ability not to cry. I knew I was in trouble when I sent a wedding gift to the mother of one of my smallest victims, a woman I had become particularly attached to, the kind of personal relationship you are sternly warned against for both the victim's benefit and your own. My department had a high burnout rate for a reason.

This book is an account of my years as a felony assistant in the Domestic Violence and Sex Crimes Unit of The Bronx District Attorney's Office. It is a memoir of my times there, and a tribute to the assistant district attorneys and their support staff, the physicians, social workers, crime victim advocates, and cops who do what I believe is truly God's work. It's also a look at the darker side of the system: those who lose track of the fact that the job is supposed to be about doing justice and those that forget that not everyone is guilty or that all guilt is not created equal. It's also about those victims who themselves aren't so innocent or sympathetic—but you do your job anyhow.

In reflecting on these cases, I attempt to be as accurate as possible, with the exception of the names of the victims and their families who, even if their cases are public record, are entitled to their privacy. Often, I don't use the real names of defendants either, even if convicted, because I am discussing matters that are not part of the public record. In rare instances, when the case was publicly reported and I am only discussing my observations or matters of public record, I do use real names of defendants. Dialogue is based upon my best recollections, while opening statements, summations, direct and cross-examinations are from my notes and actual court transcripts. I have edited these transcripts only to eliminate portions that wouldn't make sense without having witnessed the entire trial as well as areas that are redundant. Otherwise, I have done my best to maintain them in their original form. Names and descriptions of other individuals and my colleagues are generally accurate except in the rare instances where I don't have something positive to say.

1

MY AFFLICTION

A small mole in South-east Asia
is the only known rodent
that mates for life. Scientists tested that mole and
discovered a chemical in its brain
that when blocked, caused said mole
to cheat on its mate,
which set me to wondering:
What if some day a scientist
running my DNA on a gel
discovers a pattern across five loci
that matched when compared
to the DNA of my female ancestors
for who knows how many
generations back
and they discovered that this pattern
pre-determined a propensity for physical violence
by women in my family. And not knowing
whether environment caused the pattern
or the pattern was caused by environment
would I have the right to have a child
until someone found a cure for my affliction?

MOST PEOPLE WILL never go to the South Bronx. There is no reason to go there except to catch a Yankee game and some aren't even brave enough to go for that. If you do go to a Yankee game, you are unlikely to venture further than a three-block radius from the stadium because it is the South Bronx and to the outsider, it is dangerous. Once you've left, you will not say that you have been to The Bronx. You won't make that association. You will say that you went to a Yankee game. And you will be right. You will not have been to The Bronx.

The radius around the stadium is a confusing knot of roads and elevated subway tracks. The surrounding streets are a dangerous maze that you would be afraid to get lost in. There are reasons that the mayor wants to move Yankee Stadium to Manhattan. Because for most people, more than any other borough in New York, The Bronx is synonymous with danger. You live there or you work there, but you don't just go there. And when you leave there, if you are a prosecutor, you shed it like a snake's skin.

Maybe it tells you something about the promise that The Bronx once held that only four places on earth get an article before their name: The Hague, The Vatican, The Netherlands, and The Bronx. And someone who lives in The Bronx may know that other side. The side with the Botanic Gardens and the quiet and safe streets of Riverdale. Or Pelham Bay with its hundreds of acres of woodlands.

My paternal great-grandfather moved to the United States in the early 1920s and first lived in the South Bronx on the Grand Concourse. He would have described the Grand Concourse as truly grand and the Loew's Paradise Theatre as the ultimate destination for high society. Until this year, the Paradise was a lonely shell of a building sitting on the Grand Concourse like an aged debutante wondering where all of her suitors went. She was just reopened in 2005. A first step toward the dream of restoring the grandeur of The Bronx, but her tarnished image will be hard to overcome.

For the prosecutor, The Bronx is the nightmare that everyone thinks it is, even in the nicer neighborhoods that make sure not to call themselves The Bronx, like Riverdale or Pelham Bay. Death and danger are everywhere. When you are a prosecutor, you don't visit the place unless something bad happened there and then, well, it may as well all be The

Bronx that the rest of the world thinks of. And for that matter, especially for a prosecutor who deals with something as dark as child abuse and sex crimes, the whole world is a Bronx and danger is everywhere.

IF YOU DID venture just three blocks east of Yankee Stadium, you would pass the regal old Supreme Court building with its neoclassical design and perhaps think, "That's quite lovely." But if you kept going another block or so, you'd find yourself right in front of the Criminal Court Building. The Criminal Court is in keeping with what one might expect when one thinks of a place where a prosecutor works. It was designed to be locked down in the case of a felon trying to escape from the building—as one did at a late-night arraignment. In the middle of a bail application, the defendant stabbed his own attorney in the hand with a pencil that was resting on the table. He vaulted the first row of benches and sprinted down the aisle and past the audience, mostly family members awaiting the fate of a loved- or a not-so-loved-one. He shoved aside a court officer and ran out the swinging doors. The facility went into lockdown. With the press of an alarm button the whole building snapped shut like a mousetrap. Every door. Every elevator. No one could go anywhere. The man was stopped cold when he bounced off the sealed glass entrance to the building, as an army of court officers holding onto their gunbelts fell upon him.

There are almost no windows in the Criminal Court Building, certainly none in the courtrooms. A narrow, secret passageway behind the courtrooms has the only windows on the second floor of the building. It was there that we would scuttle behind the scenes from room to room or hide our coffee so that we could grab quick slugs between cases. Looking at the building, it's hard to imagine that this squat, bland tank was built by Harrison and Abromowitz, the same architectural firm who built the soaring Time and Life and the Exxon Buildings. The outside of the building is almost entirely cement while the inside is mostly composed of asbestos sheets. Any construction in the building meant sheets of plastic sealing off the work area. The workers all wore masks, but we were unprotected and signs everywhere warned of my impending doom from asbestos. The dust seeped out from around the flimsy plastic and tape and I thought of OSHA and my father treating people for lung cancer. I spent my first two years as a prosecutor in that depressing gray box deprived of sunshine and wilting like so many other flowers in The Bronx.

In my third year, I moved across the street to the Domestic Violence and Sex Crimes Bureau, or DVS, and to a brand new building that was all white and glass. Here, I sat in relative peace in contrast to the chaos across the street where the line of defendants waiting to clear security often stretched up the street and around the corner. "Across the Street" as we called it, was worse than "The Other Side of the Tracks," and, for the female prosecutor, going to work there every morning meant running a gauntlet of hoots and whistles from the dregs of society. On "This Side of the Street," the lobby was virtually free of civilians other than victims coming in for interviews. I had my own office with a window which, granted, overlooked a parking lot. But a window nonetheless, and it ran the whole length of my office. I had a built-in desk and carpeting. My office had only one previous occupant and the only sign of her occupation was the one blemish on my floor, in the form of a piece of gum. The carpet was otherwise clean enough to curl up on and take a nap. And I did. I would leave my door unlocked and a cup of hot coffee on the desk as a decoy while I slept. I was always exhausted, going from working an early morning shift to a late night shift to being awake for 24 hours or more when I was on beeper duty to preparing day and night for trial.

But worse than the physical exhaustion was the emotional exhaustion. The relative quiet of the building was a direct contrast to my growing inner turmoil. "Across the Street" was noisy and bleak and dirty. The hours and pay were worse and the caseload was heavier. But I could stomach the crimes. I could handle the petit larcenies, minor drug busts, and turnstile jumpers. But on "This Side of the Street," with the promotions and the growing confidence in my skills came the growing severity of the crimes that I was trusted to prosecute. With each promotion came greater horrors. Progress was moving from wife beater to child beater to child molester to murderer. And I knew I had reached the top echelons of the bureau when I was entrusted with my first murdered baby. So, I would curl up under my desk in a fetal position with my head on a backpack and sleep.

Why would someone do this job? Why would I spend almost a hundred grand on a legal education just to work at a job where my starting salary was $35,000, which is barely enough to live on in New York? You could not pay most people enough to do what I did or to see what I saw, so why did I want to do it so badly? I could have gone to work at a law firm in midtown Manhattan with a starting salary of at least three times that much. I would have had a window office with a real view and maybe a secretary or even, dare I dream, a computer! And I would not have had cases, I would have had clients. And it would not be about life or death, it would just be about money.

There are a lot of reasons to do this job. People do it because it is exciting. Because it is an experience that you cannot get being a drone at a law firm. Because they want to run for office or be a judge or just love being in a courtroom. Because it's certainly not boring, or because the job is way cool. I mean, who says, "Oh my gosh, that's so exciting! Tell me about it!" when you say you're a lawyer. But when you tell them you are a prosecutor in The Bronx . . .

But I did the job for a different reason. I did the job because I believed in it. I believed that I could do justice. I did it because I thought that if I could make a difference in the life of even one child, if I could stop the cycle of violence for one small soul, the suffering in my own family would not be in vain.

BELLE HARBOR, QUEENS is nothing like the South Bronx. It is a quiet, private beachfront neighborhood with small, tidy green lawns and children playing in the street. Before people recently started building McMansions on the tiny acreage, the neighborhood seemed a throwback to the 1950s—safe, quiet, and secure, with white clapboard houses. A place where the Good Humor man still came and rang his bell at the end of the block and all the children would scamper up the hot sand to get Rocket Pops. My Grandma's home was here and although it was not where my father grew up, it is where I always pictured him, with his fiery red hair, riding his tricycle up and down the boardwalk.

It was 1989 when I arrived by cab to visit my Grandma for a few days at the end of summer and before starting my sophomore year of college. The fear I had of my grandmother when I was a child had been replaced over the years with tremendous love, respect, and genuine enjoyment of her company. Time and the loss of my Grandpa have softened her hard edges and although she's no pushover, she's far less exacting than she had been when I was younger. I enjoy talking to her. She isn't judgmental and she's always in tune with the times.

My grandmother loves to reminisce and tell stories and on that day, she was talking about her mother—my great-Grandma Katie. I barely remember Grandma Katie other than a foggy recollection of visiting her once when I was a small child. She was in a nursing home and I don't think she really knew who I was. All of my impressions of Grandma Katie—her strength, her generosity to others, especially during the Depression—are based on what I've been told by my grandmother. When my grandmother describes Grandma Katie's relationship with others, she describes with great pride her mother's generosity. She told me how my Grandma Katie used to have people lined up down the block for bowls of soup during the Depression and how her mother could turn a marrow bone and a carrot into a stew that was "pure ambrosia."

That day, however, my grandmother told me stories about another side of my Grandma Katie. These were not stories about the strong, straight-backed woman in the photos that kept an entire neighborhood alive when it was starving. For the first time, my Grandma started telling me about her own relationship with her mother. It seems that my Grandma Katie saved her kindness for strangers. It became clear from what she told me that my grandmother had suffered severe emotional, if not physical, abuse.

I'm not quite sure at what point my grandmother began talking to me about her own parenting rather than her mother's. Specifically, she started talking to me about my father. I suddenly heard my Grandma say, "I will never forgive myself for what I did to him." At first, I didn't understand what my grandmother was saying. I know that she was an exacting parent, but mine is a good and loving family. My Dad is inseparable from his siblings. He adored his father and although his relationship with his mother was not always warm, he loves her and their relationship has improved over the years. But, as I processed what my grandmother was telling me, I realized that she was talking about abuse and she was talking about abusing my father.

Once, in my entire childhood, my Mom spanked me. I'm quite sure I deserved it, whatever it was, but she didn't spank me hard and it hurt my ego more than my bottom. I didn't cry, but my Mom did, and she never spanked me again. My father was more of a disciplinarian than my mother and, while I lived in utter fear that he would hit me, punishment did not take that form for my brother and me. Instead, punishment was no television or telephone privileges. Maybe we would be grounded. Never did my father lay a hand on us. Once, after I found out that my father had been abused, I asked him if he had ever had to suppress the urge to hit us. He said, "No. Not ever. Not once."

My mother was raised in a home full of unconditional love. Her father died when she was a child and her mother and her maternal grandparents raised her and her brother in a place where there was never hitting or yelling. She is a clear product of this unconditional love. She is kind and smart but, nonetheless, incredibly strong. You can't go on a walk with my Mom without her pointing out something pretty in a window or stopping to smell a flower or just commenting on the general beauty of a place. When my Mom laughs, her nose wrinkles up and her eyes disappear and her joy is contagious. But my Mom is also fiercely protective, especially of my Dad, who seems tough and sometimes unfriendly to the outside world, but who is really quite fragile and gentle-hearted.

Although my father was also fiercely loved by his parents, that ferocity was sometimes just that. There were no mistakes allowed where he grew up. As my brother and I grew up, my father struggled against my mother's lax attitude toward our antics. No matter what we spilled, broke, or colored on with crayons, my Mom thought it was great. It must have been difficult for my father to balance his desire for structure and discipline against his desire to protect us from the kind of upbringing he had.

When I began to understand my father's childhood, it was hard for me to deal with. It still is. I love my grandmother deeply and admire her strength in the difficulties she overcame. My grandmother was stifled. She is a painfully intelligent woman who was forced to drop out of high school right before graduating to support her family during the Depression by working as a waitress. She was raised in the shadows of her four brothers, who were considered more important by her mother because they were male. She went straight from living for them to living for her children and for her husband. It was not until recently that she could be herself, which meant graduating college Phi Beta Kappa in her late seventies. She's in her eighties now and walks six miles a day when she feels up to it, teaches classes, and writes down her stories.

IF SOMEONE COULD have gone back and stopped the cycle of violence, if they could have helped my grandmother fight her own demons, my father's life would have been very different. And my Grandma would have peace now instead of regret. In that moment of my grandmother's confession, everything crystallized. It suddenly seemed that my entire life was headed in the direction of fighting crimes against children. It made more sense than anything in my life ever had before. Somehow, my subconscious seemed to know that my father's childhood was not quite like my mother's or mine, but something altogether different, conflicted and painful. All these chips fell into place. When I walked through the doors of Fordham Law School, I knew exactly where to head when I walked back out.

I did it because even though it was too late for me to help my father and my grandmother, it was not too late to help another child.

2

OPERATION LOSING PROPOSITION

ON AUGUST 30, 1990, Assistant District Attorney Sean Healy took his usual carpool to work at the Bronx courthouse. He was a rookie prosecutor with a reputation for being a hard working and nice guy. The carpool arrived at the offices and Sean went to work. Each day at about 10:30 AM, someone from the car pool had to move the car to comply with the city's alternate-side parking rules. It was Sean's turn that day. He moved the car and then decided to stop at a local market to buy donuts for everyone in the office. As Healy was making his purchase, a twenty-two year old man named Jose Diaz jumped out of a car in front of the store and sprayed bullets through the storefront window with a semi-automatic weapon. Diaz was a drug dealer and was aiming for a rival dealer who was also in the store. The only person that he hit was Sean Healy. Sean fell to the floor, bleeding to death. A female cop held Sean's head in her lap until an ambulance came and took him to Lincoln Hospital. He died on his way there. Diaz eventually pled to a term of 15 years to life. In 2008, after serving 17 years, Diaz will be 40 and eligible for parole. Sean Healy was only 30 years old when he was murdered. A plaque in The Bronx Criminal Court honors his name.

On September 11, 1995, I started my first day of work with The Bronx DA's office, promising my mother that it was as "safe as any other job."

That day, my class of 25 new ADAs took our first tour of The Bronx Criminal Court. There, I saw the plaque honoring Sean Healy off to the right side of the courthouse entrance. It was a reminder that where we were and what we were doing was not your typical attorney's job. In the end, it was a lot more like *Melrose Place* without the scenery than it was like *The Bonfire of the Vanities*, but it was no cushy law firm on Park Avenue. It was The Bronx.

In reality, it is the defense attorneys and not the prosecutors who are in the most danger from defendants in the courtroom. Oddly, defendants generally do not take what prosecutors do personally. They usually think prosecutors are just doing their jobs. I even had one friend who was thanked by a defendant for a job well done after he was convicted. As the defendant moved toward the prosecutor after the verdict, several court officers grabbed him and pulled his arms back. Suddenly aware of what they must have thought he was planning, he said, "Dudes, I was just going over to shake his hand."

Perhaps you would think the defendant would blame the juries, who actually decide whether the defendant is innocent or guilty. Or even the judge, who imposes the sentence. But in the end, it is the defense attorney who is blamed if the case is lost, for not doing his or her job well enough. Or it may be a simple matter of proximity that puts the defense attorney in the most danger. The prosecutor stands at a table far removed from the defendant. The court officers stand to the side or behind the defendant. The defense attorney is right next to the defendant, usually trying to do his or her best under difficult circumstances.

In spite of Sean Healy's terrible tragedy, a prosecutor is generally not much more likely to be shot or harmed than anyone else in The Bronx. There are those rare cases that you hear about where the prosecutor or the judge is targeted. Like the case of a judge in Fulton County, Georgia, who was killed by a defendant. One woman that I worked with received bomb threats for years from a defendant on a case she had prosecuted. Finally, after the threats were all but ignored, she received a box at our office, which was ticking. Our building was evacuated and we all stood outside in the cold for about two hours before the bomb squad finally announced that it was just a regular old desk clock with some wires and chewing gum attached to it.

This doesn't mean that as a prosecutor you do not have a great fear of harm or exposure. Sometimes, when I was standing on the train platform heading home, I would be looking over my shoulder, just waiting for some defendant that I had accused in the courtroom to confront me. In those first few weeks, however, I realized that I was in more danger from having to travel by subway late nights and early mornings than by virtue of working near criminals. I recall one Sunday when I was working the 8:00 AM shift. I was heading to the subway from my safe Upper West Side neighborhood at around 7:00 AM. I think that the only time the city that never sleeps dozes off is at 7:00 AM on a Sunday. There was not a soul in sight except for a disheveled looking black man who started to follow me a block from home. I turned a corner to see if it was my imagination and he turned as well. I stepped up my pace and so did he. I started to panic. Finally, I saw a open bodega on the corner of 71st Street and Columbus. I ran and the man started to run after me. I got to the store and I told the store owner that I was being followed. She shouted in rapid-fire Spanish with a heavy Korean accent toward the back of the store. Two of her employees ran out the door and down the block. They grabbed and held my pursuer while the store owner shoved me into a cab. I still shop at that store regularly out of pure gratitude even though it's not the closest to my apartment. Although the DA's office did not supplement our meager salary to pay for early morning cab rides, I never took the subway again on an early weekend morning.

ALTHOUGH ADAS ARE technically peace officers and can carry concealed weapons, we found out on our first day of work that District Attorney Robert Johnson's policy was that we could not carry a gun or a shield. In spite of the perceived protection that a gun implies, they say that you are 200 times more likely to die from gunfire if you carry a gun. I supposed that Mr. Johnson's rationale was that guns and shields would create more problems for us ADAs than they would prevent. Some people did not appreciate this policy. In our first week of orientation, within the first few hours of our arrival, one of my classmates excitedly asked when we would get our guns and badges. When we were told, "Never," the disappointment and indignation in the room were voiced in low grumbles by all. ADAs that were in the office before Rob Johnson took the helm had been assigned badges and allowed to carry concealed weapons. Those few who were still at the office when I was sworn in were grandfathered in and often still carried concealed weapons, usually in ankle holsters. Some of us new ADAs looked at the right to carry a gun and shield as protection, while others looked forward to it as a cool perk, compensating for our meager salaries. Either way, Mr. Johnson made it clear. No guns. No badges.

As far as I know, all of my classmates abided by the "no concealed weapons policy." But, although we were not supposed to have them, almost everyone carried a shield. It was not illegal, it was just against policy, and all it took to get a shield was a valid ADA's identification and a trip to the local police supply store. We all had one within a couple of weeks of taking our positions and it seemed like a minor offense in the grand scheme of things.

To a large degree, I understood Mr. Johnson's reasoning. I saw a few ADAs abuse that shield over the years, mostly for stupid things, like getting out of a speeding ticket or jumping the line at a club. Less frequently, I saw ADAs wave the shield vaguely at someone that they felt was out of line, much the same way that a cop might and, most likely, causing people to confuse them for cops. I thought that these few vigilante ADAs were nuts for flashing a shield that they could not back up with a gun. And many of the same ADAs were the ones who complained the most about not being allowed to carry that gun. But really, why did they need it? We didn't make arrests. We weren't trained to use those weapons. Some assistants would cite the fate of Sean Healy and his inability to protect himself. But Sean was not the target of the shooting. He was an innocent victim caught in a cross-fire like so many before and after him were in the South Bronx, and no concealed weapon could have saved him.

I was one of the many ADAs who bought a shield against the orders of the DA. I used it twice in my five years at the office. Once I stopped an old lady, drunk as a skunk, from getting in her car. The second time was when a cabbie refused to drive me to The Bronx in spite of rules that require them to take you to any destination within the five boroughs. I think that both were eminently worthy uses of my shield.

IN THOSE FIRST weeks as new assistant district attorneys at the BXDA, or assistants as we called ourselves, we went through a brief period of orientation where we were introduced to the work we would be doing and the laws we would apply. Our orientation lasted about two weeks and we spent time rotating through the complaint room, arraignments, and the courtrooms being instructed by other assistants with only a year or two at most in the office.

My class was remarkably diverse given its small size and we were a very tight-knit group. There were only 25 of us, but we were 49 percent female, black, white, Hispanic, Asian, and Indian. One of my classmates was in a wheelchair and I recall going to lunch with him several afternoons. The Criminal Court Building had steps at the entrance and was not handicap accessible. He would have to take an elevator to the third floor of the building and wind his way down several corridors to a passageway that connected the Criminal Court and Family Court buildings. Often the door between the two buildings was locked and he would have to wait for or locate a court officer to let him through. From there, he would take the elevator down to the first floor of the Family Court Building and make his way outside. Once we got to the restaurant or bodega, he generally would have to place his order with one of us and wait outside, as most of the restaurants had steps or doors too narrow to allow his wheelchair to get through. I remember once in the 10 or so minutes it took just to get him out of the building expressing my frustration that a government building would be so poorly equipped for handicapped access. He shrugged and said that it was "better than most." The law required that it be accessible, not convenient.

Our two-week orientation was spent rotating through the courtrooms. We also spent time learning how to do arraignments, where defendants were first publicly charged with the crimes that the state intended to prove against them. And finally, we were sent to the dreaded Complaint Room, where cases were initiated. Each day, we would spend several hours working with a more senior assistant and learning the various skills we would need in the following months. In the Complaint Room, Marianne Connolly was assigned to teach me the ropes. Marianne was a tough talking redhead and smart as a whip. Born and raised in The Bronx, she had an easy familiarity with the place and the cast of characters that paraded through our offices. She also had a straightforward camaraderie with many of the police officers who would befriend us ADAs and use that friendship to either try to jump the line and get out of the Complaint Room sooner or to delay the processing of their case so they could make more overtime. More often than not, when they befriended a female ADA it was to get a date. The various ploys, whatever the motive, usually did not work but generally the ADAs and the cops got along well anyhow. For the most part, we were on the same side of the fence and the relationship was symbiotic. We could make each other's lives easier or harder, and as a rule, why not choose easier?

I remember writing up my first case with Marianne and a cop named Sergio Villanueva. Like many of the officers who were regulars in the complaint room, Sergio knew many of the ADAs and I came to be friendly with him. We stayed sporadically in touch after I left The Bronx, and later, after he left The Bronx too. Six years to the day after I met Sergio, he was one of the many firefighters who died on 9/11. He was a rookie with the fire department, having left the police department for the better hours and pay. When I sang at his memorial service the church was filled with cops and firefighters each saying that their work was Sergio's true passion. I cannot speak to his passion as a firefighter, but I can say that Sergio was a good cop and, more than that, a good person. All of us who worked at the DA's office lost at least one friend on 9/11 and most of us lost many more. Like I said, the job was fairly safe for ADAs, but it is not so safe for some of the many friends that we made in law enforcement's other roles.

AFTER ORIENTATION, OUR class was divided into sections. About 80 percent of us went to the Criminal Court Bureau where we handled various misdemeanors (meaning crimes punishable by up to a year in jail), including assaults, petit larcenies, narcotics, trespasses, and so forth. The other 20 percent of our class was divided between the specialized bureaus including Investigations, Appeals, and the Domestic Violence and Sex Crimes Bureau ("DVS"). When I starting working in The Bronx, domestic violence, sex crimes, and crimes against children were all handled by this one group of prosecutors, and this is where I desperately wanted to work. At the time, there were only about seven assistants in DVS and a position there was not easy to obtain. I interviewed for DVS in my first week, but was not accepted, losing the one coveted space that year to the rare male who wanted to work there. The next available spot went to my friend Asha in year two. I would not get into DVS until my third year at the office. I therefore, like most of my classmates, began my career in the Criminal Court Bureau.

Criminal Court assistants have several basic functions. They are responsible for doing the initial screening and processing of misdemeanors in the Complaint Room, they handle arraignments for misdemeanors and felonies, they stand up in or "cover" the various misdemeanor court parts, and they handle their own caseloads of as many as a hundred cases.

In The Bronx, if a case survives initial processing and scrutiny by the police, it is brought to the Complaint Room where initial assessments are made by ADAs as to whether to prosecute the case and what crimes to charge. This decision is based upon whether the ADA reviewing the case believes that the initial crimes charged by the arresting officer are justified by the facts. For example, sometimes the arresting officer would charge a certain felony on a case and the assistant would "D it out," which means charging a lesser felony or reducing the crime to a misdemeanor. No one was ever able to satisfactorily explain to me why we called it "D'ing it out," but, nevertheless, sometimes the arresting officers didn't care what we did with the charges and sometimes they cared very much. What to charge and whether or not to reduce the charges led to some pretty heated debates between the officer, who considered it his case, and the ADA, who considered it her case.

My first such confrontation occurred when Danny Withers, who several years later was the detective on the Esmeralda DeJesus murder, charged both a burglary and a robbery on a case that I wrote up in the Complaint Room. A person is guilty of burglary when he knowingly enters or remains unlawfully in a building with intent to commit a crime therein. Robbery is forcible stealing. One can commit a burglary without committing a robbery or vice versa. When I reviewed the case, I did not think that the robbery charge was warranted and intended to charge only the burglary. Danny strongly disagreed with me and a huge battle ensued first between Danny and me, and then later, between our supervisors. Such disputes between cops and ADAs only continued when the ADA who was eventually assigned the case would, after a more extensive interview of the officer and victim than the Complaint Room assistant was able to do, alter or reduce the charges yet again.

When I started working in The Bronx, a case was not processed unless the victim personally appeared in the Complaint Room. The theory was that the victim (or complainant) should be present at the DA's office to write up the complaint based on direct information because if someone is willing to show up at the Complaint Room, that person would be more likely to show up later on when he or she was needed for further prosecution of the case. Exceptions were, of course, made for victims who were in the hospital and so forth, but generally speaking it made for a lot more waiting around for victims to show up and for a lot more dismissed cases when victims did not show up.

Shortly after I started in the office, we began installing videoconferencing, which allowed us to interview the victims remotely from the precincts rather than making them come in all the time. The hope was to streamline the process a little bit. It would mean a lot less traveling back and forth for the cops and the victims and, hopefully, faster processing of the cases. In the interim, all victims came to the Complaint Room to be interviewed personally by an ADA and to sign the complaint. On cases where there was no specified victim, other than society (such as in narcotics cases), and the complainant was a police officer, we used a system called "BLAP." BLAP meant that information was faxed back and forth between the complaint room and the precinct for signature by the cop rather than the cop having to come to the DA's office just to sign the paperwork. The technology may sound dated, but keep in mind that most of the ADAs in the office did not even have computers until about three years ago.

I don't think anyone knew what "BLAP" stood for, but it was a sort of emotional onomatopoeia for how we felt about it. The cops hated the system because it meant less overtime and because it did not work well. In fact, it stank. We hated the system because it meant more delays and ADAs don't make overtime, so delays were not rewarding for us. And, it stank. The fax machines would break. The line at the precinct would be busy. The papers would get lost. The whole thing just made you want to stick your finger down your throat and go "BLAP."

There was a "BLAP Sergeant," a member of the police department who was permanently assigned to BLAP. I can't recall his name, but he was a burly officer with a crew cut and a terse manner. He barked orders and resented his crappy assignment, which was basically to fax papers back and forth between the DA's office and the precincts and to yell at ADAs and cops for not being expeditious. The BLAP Sergeant had been accidentally shot in the big toe by his partner, which was bad enough, and now he was stuck working in his windowless cubicle full of fax machines until his case finally wound its way through the bureaucracy, which may have been worse. He would eventually be retired early with three-quarters pay since he had been hurt on the job but, in the meantime, he was stuck working at the DA's office in the crappiest assignment possible. I am sure it isn't what he imagined doing when he first signed up for the police department. He looked like a marine and ran his cubicle like a barracks, which meant being tidy, efficient, orderly, and not allowing any eating in the Complaint Room since it was not the mess tent.

Once, when I was working in the Complaint Room at night, several of us got stuck late when the computer systems went down. We were working a 4:00 to 12:00 shift and it was already well after midnight before the systems were brought back up and we could finish processing any cases that could not wait until morning. I guess we should have been grateful that, unlike the Manhattan ADAs, we did not have a midnight to 8:00 AM shift. They call that the "Lobster Shift," a term used by newspapers writers to describe the overnight shift. The origin of the term is subject to many theories, but all I knew is that I did not want to work it and I seemed to be headed that night toward not just a Lobster Shift, but a double shift.

Looking for some comfort food and some sugar to keep us going, I ran across the street to the supermarket and picked up several boxes of ice cream sandwiches. I thought it would be a nice thing to do with everyone stuck at the office late. I left the boxes of ice cream on the counter near the entrance to the Complaint Room, took one with me, and went back to my cubicle to start grinding through the rest of the cases so that I could go home. A few minutes later, the BLAP Sergeant stormed back to the area where the ADAs were working and, holding an ice-cream sandwich box with two fingers like it was a dead rat, sneered, "Who bought these!!" Shrinking, I timidly raised my hand and said, "I did?" He stormed back to me, leaned over my desk and said quietly, so that no one else could hear, "I don't eat this crap, but that was real nice of you." He winked. Walked away. And after that, we were friends.

. . .

MY FIRST CONTACT with DVS-type cases occurred when I was assigned to the Complaint Room in that first year. Unlike some other boroughs, and something that has been changed since, assistants from the specialized bureaus were not assigned to the Complaint Room. As a result, all cases were processed by criminal court assistants in the case of misdemeanors and by Grand Jury assistants in the case of felonies. Since I knew that I wanted to go to DVS, I often made an effort to take cases out of the bin that would land in DVS, eventually. It was not a problem as most people avoided the sex crimes like a plague, mostly because they were time-consuming and cases with victims were generally harder to deal with than those with just a cop. I hoped that by writing up a lot of DVS cases, I could develop a relationship with supervisors in DVS that would help my chances of getting into the bureau when the next round of promotions came up.

My first official contact with sex crimes came by writing up prostitution charges. These cases are not sent to DVS and were actually normally pled out with "time served" and maybe some (other kind of) community service during arraignments. But they were my first insight into the world of sex crimes and the blunt manner in which such cases are dealt with. Since prostitution, or "pross" cases, rank among the lowest level of crimes right next to fare-beats, many assistants get broken in with them. Sometimes hundreds of these pross cases would be brought in over the course of the night if a precinct was targeting streetwalkers or their customers or "Johns." These arrest operations, dubbed "Operation Losing Proposition," would occur every so often as part of then-Mayor Rudolph Giuliani's quality of life campaign. To the city, operations "Losing Prop," "Clean Halls," and "Get Rid of the Squeegy Guys," and whichever other quality of life campaigns Giuliani came up with, meant cleaner and safer streets. To us, it meant longer nights and smellier holding pens.

In undercover pross cases, undercover cops, or "UCs," pose as prostitutes, wearing wires to record conversations between themselves and any potential customers. Once these UCs are solicited for sex and a money offer is made, the John is arrested. I had one case that I handled as a misdemeanor assistant where the John was claiming that the cops just picked him up as part of a general roundup and that he hadn't solicited the prostitute, who was really a UC, for sex. The man claimed that, in fact, he couldn't have solicited the UC and that the police were fabricating the charges because he was both deaf and mute. The case went on for several months as I attempted to get a copy of the recording to see what was on it. Matters were further complicated by the fact that the man signed in Spanish and every time I ordered a Spanish sign interpreter for court, one that only knew American sign would show up. Finally, after several months of waiting, I got the recording made by the UC. The next day in court, I smugly handed the tape to the deaf man's lawyer as proof of the crime saying, "Well, he's deaf, but on the mute part, your client has you fooled!" Not only did the recording pick up the man asking, in Spanish, "How much for a blow job," but you could tell from the speech pattern that it was a deaf man talking.

Real prostitutes are also arrested during "Operation Losing Propositions" after being observed soliciting civilians or after soliciting UCs posed as Johns. Once a certain number of arrests are made, the operation is shut down and a detective comes into the DA's office with a whole pile of reports written up by the UCs. Narcotics operations, also known as "Buy and Busts" (or "B&Bs"), are handled in much the same way.

In order for a pross complaint to be legally "sufficient," the sexual act had to be described explicitly and not just in generalized terms. When my first pile of pross cases came in, I found myself sitting across from a veteran detective with at least 15 years on the job. I wasn't the first rookie ADA he'd dealt with, so there were few surprises at my reactions.

In a UC's report, the suspect is often referred to as a "JD," or John Doe. The JD will be followed by a description or identifying characteristic, i.e. "JD Red Shirt" if the suspect is wearing red, or "JD Braids" if the suspect has hair plaits. I once had a "JD Sores," which I don't care to elaborate on. The detectives came in with an initial write-up of the case on a form called a 41 or a 55 or something like that, I don't recall. My job was to translate cop-speak into ADA-speak, which meant translating the UC's description of the events that unfolded during that night's "Operation Losing Prop" onto one of the white folders that our case summaries were written on. The white folder contained the "story," and was mainly intended to help the ADA in arraignments, and then the one who was eventually assigned to the case, understand what had happened. My job was then to translate this story from ADA-speak to judge speak and succinctly put only that information that made out the elements of the crime onto a complaint form, which would then be signed by the detective. As you can imagine with all of this paperwork and duplication, errors in the translation often became fuel for the defense at trial and the job had to be done with care. From cop jargon to legalese to judge-speak onto the official complaint without changing the facts, my first pross case turned out like this:

> *At T/P/O* [time and place of occurrence] *UC 23456 was approached by JD Red Shirt who did ask, "how much for half and half."*
>
> UC 23456 did reply, $10.00. JD Red Shirt then did ask "how much for an around the world." UC 23456 did reply $20.00. Deponent states that based upon his training and experience in the area of prostitution that 'half and half' mean. . . .

> "Uh . . . detective, uh . . . what's 'half and half'?"
>
> "Rookie, huh?"
>
> "Well, I've been here like two weeks."
>
> "'Half and half' means dat he wants a blow job and regula' sex. You gonna' wanna' know what 'around the world' is?"
>
> "Uh . . . yuh. . . ."
>
> "Well, 'aroun da' world' means he wants ta put it in all a her ora-fices. Don' worry about it. You ain't the first rookie ta ask me that."

And so I was initiated into a world where things that no one else wants to say are so much a part of the daily vocabulary that words I would never have said in public in my pre-ADA life rolled off my tongue like I was reciting the weather forecast.

MY FIRST LEGITIMATE domestic violence case came only a short time later. Although for my first year I was generally allowed only to write up misdemeanors, sometimes a supervisor would hand me a felony when he or she thought it should be reduced to a misdemeanor. This was such a case. The case was written up as a felony assault with a deadly weapon.

I sat down with the cop and a pretty Hispanic woman of about 22. She had a fairly bad black eye. I read over the police report, which said that the woman's boyfriend had punched her in the eye. No matter how serious a bruise, if it is caused by someone's hand, the injury is a misdemeanor assault. I asked the officer why he had written the charge up as a felony assault with a weapon when the injury was caused by a punch. Cutting off the cop just as he opened his mouth, the woman stuck her finger in my face and waved it back and forth in front of me. At the same time, she moved her head back and forth on her neck in the opposite direction: a trademark Bronx move. "Nuh ... you don' unda' stan'.....Mah boyfriend be Golden Gloves champion. His haaaaands be regista'd lethal weapons."

Although there were moments of levity in my job, more often than not it was sad and frustrating. With few exceptions, no ADA was forced to come to DVS. Part of the reason was exactly what you'd suspect. Some are not comfortable with the subject, some would rather work with police witnesses than with civilians, and some simply feel that they can't deal fairly with people who abuse kids (especially sexually). More than once, my office colleagues told me that they were afraid if they handled one of these cases, they would just "jump across the table and strangle the guy." Sometimes our non-DVS colleagues criticized us for what they thought was too lenient plea bargaining. But they had no idea what the obstacles were like in DVS.

I HADN'T BEEN working in the Complaint Room for more than a few days before I wrote up my first battered woman case. By week two, I had written up dozens, and by a couple of months into the job, hundreds. The scenarios and responses were similar from case to case and my expectations of the victims were formed rather quickly. I found that a large percentage of the abused women who came into the Complaint Room refused to press charges and most of them would return time and time again. Many of these women were known to their local precincts as they were constantly calling 911 for help. Many also became known to the DA's office. The story was often the same. They loved the guy. They knew he wouldn't do it again. He said he was sorry. He bought them flowers.

It was their fault because they provoked him. We would see the same faces over and over again, each time more seriously injured than previously. We were always concerned and knew that, most likely, it would only get worse. Sometimes we would try to force these women to press charges or would try to charge the man with a crime for which the woman would not be needed in order to prosecute. Most often, we would admit defeat and just let the victims drop the charges, having them sign a statement saying they refused to proceed.

I was once particularly frustrated with a domestic violence victim who wanted to drop charges. She was a second-year law student and I thought that she should know better. I tried to talk her into proceeding with the case but, when she continued to refuse, I had her sign a statement before I would dismiss the case that said, "I don't mind being a punching bag." When the victim of a crime, especially domestic violence, wanted to drop charges, they would first have to sign a statement to that effect. It was a big CYA, or "cover your ass" move. On the one hand, we wanted to make sure that they really wanted to drop charges and sometimes, putting it in writing brought it home. On the other hand, we needed to cover our asses so that if the victim was beaten up again, or even killed, we had a record of our efforts to prosecute and of her decision not to.

In the case of my second-year law student, when I insisted that she sign this statement in order to drop charges, she threatened to report me to the Bar Association, saying I was forcing her to sign it. "Go ahead," I told her, "I'm not forcing you to do anything. However, if you don't sign this, he'll stay in jail and if you want him out of jail, well, then you need to sign it." She signed and he was released. I thought that my supervisor would kill me for pulling that stunt but, to my surprise, instead I got an "atta' girl." Everyone got sick of dealing with it after a while. I know you aren't supposed to say that but it's the truth. It was frustrating, time consuming, disheartening, and depressing.

I found out later that a large percentage of cases written up after much cajoling and pleading by the Complaint Room assistants were unceremoniously dropped by DVS when the women again changed their minds. Not only did DVS lack the manpower to pursue each and every case, but there was a point where we simply had to pick and choose our battles. I wish that I could count the number of times that women who begged and pleaded with me to help them and swore that they wouldn't drop charges ended up in court telling the judge that I forced them to prosecute. The psychology of the battered woman is something that I eventually understood very well in theory but never really understood in practice.

AFTER A YEAR in Criminal Court, I was promoted. In my second year at the office, all I did was present cases to the grand jury as an assistant in the Grand Jury Evaluations Bureau, or "GJE." Our job in GJE was to indict all non-DVS and non-narcotics felony cases such as robberies, assaults, murders, and burglaries. While DVS and Narcotics indicted their own cases, the "Trial Bureaus" did not. Instead, GJE assistants would indict and then send the cases "Across the Street" to the Trial Bureau. For an entire year, except when I was in the Complaint Room writing up felonies, all I did day in and day out was indict cases. And indict I did—hundreds of people. . . .

3

THE CASE OF THE GOLDEN DILDO

My Daughter Graduated from Law School Today

I pulled out an old photo. This is July
in St. Louis. She's wearing
her Raggedy Ann dress and her mother's

blue straw hat. Each time I aimed the camera
she looked away, so I lay back and watched
the sun creep over the asphalt roof

and dip beneath its peak. Just as I turned,
I caught the last light as it filtered through the hat
across her cheeks. Her eyes were dark

and translucent as sorrel agates, and her chin
tilted forward as if to contest the axis
of the earth. She was two years old.

—MARC J. STRAUS

IT IS NOT in my nature to take things at face value. Whether that is built into my personality or a characteristic that I grew into because it was expected of me, I don't know. What I do know is that this is who I am. I have always questioned and defied, for better or for worse.

My family loves to tell a story about how they knew I was going to be a lawyer from when I was just two. It was 1972 and I was sitting in the back of my parents' Dodge Dart. I remember that car like it was yesterday. We had it for at least a decade and by the time my father got rid of it, rust had eaten all the way through the floorboards and there were mushrooms growing on the rugs. My brother and I would kick the mushrooms off the rug and push them through the holes in the floor. Then we would turn around quickly and time how long it would take for the mushroom to appear on the road behind us.

But back then, the car must have been pretty new. My parents were in the bench seat in the front and my uncle Stephen, who was then about 22 and had just graduated from MIT, was next to me. My uncle was telling me not to do something and I was ignoring him. After several requests from my uncle for me to "stop," my father told my uncle, "Give up. You won't win."

My uncle retorted, "What are you talking about? She is two. I'm not going to argue with a two-year-old!"

My dad just shrugged his shoulders and kept driving. Whatever it was that I was doing, I kept doing it, and my uncle kept telling me to stop.

Finally, I looked at him and as he put it, "sassed my shoulders," and said, "The more you say it, the more I won't."

Maybe I was born to be a lawyer. By and large, I have always believed in the criminal justice system, but never without questioning it. It's full of flaws, but it is what we have and you have to work with what you have or work to change it. No use in complaining about something that you intend to do nothing about. Sure, there are bad eggs everywhere. There are bad cops, there are bad prosecutors, and there are bad judges. But most of the people I worked with were good people and they were trying to do the right thing. You hear about the bad people more, so it may seem like there are a lot of them, but you don't hear about the good people that often and in The Bronx, I met many more good people than bad ones. It gave me faith and drove me to stick with it. But if I have to select one thing that discourages me the most about the criminal justice system in New York, it's the Grand Jury. And I developed this cynicism about the process during that year in GJE.

THE ORIGINAL PURPOSE of the Grand Jury was noble, both in design and literally. King Henry II established the "Grand Assize" in 1166 to gather information about criminal activity from the citizenry, mostly for his own selfish purposes. About five centuries later, a more righteous function of the Grand Jury grew out of a case from the late 1600s in which an English grand jury refused to grant the request of the king's prosecutor for an indictment against a nobleman accused of treason. Since then, the grand jury process has been favored based on the belief that the grand jury prevents the prosecutor from bringing an unfounded charge against an innocent person for improper or malicious reasons or without sufficient cause.

Grand Juries became popular here during the American Revolution because they often stood between American patriots and the crown's prosecutors. Some of the decisions of those colonial grand juries may have been for good reason and others may have been examples of the first "jury nullifications" in the new world. Jury nullification is when a jury (or Grand Jury) comes to a verdict not based on the law as given to them, but because it feels like the decision is morally right—somehow justified even if contrary to the law. Simply put, it means that sometimes a jury will vote against an indictment (or conviction if a trial jury), even if the crime is supported by the evidence, because they think it's the "right thing to do." The danger of a jury deciding what was right over what a judge or prosecutor tells them is much higher in The Bronx than in most places because there is so much suspicion of law enforcement. But the decisions of the Colonial Grand Juries against the crown remind us that we have a rich history of juries making decisions founded in politics rather than in the law.

As a result of the popularity of Colonial Grand Juries, when the US Constitution was drafted, the grand jury system was incorporated into the Bill of Rights. The US Supreme Court has repeatedly upheld the right to a Grand Jury, stating that, "The most valuable function of the Grand Jury is to stand between the prosecutor and the accused." Many of the states in the Union, including New York, followed suit in their state charters.

Since that time, however, the feeling has developed that, in the hands of a determined and/or publicity-seeking prosecutor, the Grand Jury has become a sword for the prosecution rather than a shield for the citizen. It has become easier and easier for prosecutors to use the Grand Jury as an instrument for their own purposes and many feel that the Grand Jury simply acts as a "rubber stamp" for the prosecutor. This ease of obtaining a conviction led Judge Sol Wachtler, the former Chief Judge of New York, to famously say that, "A grand jury would indict a ham sandwich."

On a positive note, the Grand Jury system certainly does represent an attempt to involve citizens in the administration of criminal justice. In theory, the Grand Jury is comprised of a panel of the community's citizens. Their job is to act as impartial overseer of the criminal justice system. The grand jury is also intended to serve as quality control for local government—to ensure that justice is being properly administrated during this "secret" proceeding by law enforcement and prosecutors.

The job of the modern Grand Jury is to review the evidence presented by the prosecutor and determine whether there is probable cause to return an indictment, which is essentially a document ratifying the charges. The effect is that the Grand Jury decides if the case will continue or not. In an ideal world, the system should help avoid situations where individuals who aren't at least more than likely to be ultimately found guilty of a crime continue to stand charged for as much as a year or more until a case goes to trial (which can also mean sitting in jail). However, since the role of the Grand Jury is only to determine probable cause, there is no need for the jury to hear all the evidence, or even conflicting evidence. It is left to the good faith of the prosecutor to present conflicting evidence. What constitutes good faith can be open to interpretation, and some would consider the interpretation of certain prosecutors quite unforgiving.

THE TARGET OF a Grand Jury investigation in New York has the right to testify before the Grand Jury, to tell his side of the story. Many Bronx defendants could avoid indictment, or persuade a jury to nullify, by refuting the claims of the prosecutor. Often it doesn't take much more than some wild story to do just that. I had only one case in five years where the Grand Jury voted "no true bill." I presented the case to the Grand Jury early in my career with DVS. It was one of my rare cases where the defendant testified in the Grand Jury. Her story was ridiculous and the Grand Jury's decision to vote "no true bill," dismissing the charges, was mind-boggling.

I was assigned an "in" case, meaning that the defendant was in jail and did not make bail. This meant I would have to present the case to the Grand Jury for indictment within six days. My victim, Charles, was in the hospital with a stab wound to the side, a punctured lung, and an infection from the dirty knife he was stabbed with. I went to the hospital to interview him. He was a soft-spoken black man of smallish stature with a sweet face and a calm demeanor. He seemed like a kind, easygoing person and a good family man. Charles worked full-time to support his wife and son and I gathered, after a short talk with him, that he was the frequent victim of abuse by his wife. The man was embarrassed about being battered by his wife and had never called the police. This was typical of abused men, and there are more than you would think. He also said that his wife did not hurt their child and that he didn't want to break up the family, so he did his best to make it work. The only reason that this incident had been reported was because this time he'd ended up in the hospital. Charles did not want to press charges but his injury was quite serious and I could not let it go that easily. I persuaded him that his wife was a danger not only to himself but also to his son who she would likely eventually hurt. I told him that it was time to do something about it. It took a lot of cajoling but, finally, the man agreed to testify before the Grand Jury after his release from the hospital.

Charles went before the Grand Jury and told the jurors how he and his wife got into a fight because she was drunk. She had another beer in her hand and was about to open it. When he tried to take the beer away from her, she stabbed him with a knife that had just been used to cut raw fish. The knife went into his side under his left arm, through his ribs, puncturing his lung. He developed an infection from the wound because the knife was dirty. The couple's son had witnessed the entire event.

Charles's wife opted to testify before the Grand Jury as well and, later that day, she came into the chambers with her lawyer. She was a very pretty petite woman with large, doey brown eyes. The defendant told the jury a very different story than Charles had. She claimed she was trying to open a beer and that the tab broke off, so she had tried using the knife to push in the tab. She said her husband got angry because it was the last beer and he wanted it, so they started to tussle over the beer. She claimed that at this point, the knife fell out of her hands and her husband slipped and fell onto the knife, which went through his ribs and punctured his lungs.

I can't tell you how many times in my five years I heard the "he fell on the knife" story. I found it to be the lamest of all defenses and I would think that the impossibility of what this woman described would have been apparent to the Grand Jury. I questioned the defendant, who by this time was crying a river of crocodile tears, about how Charles could possibly have fallen onto a knife at such an angle that it would actually penetrate through his ribs and into his lung. The sheer absurdity of her story seemed incredibly obvious and, after just a few questions, I dismissed her from the Grand Jury room and took a vote. I was confident of the Grand Jury voting a true bill and when they told me they reached a decision a short time later, I truly thought I misheard when they informed me that there was no indictment. I knew I wasn't supposed to say anything to them about it, but I could not control myself. I looked at them with my mouth agape in utter amazement and said, "How could you have possibly believed that load of crap! Do you actually think that a woman isn't capable of harming a man!" One of the Grand Jurors followed me out of the room and complained, really rightfully so, about my outburst. The court officer that the juror complained to promised he would take care of it and as soon as the door to the jury room closed, he put his arm around my shoulders in empathy and said, "Some day, nothing will surprise you." It was with such shame and mortification in the system that I went back to that poor man, whom I had begged for the sake of his child to press charges, and told him that his wife was going to be released. He was not surprised either. It was one of the reasons he didn't want to press charges in the first place. He thanked me for even caring and took his son home.

. . .

IN MY FIVE years with the DA's office, I indicted well over a hundred cases. In that time, only five defendants actually testified in the Grand Jury and that one case was the only "no true bill" that I ever got. I think that I could have in fact "indicted a ham sandwich." And although it would more likely lead to more "no true bills," it is still rare for defendants to testify before the Grand Jury. It is risky for an accused to talk to anyone but a lawyer before trial and few defendants, especially in DVS-type cases, would avail themselves of the opportunity to testify. Also, Grand Jury testimony is admissible against the accused if he testifies at trial.

Testifying in the Grand Jury, especially in The Bronx, started to become more common by the time I left the office, especially in drug cases where the cry of police conspiracy goes a long way in persuading people not to indict. But in the end, the system seems fatally flawed regardless—either because it's too easy for the prosecutor to obtain an indictment or because the Grand Jury abuses the process by making a political statement rather than by following the law. Most of the time, however, the Grand Jurors fail by simply not caring.

MY FIRST EXPERIENCE drafting a felony DVS complaint in the Complaint Room ended up leading to my first time in the Grand Jury. It was a few months before I was promoted to GJE and I was interviewing a 13-year-old girl who claimed that her stepfather had put his finger in her vagina. It seemed like your typical misdemeanor sex abuse case. I spent some time chatting with the child about school and friends, trying to make her more comfortable. Then I went over the facts with her and wrote everything down. The whole thing took only about a half hour, which made me happy because I was working the night shift. It was midnight, and this was my last case of the evening. As soon as we were done, I could go home. I shook the girl's hand, and she got up to leave.

Just before she walked out of the cubicle, the girl turned to me and said, "Ya' know, the thing I think made him do it was all those naked pictures my mom took of me that he's always lookin' at." I heaved a sigh and settled back in my chair for a long night. "All right," I said, "lets start again."

The girl proceeded to tell me that her mother took naked photos of her, the girl's two older sisters, and a 12-year-old friend in various poses and in such lovely locations as the shower, the kitchen, and the bedroom. Apparently, she took these photos so that the older sister could send them to a boyfriend in jail. The girl was very specific and credible with her details about what, where, and when. She told me that the photos were kept in a shoebox in the closet, and that her stepfather also stored a gun there. I brought in the cop who had made the collar, or the arrest, telling him what happened. We quickly drafted a search warrant so that we could run it upstairs and get it signed before the judge in Arraignments went home for the night.

The next day when the cops executed the warrant, they weren't able to locate the gun but found the shoebox right where the girl had said it was, filled with nude photographs. Also in the shoebox was a giant gold dildo, which was apparently a favorite photo prop. The mother was arrested.

The case was assigned to a senior assistant in DVS named Robert Holdman (now Judge Holdman). Holdman called me up and asked me to sit in on his interview of the girls. He said that the girls were uncomfortable with having to speak to a man and that the girl I had met two days earlier specifically requested my presence. It was quite a compliment to me. I was nervous and excited about participating in my first felony. I also desperately wanted to impress ADA Holdman in the hopes that he would some day put in a good word for me with the bureau chief at DVS.

When I arrived in his office, Holdman again went over the facts of the case with the girl I'd interviewed, and also interviewed her 12-year-old friend. The sisters were not minors and they had the right to consent to having their photos taken, so we didn't interview them. We went through the photographs with the girls one by one to find out where each was taken. We got the girls' ages at the time of each of the photo sessions. Privately, Holdman later told me that the pictures might do more harm then good because the girls were apparently having fun when they were photographed. Although the crime was statutory (based on the ages of the girls) and therefore it didn't matter whether they had consented to have the pictures taken or not, Holdman was concerned about getting the Grand Jury to indict or to "vote a true bill" if they became unsympathetic after seeing the pictures. One photo in particular raised concerns. It depicted the 12- and 13-year-olds nude and posing suggestively with the gold dildo. They were facing the camera with their arms around each other, butts stuck back, chests stuck forward, and big smiles over that giant gold dildo. It was going to be hard to get the jurors to put aside their impressions that these young women consented to have the photos taken and, in fact, enjoyed having them taken, and apply the law, which says that they aren't old enough to consent no matter how mature they are or how fun they thought the game. It also did not help that they looked much older than their years.

As we reviewed the picture with the girls, one of them inquired, "What's going to happen to it?"

"What?" Holdman raised an eyebrow, "The dildo?"

"Yah."

"It was vouchered for evidence. Don't worry, you'll get it back."

It often seemed to me that in spite of the law, the age of consent in The Bronx was about 12. I could not have imagined myself or my friends behaving in such a provocative manner at that age.

As a result of my involvement in the case, I was invited to sit in on the Grand Jury presentation. It was the first Grand Jury presentation I had seen. The large Grand Jury room was set up somewhat like a college lecture hall, with seats going upward toward the back. On the floor was a table where four people sat, including the foreperson. The witness chair was next to the foreperson, and a court reporter or stenographer sat in front of the witness chair. Ideally, there are 23 people in the Grand Jury room. In The Bronx, they sit for one month, four days a week, from about 10:00 AM to 5:00 PM.

By the time the Grand Jury has been seated for about a week, it is already jaded. People sleep or read papers through cases. They fight, they laugh at inappropriate things, and worst of all, they get tired of being there and stop giving a crap. One of my friends recently sat on the Grand Jury in Brooklyn. She said that it was one of the most disheartening experiences of her life. "They simply did not care," she told me. She knew that I was writing a book about my experience at the DA's office and she informed me that it was no better in Brooklyn than in The Bronx. "They think everything is police conspiracy no matter how farfetched that might be." She said that the jurors were far less concerned about punishing the criminal than about teaching a lesson to the cops and that often when she voted to true bill a case, especially when it was a narcotics buy and bust operation, they accused her of being racist.

The Grand Jurors groaned when we walked in to begin our presentation. We were interrupting card games, lunch, and naps. To our advantage in DVS, our cases were intriguing and different from most of what a Grand Jury heard. Since 50 percent of the cases in The Bronx deal with narcotics, the first thing these jurors would mutter when new people arrived was, "Not narcotics again?" When they heard DVS, the first response was usually "thank God." But when we brought in a kid who had been beaten or sexually abused, most of them wished for narcotics cases again. On the other hand, it was less likely that the Grand Jury would give us a hard time than it would on a narcotics case. Hating the system and punishing a cop for it was one thing, but taking that hatred out on a child or a battered woman was another and it was much harder for a defendant to cry "police conspiracy" in a case with a victim who was one of their own.

This presentation went fairly smoothly. I sat off to the side near the jurors. Holdman first came in alone to introduce himself and put some basic information on the record—his name, the name of the defendant and witnesses, the location of the crime, and so forth. He also noted that my presence in the Grand Jury was for observation purposes only and that no inference was to be drawn from my presence. Once he'd done that, he called the girls in one at a time to tell the Grand Jury what had happened. He also put the cop on the stand to describe what he recovered pursuant to the search warrant and to tell what statements the defendant made.

The Grand Jury seemed disturbed by what they heard, but our guess was right. Once they saw the pictures, they sang a different tune. They commented about the girls seeming to enjoy themselves. Although they had been carefully instructed on the girls' inability to consent due to their ages, this did not seem to matter. We walked out of the Grand Jury fairly certain that we were about to face jury nullification. Even knowing that the law said the girls could not consent due to their age, these were not naked five year olds. They were naked teenagers and due to their demeanor and willingness, the Grand Jury likely would not true bill the case. The mother pleaded guilty before we could discover for sure whether the Grand Jury would vote a true bill or not, but I felt badly about this, my first exposure to the idea that sometimes, even if you've met your burden legally, the Grand Jury may not follow the law. They were the first people that you faced. The first that you had to prove yourselves to. And if you could not prove yourselves to them, everything could be lost.

4

QUANIE

It's February in Boston.
I'm at the barre in my navy blue snappy-crotch leotard,
red tights and black canvas shoes.

My hair is fastened in two pigtails with
yellow-plastic-ball ties. I'm standing in profile:
two skinny girls on either side of me.

My s-shaped body, clearly not made for ballet,
points belly forward and butt back.
They sent me because I was pigeon-toed.

Two weeks later I will break my left ulna
while doing a round-off. My teacher will keep me in class
in spite of a triple-sized arm. I never went to ballet class again.

I think of this photograph as Quanie sits in front of me, left arm hanging
useless at her side. Spiral fracture of the humerus
sustained in the course of punishment for a bad report card.

IT WAS SUMMER, with several felony DVS assistants on vacation. The bureau was having a particularly bad week. It was so bogged down with new cases and so short of staff that it had to ask for assistance from GJE to indict some of its jailed defendants within the allotted six days. My supervisor knew that when promotions came around, I was hoping to move to DVS and I was thrilled to be assigned this fairly simple sex crime. A black man in his forties or fifties had exposed himself to a teenager who lived in his building. The odds were that we weren't going to indict the case and would reduce it to a misdemeanor since the girl was not harmed, but we needed to do a thorough interview first.

I was in the middle of interviewing the teenager when Rosemary Harlem, a senior assistant from DVS, came into my office along with a detective from the Bronx Special Victims Squad (BXSVS). They told me they needed to interview my witness. It seemed that the night after my teenager was flashed, an Hispanic woman who lived across the hall from my witness was raped by a black man fitting the description of my defendant, at least to the degree the woman could describe him. She could only give us the man's build and race because he had worn a mask and gloves. The woman begged her attacker, in her poor English, to wear a condom since she was pregnant. For whatever reason, the rapist had complied.

Rosemary and the detective told me that my defendant had several prior rape convictions, including one for raping the actress Kelly McGillis in her Brooklyn apartment in 1982. They also said that they had recovered a torn condom wrapper from inside the pregnant woman's apartment and a used condom outside the defendant's apartment. Whether or not he had actually raped Kelly McGillis, I could not tell from his rap sheet, but I could tell that he had been convicted of rape before and he seemed to have some experience with evidence collection because he shaved his pubic hair, wore a mask that covered his face and hair, and wore gloves in order to reduce the risk of leaving behind fingerprints or hair samples. It was odd, however, that he wasn't clever enough to properly dispose of the condom full of semen.

In April of 2000, shortly before I left the BXDA, the New York State DNA Databank became fully operational. The databank is part of a national system called CODIS, which is a searchable software program. In New York State alone there are eight DNA laboratories. All of these laboratories maintain a forensic index which is comprised of DNA profiles from crime scene evidence. These profiles are routinely inter-compared in order to identify and link criminal incidents that may involve the same perpetrator. Offenders convicted of certain qualifying offenses must provide a DNA sample for inclusion in the databank. The list of designated offenses currently includes violent felonies, sex crimes, felony crimes of terrorism, and felony hate crimes. Any offender convicted in a New York State court who is required to register as a sex offender must also provide a DNA sample for inclusion in the databank. DNA has been much in the news lately not only as a powerful tool for law enforcement, but also as a means of exonerating the falsely accused. At the time this case came in, however, there was no such thing as the DNA databank. We could not take the DNA sample from the condom and compare it to anything in the database to see if we could match it to a known sex offender or to our suspect. So the Special Victims Squad detective had to determine the truth by more traditional methods.

The detective purchased a condom that was the same brand as the one found in the hallway. He tore the wrapper the same way as the one he found in the hallway, unrolled the condom and, dipping his fingers in print powder, put prints on the surface of the rubber. He placed the two items in an evidence bag, sealed them, and left them on top of the desk and in plain view in the interview room. The suspect, who was still in jail on my case, had not yet been arrested on this new charge and, therefore, could be questioned about it. The detective brought him into the interview room and sat the defendant across the desk, speaking without acknowledging the "evidence," and questioned my defendant about the rape of the pregnant woman. Although the man repeatedly denied knowing the Hispanic woman or anything about the crime, his eyes kept gravitating toward the bag. Eventually, when questioning alone got the detective nowhere, the detective pushed the bag toward his man. "You wore gloves when you went into that apartment, but you weren't wearing gloves when you took the condom off!" he yelled. Believing that the fingerprints on the condom were his own, the man finally admitted to having sex with the Hispanic woman, claiming they were having an affair and that he only denied it so his wife wouldn't find out. But his admission of sex, coupled with the woman's accusation of rape (plus the fact that he spoke no Spanish and would have been hard-pressed to communicate with this female he was having an "affair" with) were enough to arrest and indict him. He eventually pled guilty to both my indecent exposure case and the rape. And, given his prior convictions, he will be in jail for a very long time.

I spent a year in the Grand Jury Evaluations Bureau indicting case after case after case but finally, when promotions came around, I got the news that I would be going to DVS. I was finally getting my wish.

BECAUSE I HAD the year of misdemeanor trial work and a year of Grand Jury under my belt when I got to DVS, I came as a felony assistant who was expected to know what I was doing. Nothing could have been further from the truth.

If a person is accepted into DVS at the outset, he or she goes through in-bureau training. Things no one else deals with become a part of daily vocabulary in DVS, so the training is a little different from what the Criminal Court assistants got. I walked by one new class that was sitting through such a training session and heard the supervisor saying, "Okay, everyone, on the count of three; one, two, three, PENIS! One, two, three, VAGINA!" Such an indoctrination is necessary because DVS cases require a witness to be very specific about the crime. It isn't sufficient in a rape case for someone to testify, "He had intercourse with me." She has to say "He put his penis in my vagina." For obvious reasons, not everyone is comfortable having such a blunt discussion, let alone with a stranger, adult, or child. In a way, therefore, the DVS assistants have to go through lack-of-sensitivity training to learn how to stop beating around the sexual bush and just tell it like it is.

The work of misdemeanor assistants in DVS is substantively and cumulatively daunting. When I came to understand the fundamental difference in this caseload versus the caseload of the Criminal Court assistants, I was glad to have been passed over those first two years. Like Criminal Court assistants, DVS misdemeanor assistants handle over a hundred cases each. And while I believe that DVS was the best place to be a felony assistant, it was the worst place to be handling misdemeanor crimes. The bulk of the hundred or so cases handled by Criminal Court assistants don't have any victim and can be easily disposed of. The victim is society at large and the prosecutor alone is entrusted with deciding what punishment fits a crime like a fare-beat or a drug buy or getting caught smoking crack on a stoop. When there is no victim, there is no one to consult before an offer is made to the defendant. In DVS, on the other hand, 100 percent of the cases involve a victim. This means keeping in touch with hundreds of people, discussing offers, and often dealing with reluctant victims, which is some of the most trying work in the bureau.

Obviously, misdemeanor DVS assistants, while phenomenally overburdened, also receive a tremendous amount of experience by the time they are promoted to felony assistants. I, having spent my initial term elsewhere in the office, did not have the benefit of such DVS-specific experience. I did have the advantage of already knowing how to indict a case. DVS assistants indict their own cases once they are promoted to felony assistants, so most spend about two years just prosecuting misdemeanors. When they are promoted, they then have to learn how to present a case in the Grand Jury.

But that part is easy to learn and I did not have the benefit of all of that other valuable and specific knowledge that my colleagues who started in DVS had. New DVS lawyers learn what questions to ask children to determine if they can be sworn in and how to run AP10, the court that handles misdemeanor DVS cases. They learn in detail about the sections of the penal law typically charged in the bureau. They are taught about the Administration for Children's Services (ACS), an agency that investigates reports of abuse and neglect and, as a result, has close contact with DVS. They are also counseled to work closely with crime victim's services to help victims get counseling, have their locks changed, and be admitted to shelters. They receive training on battered women's syndrome, child sexual abuse syndrome, post-traumatic stress disorder, Munchausen by proxy, pedophelia, hebephelia, and the like. They are given information about the Montefiore Child Protection Center and the other child advocacy centers at hospitals throughout The Bronx where DVS refers children for medical examinations. These centers, in turn, refer to DVS youngsters they suspect have been abused. Throughout the remainder of their careers, DVS assistants are continually sent to hear local and national lectures to further their education in relevant areas. They are taught how to interview child and adult victims of sex crimes. They are taught anatomy relevant to the rape. They are warned not to talk about the cases in the elevator because their discussions will make other people uncomfortable.

When I came to the office in 1995, there were between five and eight misdemeanor DVS assistants and maybe 20 assistants in the entire bureau. By the time I left in 2000, those numbers had doubled. Increased reporting of sex crimes and domestic violence as well as expansion of our office's definition of what constitutes "domestic" violence were responsible for the additions. The expansion of the bureau is reflective of a nationwide trend to treat domestic violence and sex crimes more seriously as well as treating the definition of a "relationship" more broadly. When I started in the office, DVS pretty much only took cases that either involved sex crimes or crimes between people living together or married. Domestic violence was primarily only between people who were legally married. By the time I left, DVS handled crimes where couples were of the same or different sex, still living together or having once lived together, or where there was a child in common even if the people never cohabitated. They also handled all cases where the parties were related by consanguinity. In 2003, the load finally got too large and DVS was split into two bureaus. The Child Abuse/Sex Crimes Bureau (CAS) prosecutes all sexual assault cases involving both child and adult victims, as well as all misdemeanor and felony physical abuse involving child victims under the age of 17. The Domestic Violence Bureau (DV) prosecutes felonies and misdemeanors involving family violence by one family member against another where these members are adults.

Even though I came to DVS as a felony assistant (or "lateral") and my experience was somewhat different from the majority of my colleague's, and in spite of the fact that I received none of their training and lacked their experience, I was still supposed to know what I was doing. Criminal Court and Grand Jury prepared me for many things, but it did not prepare me for the first challenge I would face as a DVS assistant.

THE FIRST CASE assigned to me as a DVS assistant involved a girl named May, an eight-year-old from Guyana who was sexually abused by a Guyanese male tenant who rented a room in her mother's home. The man denied touching the girl. I began my case by speaking with the mother, who immediately and aggressively informed me that the child was lying and I must drop the charges. While I was off to a bad start with the mother, I could not have bungled things with the child much worse than I did.

CONTRARY TO WHAT common sense dictates, there is rarely medical proof of the sexual abuse a child alleges. One would think that since children are small and their attackers are big, there is likely to be more damage than in an adult, but often the opposite is true. In prepubescent females, the hymen is extremely elastic. It tends to stretch rather than break, often leaving no tears or lacerations as evidence of penetration. The hymen does not thicken or "estrogenize" until puberty. So many times there is no evidence of penetration of young female victims. The rectum is also an elastic muscle and often does not show signs of penetration. Even when the rectum is somewhat stretched from penetration, the elasticity returns within days. Therefore if a child is penetrated rectally and does not speak about it immediately, the muscle will often have returned to normal by the time that child is examined.

Additionally, most pedophiles don't want to be caught and therefore avoid physically harming a child. They are often not violent in the traditional sense; i.e., they are not seeking to physically harm the child. Most pedophiles want an ongoing relationship and are often as gentle as possible to avoid scaring the child away. They also bribe their victims with gifts and treats in order to persuade the child not to tell anyone about the abuse. The scariest thing about dealing with pedophiles is that they turn out to be the last person you would expect. They gain access to children by winning over both their victims and the parents. They are often the people everyone believed to be the "nicest person," who "just loved kids." It makes sense when you think about it. Why would you leave your child with someone you didn't trust? Also, for obvious reasons, there are usually no eyewitnesses to sexual crimes against children. So, with no medical corroboration and no witnesses, we were taught how to best determine if a child was being truthful in the absence of that corroboration. We had to get as many details as possible from the young victim, the theory being that a child cannot know certain things about sex unless he or she experienced it.

Since defense attorneys don't want to attack children on the witness stand, mostly because it would make them look bad in front of the jury, a common theme is to claim that an adult had the child make up the story, coaching him or her on what to say. Although this happens, it does not happen frequently and is usually pretty simple to figure out because a child won't be able to give details about something they haven't experienced. Additionally, children are not as easy to manipulate as most people assume. Few children will say that something terrible and embarrassing happened to them unless it really did. And even if they can be convinced to tell such a lie, the lie is usually transparent. This is why we would get details about such things as position, taste, texture, and appearance—to discover if a child was really abused and to disprove any claim that he or she was coached into lying. If a child was coached, he or she could not know all these details because the child would be too young to retain all the information, and because it is difficult for anyone, especially a child, to sustain a story about something that was not experienced by him or her.

An adult might know how to coach a boy into claiming that he was forced to perform oral sex and say, "White stuff came out," but that boy was not likely to describe the taste or texture of ejaculate with any accuracy. A young person could not review the details of the position he was in while the abuse occurred, making sure it was feasible. An adult might tell a kid to say he was bent over a chair, but I would ask, "Where was he?"—(meaning the perpetrator)—What kind of chair? Where was the chair? What position was he in?" A four-foot tall child would have to be able to explain in detail how a six-foot tall man was able to do what was being alleged.

A perfect example is that of a boy named John, a seven-year-old I interviewed toward the end of my career at DVS. John claimed that his aunt's boyfriend sodomized him in the bathtub. The story was very basic and full of inconsistencies. I was pretty sure that John was making this up. When he was five, John had been sexually abused by his uncle's friend. In that case, John truly had been abused. The defendant confessed and was still in jail at the time that I met John. Even with this prior sexual experience and some age-inappropriate knowledge because of it, it was clear from what John told me that the boy wasn't being truthful. He was confused about his new story, describing physical positions that were impossible. When I confronted him about the impossibility of what he described, he changed his claim about how he was positioned, or how the aunt's boyfriend was trying to make the sodomy work. Nevertheless, while John continued to be inconsistent in his description of the events, he refused to admit he was lying.

John seemed like a good boy. He was a chubby child with a sweet disposition and a good and well-developed sense of humor. Although he was clearly scarred by his earlier abuse and remembered it well, as was apparent from his current claim, I could tell that he received love and support in his home. It did not seem likely that his lies were purely malicious. But he was lying for some reason. Just like adults, children don't lie without a motive. That motive can be simple or complicated. The key to getting John to admit that he had fabricated this claim of abuse was finding out what John's motive might be to accuse this man of sexually abusing him.

I brought the child's aunt, the girlfriend of the defendant, to my office to talk to her about the allegations and to find out a little more about the defendant. It turned out that John's aunt was his favorite person on earth. She and the boy were very close and John often spent time with her and, consequently, with her boyfriend. As we continued to talk, the aunt confessed to me that while she did not believe her boyfriend sexually molested John, she was a battered woman. John had seen the defendant beat his aunt on more than one occasion and it was very upsetting to the child. It became clear that John was lying to try to protect his aunt.

We brought John into the room and seated him in one of the chairs. His aunt kneeled down on the floor next to him so that they were eye to eye. She told him she knew that he loved her and wanted to protect her, but that lying was not the way to do it. I promised John that if he would tell me the truth, his aunt and I would work together to find some other way to make sure that she wasn't hurt again, but that telling a lie like this was not the right way to help her. John began to cry and said that he didn't want his aunt to be hurt anymore. He knew from his prior experience that this sort of tale would make his aunt's abuser go to jail and he just wanted to protect her. It was the most forgivable lie a witness ever told.

John's case is a perfect example of how difficult it is for children to tell a convincing lie. With perseverance and attention to detail, we could usually figure out they were doing so before a case ever got to a jury. With little physical evidence and no eyewitnesses in most cases, interviews with these children were crucial.

But, in contrast to how experienced I was when I interviewed John, when I met that little girl named May, during my first case in DVS, I had no experience with children or with sex crimes. I did not know what to ask her or even where to start. I brought May into my office and then made the huge error of trying to jump right into the accusation and get her to talk about what happened to her. Naturally, she clammed right up. A child like May may not completely understand what is going on when she is sexually abused, but she still has some sense of right and wrong. Children know that sex is "bad" and if they are sexually abused, they know that something wrong has happened. But often they believe they are somehow responsible for what happened to them. In fact, often the defendant convinces them it is their fault and tells them they will get in trouble if they tell anyone. Therefore, they are very reluctant to speak about abuse, thinking they will be punished if they reveal the truth. In May's case, aside from whatever the defendant told her, May's mother was calling her a liar and telling her that she was bad. It was going to be especially difficult to get May to talk. By approaching the girl so aggressively, I had only succeeded in making her totally withdraw. I did what any intelligent person in my situation would do. I ran to get help.

Mary Clark-DiRusso is the kind of senior assistant everyone dreams of. She was the head of the unit that investigated crimes against children reported directly to us by schools and hospitals (rather than to the police). She had been working with kids for years, her door was always open, and she had the patience of a saint. Mary came to my rescue armed with a box of crayons and a roll of stickers. (I made a purchase of my own that afternoon.) I learned more about how to talk to a kid from watching her for 10 minutes than any amount of lecturing could possibly have taught me.

Mary began by talking to May about benign things, like where she went to school, who was her favorite teacher, and which was her favorite color in the entire box of 100 Crayola Crayons. In short, Mary started getting May to talk, play, and laugh. To just be a kid. She waited until May was comfortable to broach the topic of the accusations. She did not lead the child, but asked open-ended questions without implying answers. She promised that May would not get into trouble and asked, "Do you know why you are here, May?"

As the interview proceeded, Mary assessed this little girl's credibility by asking her for extreme and minute details. Even though I wanted to be in DVS and thought I knew what I was getting myself into, I was not prepared at all for what it was really like. I was horrified. To hear an eight-year-old talk about the taste and texture of semen is an experience I am at a loss to describe and one that did not get easier with time. In fact, it only got harder for me. But I understood immediately that no amount of coaching would have given this child the information she had. There was also no motive for her to lie and no adult available to have coached her, besides a mother who didn't believe her. It was very clear that May was talking about something that had really happened.

Unfortunately, there was nothing I could do to convince her mother that May was really abused. I went through everything with May's mother—the detail of her knowledge, the scenarios that she described. But May's mother continued to insist that the girl was lying. She said that the girl was possessed by demons and that she was sending her to Guyana to see the witch doctor who would exorcise the demons from her. Finally, I had to put the child before a Grand Jury without her mother's permission. The Grand Jury indicted the case within seconds. A week later the mother shipped May back to Guyana.

THERE WAS A hypothetical question that was posed to me at each of the four DA's offices that I interviewed with when I was coming out of law school. The line of questioning went something like this: "What if you are starting trial in the morning on a case with just one witness. Without that witness, you have no case. The morning of the trial, you get a call that your witness died. When you go into court that morning, and before you have a chance to tell the court that your witness is dead, the defense attorney tells you that his guy wants to plead guilty. What do you do?"

They tell you there is no right or wrong answer but the right answer is that you let the guy plead guilty. Legally, you have no obligation to tell the defense attorney you cannot go forward with the case. Morally, you justify your behavior by believing that the guy must be guilty, otherwise he wouldn't take a guilty plea. So you refrain from mentioning that your witness is dead. When I answered this question during my interviews in 1994, I said that I would not tell the defense attorney because that is what I thought they wanted me to say. In truth, I did not think that I could really do it. I thought that it was unethical or immoral and that my conscience wouldn't allow it. I worried, "What if the guy is not guilty and is only taking the plea to avoid the risk of higher sentence after conviction at trial?"

It turns out that I had no qualms when faced with this scenario in May's case. Several months after the case was indicted, the defense attorney asked me for a plea offer. He never asked me if the girl was available to testify and I never volunteered that she was in Guyana and I did not know if I could get her back. I knew more about the case than a jury would ever be allowed to hear and I had no doubt about the defendant's guilt. I took the plea without remorse. The defendant served his time in the New York prisons and was then deported to Guyana. I only can hope that May never saw him again.

I ENCOUNTERED MANY parents in my three years in DVS who either didn't believe their children or who put the abuser ahead of their child in spite of what he or she had done. The reasons varied. Often the person who hurt a child was a relative, a sibling, or boyfriend. Sometimes it was simply easier to believe that what had occurred could not be possible.

Sometimes, there were cultural matters that interfered with the prosecution. Shortly after I handled May's case, I was assigned a case with an Ethiopian girl who was raped by a family friend. She was only 14 years old. Initially, the parents were anxious to prosecute their daughter's rapist but when the case landed on my desk just three days later, the parents informed me that they wanted to drop charges. I explained that this was a statutory rape case and that we would prosecute regardless of whether they wanted to or not. I steeled myself for another set of parents who thought their girl was a liar. Instead, the parents calmly explained to me that the rape was no longer a crime. It seemed that in the village they were from, rape was not a crime if the rapist offered to marry the victim. In their culture, the damage to the girl's value due to the loss of her virginity was repaired by the offer of marriage. So what would normally be a crime on the part of the man becomes a life sentence for his victim and he is considered to have righted the wrong. I did not mince words when I told the parents that this is not Ethiopia.

The decision to prosecute in the Ethiopian girl's case was easy, but sometimes the cultural difference led to more complicated issues. I was contacted by detectives regarding a statutory rape where the victim was a 14-year-old Mexican girl. She was about eight months pregnant and had just moved to the States with her parents and the baby's father. When neighbors reported to the police that a child had just moved into their building and was pregnant, they went to the apartment to investigate. It turned out that the father of the child was 21, but was legally married to the girl under Mexican law. The girl and her family all reported that the husband treated his young wife well. That he was a hard worker and a kind person. The being married part wasn't a crime, but the sex with a minor was, so the detectives called me for advice as to how to handle the matter. We refused to press any charges and had to settle with telling the husband that under US law, he couldn't have sex with his wife until she was old enough. It was implicit that we were telling him just to keep it behind closed doors and not get her pregnant again for a few years.

But sometimes the push-back from parents to not prosecute went to extremes. Jamal Darden's case was still pending when I left the office. He had sexually abused his seven- and twelve-year-old sisters. The seven-year-old had severe sores around her vagina, which turned out to be the result of a sexually transmitted disease. She described the abuse to the doctors when her mother took her to the hospital. She also revealed seeing the older sister attacked.

When Jamal was arrested, he made a full confession. He provided a detailed statement about what he had done, complete with approximate locations, times, and dates. He accused the seven-year-old of having seduced him, not an uncommon claim or belief among pedophiles. The older girl admitted that she had also been abused by her brother. She was HIV positive and her hymen was torn (a condition consistent with penetration). She was pregnant with another man's child and we believed that Jamal, who was also HIV positive, had transmitted the disease to her but, fortunately, not to the seven-year-old. The older sister ran away from home before we were able to put her in the Grand Jury.

By the next court date, the mother had lost custody of both girls because she refused to believe that Jamal had abused them in spite of his own confession. Jamal was now claiming that the police forced the confession out of him. The mother reasoned that the seven year old must have gotten the sores off a public toilet and the older sister was promiscuous and got HIV from someone else. Denial is a powerful emotion. No amount of evidence or corroboration was going to convince Jamal's mother that her son was guilty.

Often, refusal to admit that there is abuse in a home is coupled with other problems. I had a case with three children who were being severely beaten by their father. The mother was a battered woman. When the school finally reported the abuse to the police, the mother refused to speak to the authorities. Initially, the children also denied their father's beatings in spite of the obvious cuts and bruises. Eventually, the youngest child, an 11-year-old, confessed that the abuse had occurred, telling me that all of the children were afraid because the father threatened to kill the mother if his behavior became known. The mother refused numerous attempts on our part to help her. Eventually the children were removed from the home and placed in foster care. Even faced with losing her children, this woman stayed with her abuser.

A famous example of this is the Heda Nussbaum/Joel Steinberg case. Heda had suffered intolerable beatings at the hands of her husband, yet she was no more able to protect herself and leave him than she was to protect her daughter. The story only came to light when the little girl died.

There are degrees of abuse and often, as prosecutors, we came into conflict about where to draw the line. A prosecutor wields a tremendous amount of power. She has discretion that can vary a considerable degree in matters of sentencing and punishment. The decision often rests with the prosecuting attorney alone—who may be as young as 24 years old and never have held a prior job—as to whether someone deserved to go to jail or just needed to attend some corrective classes.

For example, I had a case in which three children were beaten with a belt by their stepfather, leaving buckle-shaped marks all over their bodies. The bruises were bad enough that the school reported them to our office. However, the children and the mother described the defendant as a very loving parent who never abused narcotics or alcohol and only hit his kids when they misbehaved. They also said that he had been disciplined this way as a child. The defense, of course, was that this was appropriate corporal punishment. I felt that it crossed the line and that although the man perhaps didn't deserve to go to jail, he certainly needed to learn parenting skills. Ultimately, in exchange for voluntarily attending such classes, he received neither jail time nor a criminal record. Hopefully a good man was allowed to stay with his family, be a better parent, and justice prevailed.

A judge's sentencing power is very different from a prosecutor's. If a person pleads guilty to the most serious crime with which he or she is charged, or a person is found guilty after trial, the judge can sentence that defendant within state-mandated guidelines. In other words, there is a legal maximum and minimum that a judge can hand out based on the crime for which a person has either been convicted or to which he pled guilty. In this scenario, the prosecutor can make a recommendation, the victims and their families can appeal to the court for a specific sentence, but it is totally up to the judge to decide what the appropriate sentence is within the statutory limits. But only the prosecutor can agree to a "plea bargain," which is basically an agreement between the prosecutor and the defendant that if the defendant pleads guilty to a lesser charge, he will get an agreed-upon sentence that is less than he might get for the highest crime with which he is charged. The judge must agree to accept the plea bargain, but a judge alone cannot reduce the level of the crime without the consent of the prosecutor.

The purpose of plea-bargaining is manifold. For a defendant, it guarantees a specific punishment and avoids the gamble that a conviction could earn greater punishment. So a person will often weigh the strength of the "People's case" and the potential punishment in considering the "People's offer." An example would be a death penalty case where the prosecutor agreed that the defendant would not face death if he pled guilty. If the defendant went to trial, the possibility of dying would be left in the hands of a jury. For a prosecutor, a plea bargain guarantees that a defendant will be assured punishment with the conviction noted on his rap sheet. Even with a seemingly strong case, there are no guarantees of conviction at trial—especially in The Bronx.

In child abuse and sex crime cases, there are strong additional factors in favor of a plea bargain. In a sex crime, the victim is spared the ordeal of having to publicly recount an embarrassing and traumatic experience. It also spares her from having to face her attacker in court or having to deal with all of the accusations that come with cross-examination. In child abuse cases, there are similar factors, along with the additional emotional trauma testifying can cause a minor. There is also the difficulty of obtaining a conviction for sex crimes and crimes against children. It can be difficult for people to understand the lack of corroborative evidence in such cases. Also, conviction rates vary from county to county, and from state to state. In The Bronx, unfortunately, the low conviction rate often forces prosecutors to provide a low plea offer that is both unfair to the victim and unjust punishment for the crime, but better than nothing.

QUANIE HARRIS'S WAS the second case I handled in the DVS Bureau and she remains one of the children who weighs heaviest on my heart. Quanie's mother—we'll call her Mrs. Harris—brought Quanie to the hospital claiming that Quanie fell off the bed and broke her arm. An X ray revealed that the fracture to Quanie's arm was a "spiral" or "torque" fracture. A spiral fracture appears just as it sounds, and its unique form is the result of a twist injury. Since such fractures can occur in nature, especially with children, it is usually not the injury itself that signals abuse but an explanation offered for the injury which is not consistent with the injury. At that point, the question is why someone would lie about the cause of the injury if there is no foul play.

It was almost impossible that Quanie would have sustained a spiral fracture to her ulna from falling off a bed, especially as Mrs. Harris described. When hospital personnel confronted Mrs. Harris with this fact, she then claimed that it happened when Quanie brought home a bad report card and was twisting away from her mother's grasp, also an unlikely way for the injury to have occurred since a child wouldn't twist her own arm to the breaking point. We ran a check on Mrs. Harris with the Administration for Children's Services and found out that Quanie had already been removed from the home twice due to abuse. The second time, Mrs. Harris simply brought Quanie to the hospital, shoved her at the social worker, and said, "Take this child before I hurt her again." Quanie was returned to her mother after the mother successfully completed voluntary parenting skills courses. She married a man who was not Quanie's father and they had a son together who was about a month old when I met Quanie.

The first time that I spoke to Quanie, it was immediately clear that she was an extremely intelligent child. Although she was standoffish at first, her kind nature surfaced once she got comfortable with me. At first, Quanie adamantly denied that her mother had abused her. Having clearly been rehearsed, she claimed that she was being bad and jumping up and down on the bed when she fell and broke her arm. This was the first story that the mother told the hospital. Mrs. Harris obviously had no time to prepare Quanie with a new story before she was arrested at the hospital. I confronted Quanie with the fact that her mother admitted to having "accidentally" twisted her arm. Quanie continued to deny this for about an hour.

We stopped talking about the case and played for a while. I let Quanie use my computer and we drew with crayons together. I was probably the first person who had paid any genuine attention to the child in months. The cautious child disappeared during that time and was replaced by a clever, sweet, and normal child. I won Quanie's trust. She brought the case up again on her own, but she told me that the stepfather, not the mother, had twisted her arm when he found out about the report card. I still thought Quanie was trying to protect her mother but, nonetheless, I followed up on her new claim. I ran the stepfather's name to determine if he had a criminal history and found out that he was on probation for robbery. If he committed another crime, it would be a violation of his probation and he would likely go back to jail. Conviction on a new felony would also result in a longer sentence since it would make him a second felony offender. It was very possible given this new set of facts that Mrs. Harris, who had an ACS history but no criminal history, was taking the rap for her husband. Since this was her first offense, the likelihood of her being sent to jail was slim to none.

I spoke with Mrs. Harris's attorney and I explained the situation to him. I told him that between the medical records and the mother's "confession," I had more than enough evidence to indict her. On the other hand, if she was willing to talk to me and tell me what really happened, I told her attorney I would consider dropping the charges against her. We agreed that I would give her what we called "Queen for a Day."

She would come to my office with her attorney and tell me the whole story. Anything that she told me during this one session that was self-incriminating could not be used against her. After this meeting, all bets were off and I could prosecute her with any other information that I had or that I subsequently gained.

Mrs. Harris was one of the most arrogant women I had ever met. She was on welfare and had never worked a day in her life but her intelligence, or shrewdness, was apparent and biting. I began by telling her that she had a brilliant child who had a chance to succeed in this world with proper upbringing. Mrs. Harris replied, "Where do you think she got it?" I stared at this woman, trying to size her up.

"Well, she certainly lacks your charm," I said. I laid out my theory on the table for Mrs. Harris and explained to her the various possible roads we would go down depending on what she told me.

Mrs. Harris admitted to taking the rap for her husband to avoid his probation being violated. However, Mrs. Harris's concern was not with Quanie at all. It was with the custody of her son, which she had also lost when Quanie's arm was broken. It was immediately clear that she would put on whatever display of good parenting and concern she had to in order to get her son back but that she couldn't care less about her daughter. I knew that if Quanie ended up back in her mother's home, she would continue to suffer—and suffer worse, for having been the cause of her brother's removal. We dropped the charges against Mrs. Harris and the stepfather was arrested. Before the mother could convince Quanie to stop talking to me, I presented the case to the Grand Jury. The Grand Jury indicted.

A few months later, I called Quanie's foster parents and had them bring Quanie back to my office. I had not seen Quanie since the Grand Jury presentation. Although we were several months from going to trial, I was concerned that if Quanie forgot me, I would lose her trust. I was right. In the several months since I had last seen her, Quanie's mother was working her poison twice a week during visitation sessions, telling Quanie that if she told me the truth she would never come home again. That Daddy would go to jail and that Mommy would never see her again. That she and her little brother would be separated and never see each other again. Quanie recanted her story and told me that she only said the stepfather twisted her arm because she was mad at him. It took me hours and several visits to persuade her that what her mother said was not true and to convince her that helping me was the only way that she would not get hurt again.

It was a constant uphill battle and try as I might, Mrs. Harris did not lose her visitation rights because Quanie begged to see her each time the family court judge threatened to take them away. Quanie would even try to bribe me by saying that she would not talk unless I let her continue to see her mother. By the time I brought Quanie in to prepare her for trial, she was lost. The last glimmers of the amazing child I had met a year earlier were totally gone. She was replaced by an angry, bitter, violent girl with no trust for anyone or anything.

When the foster parents first arrived at my office for Quanie's last visit so that I could prepare Quanie for trial, I saw that Quanie's little brother had a black eye. My knee-jerk reaction was to think that the foster parents were abusing him. I asked Quanie first, in private, what had happened to her brother. The familiar lie rolled right off her tongue when she told me that he fell off the bed. When I confronted the foster parents they told me that Quanie was the one who caused her brother's injury. I confirmed with ACS that it was not the first time Quanie had bruised or bloodied her brother and that they were going to have to remove Quanie to a home for disturbed children since the foster parents could not control her anymore. It was the first time I felt that I had truly lost a child. Worse yet, the parents got their way in spite of me. They would get their son and their daughter would remain in foster homes for the rest of her childhood.

Even in retrospect I don't know how I could have handled the situation better. I used to have nightmares that Quanie was living on the streets and telling me it was all my fault because I took her away from her mother. I still wonder if what I did was right or wrong and I don't think there is any way for me to know the answer. I do know for certain that had I left her in the home, the abuse would have continued and gotten worse. Then again, what if, as with my father, leaving her at home would have given her the strength to fight back and to be different. I hope that she finds that strength anyhow, but in my heart, I doubt it is possible.

5

THE LITTLE CHESTER'S SHOE STORE MASSACRE

Black Air-Jordans (size thirteen)

Five days before Christmas
five people died
when Michael Vernon
walked into Little Chester's Shoe Store
claiming to be driven by the voice of Simon
from "Alvin and the Chipmunks"
to "shoot 'em, shoot 'em"
for not having Black Air-Jordans in a size thirteen.

Only two bullets found
near the owner's wife
though she had three holes in her body.
Gun-powder stippling
on the back of her right hand
indicated she was shot at close range
and was covering her head
when she was killed execution-style.
The bullet's trajectory

showed it entered her skull at the base,
angled upward splitting her palate,
blew out her two front teeth,
exiting through her upper lip,

One of two brothers killed
was wearing a toy called a "Yack-Back,"
which recorded for fifteen seconds
the moment he was shot.
In sing-song (sounding like a chipmunk)
he can be heard saying: "Please don't hurt me,"
then a bang, then static.
Shot through the front of the head
he slumped off a stool
and onto his mother's legs.

Crime scene footage shows
her nails were perfectly manicured that morning.
The deep enamel is smooth and chip-less
with no smudges on her cuticles
and with little gold flecks
that would iridesce if she could
turn her hand in the camera's light.

IT IS DECEMBER 19, 1995. It's snowing heavily outside, and the streets are filled with holiday shoppers. Little Chester's Shoe Store, at 2186 White Plains Road in The Bronx, is crowded. It's a tiny store full of racks and boxes of shoes—mostly expensive sneakers. Inside the store is Choon Bae, the owner. His wife, Kyong Bae, is behind the cash register gossiping with her friend, Janet Ham. Juan Dones, a 30-year-old father of two, is working in the store and Jae Moon Chae is buying a large supply of sneakers to re-sell at flea markets for a small markup. Maria Carrasquillo is with her 12- and 14-year-old sons, Rafael and Ricardo, buying them Christmas gifts. Her teenage daughter is at a friend's house watching TV. She did not know that when she watched the six o'clock news later that night, she would find out that her whole family had been killed.

Henry Lucero Inca and his cousin Gonzalo Saed Galvez, two immigrants from Peru, are also shopping that morning. Two doors down, in the Twin Dragon Restaurant, three plainclothes police officers are eating their lunch. Police Officer Leonel Quinones, from the NYPD Highway Patrol, is driving down the block in his marked patrol car. He is wide-faced and sweet-looking in spite of his Gestapo-like uniform with high-lacing boots and pants that flare out at the thighs. PO Felix Vasquez is off-duty and is a block away, Christmas shopping with his wife. In the habit of most Bronx cops, his personal sidearm is shoved in his waistband even though he is not working.

At about 11:45 AM, 22-year-old Michael Vernon, a tall, gaunt, black man with haunted eyes, walks into Little Chester's. In his pocket are a loaded 9-millimeter containing 16 rounds, matches, and a bottle of lighter fluid. There is a round ready in the chamber. Michael Vernon wants black Air Jordans in size 13½ and has repeatedly come into this little mom-and-pop store asking for them. Vernon walks into the store just as Janet Ham walks out. Janet hears gunshots as she exits the store and she runs down the block looking for help. She sees PO Quinones driving by in the squad car and frantically hails him, telling him about the black man who entered the store as she exited. Quinones races down the block, parking his squad car in front of Little Chester's and radioing for backup as the carnage commences inside.

The order of events is not clear to anyone that survived the massacre that day, but how each person is killed and the position where they fell are apparent to all at the crime scene. Michael Vernon walks up to the register. Kyong Bae is on her knees behind the counter with her hands behind her head—as if they could protect her. Vernon shoots at her from a few feet away, hitting her in the elbow. He then puts the gun inches from her hands, shooting her execution-style at point blank range. The gunpowder leaves a speckled burn as the bullet goes through her hand, then her skull, and exits through her right cheek. I picture her crouched behind that register, terrified, instinctively covering her head to protect herself when he shoots her.

He shoots Maria Carrasquillo in her back. The bullet goes in through her spine and exits through her mouth, crushing her larynx. Fourteen-year-old Ricardo is next. He is shot once in the right elbow as he tries to defend himself. The second bullet goes through his pulmonary artery, his lung, and his spine. The medical examiner will testify at trial that Ricardo was immediately paralyzed when the bullet hit his spine and then suffocated to death from the perforation of his lung.

Rafael is the last member of the Carrasquillo family to die. One bullet through the brain and he slumps on top of his mother on the floor. When I look at his crime scene photo a year later, I see a hole so small and so little blood that it is impossible for me to imagine that it could have killed him. His eyes are slightly open and shining under his long dark lashes as if he is just waking up from a nap. Around his neck is a toy called a "Yak-Bak" that records sound bites in a distorted voice. It is meant to be funny. It is somehow triggered just before he is killed and records in a sing-song voice the last words from his mouth- "Please don't hurt me," then a gunshot, then static.

Vernon shoots Henry Lucero Inca in the back. This single bullet perforates his spine, spinal cord, lung, heart, and liver, before exiting through his abdomen. He bleeds to death. Jae Moon Chae is shot in the upper chest and the leg. He survives his wounds, paralyzed on the right side. Juan Dones is shot in the back of the head. In a year, we'll bring him to court from the nursing home that he now lives in. He testifies at trial from his wheelchair—blind, deaf, and paralyzed.

By the time that Vernon has only one person left to shoot, PO Quinones is in position behind a blue Volvo that is parked in front of the store. He aims his shotgun over the top of the car and looks inside through the glass storefront of Little Chester's. He sees two males in the back of the store, a light-skinned male lying prone on the floor and a dark-skinned male on top of him, pointing a gun at his head. The light skinned male is Gonzalo Saed Galvez. Galvez looks toward the front of the store and locks eyes with Quinones. Galvez sees salvation. He jumps up and breaks for the door. Vernon calmly follows him out, shooting him twice. One bullet hits him in the back and the other bullet goes through his left arm. Galvez falls face down in the snow on the sidewalk in front of Quinones and rolls over on his back. Vernon stands over him and shoots him in the stomach. The snow is stained with blood. Now Vernon's attention turns toward the sweet-faced cop. Quinones is yelling at Vernon, "Police, don't move!" but Vernon continues toward him with his gun aimed, pulling and pulling the trigger. Quinones aims his rifle across the top of the Volvo and pulls his trigger. Nothing happens. He pulls again and again, but his weapon does not fire. In his panic, he forgot to take off the safety. Just as he realizes this, Vernon leans over the top of the car, points his gun right at Quinones's head, and pulls the trigger. Quinones hears the click, but feels nothing. The gun is empty. Vernon runs. Quinones shoots Vernon as he flees, hitting him in the left chest, the left buttock, the left side of his abdomen, and his right hand. Quinones is unharmed. Galvez, bleeding in the snow, miraculously survives his wounds but emotionally, he never recovers.

Hearing the gunshots, the plainclothes officers in the Twin Dragon Restaurant abandon their meal without thought and run out. They pull out the shields hanging on chains under their shirts to identify themselves as they give chase. At the same time, PO Vasquez sees Vernon coming around the corner with a gun in his hand and blood pouring down his leg. His training kicks in. He reacts. He pushes his wife into the vestibule of a bank and tells her, "Call 911!" Vernon is running down the sidewalk. Vasquez screams to all the last-minute Christmas shoppers, "Clear the area! Gun! Gun!" He gives chase down the middle of the street, keeping the cars parked along the curb between himself and the armed, bleeding man. A block and a half later, Vernon drops on the sidewalk from loss of blood.

THIS IS MY training ground. Before doing a felony trial of one's own, each ADA "second-seats" an experienced attorney at the office. Second-seating has different meanings depending upon the case and the lead prosecutor. For some it means basically being a gofer, staying up late nights doing research, and photocopying. For me it was literally trial by fire. By the time I resigned from the DA's office, William Flack, now my mentor and good friend, had been at the Bronx DA's office longer than any other trial assistant. He'd been through three district attorneys and, in fact, started at the office before District Attorney Robert Johnson was even an ADA. At age 49 when we tried the case, he was five years from retirement and Methuselah by our office standards. For most people, being a prosecutor is a stopover to get experience before moving on to higher-paying private or defense work. For Flack, it was a career. Bill was assigned the Vernon case on the day that the shooting occurred and he did not rest until he knew that Michael Vernon would be somewhere that he could never kill again. In the months that I worked with Bill Flack on the case of *People v. Michael Vernon*, I got to do more in a courtroom than most attorneys do in a lifetime.

October and November of 1997 were eventful months for me. I was still assigned to the Grand Jury Evaluations Bureau when I was told that I would be second-seating Bill about two months before the trial against Michael Vernon started. All of my pending Grand Jury cases were reassigned so I could devote my full attention to assisting Bill. We worked together on a daily basis preparing the case for hearings and trial. Two days after being told that I would second-seat Bill on the biggest case in The Bronx DA's office that year, I was told that I was finally accepted into DVS. I would start there as soon as the trial was over but, in the meanwhile, I would move to my new window office in the just-completed office building across from the Criminal Court. I was elated. I would be helping Bill most days of the week, and on my days off from working on the Vernon case I would ease my way into working for DVS. Everything finally seemed to be coming together.

ASIDE FROM THE amount of press a tragedy of this magnitude would normally receive, add the following morbid TV appeal: It was five days before Christmas. Along with everyone else he killed, Vernon had killed a mother and her two sons. Finally, this was the first potential death penalty case since the law had been reinstated in New York three months earlier. Although the district attorney announced early on that we would not be seeking the death penalty due to Vernon's history of mental illness, the potential put the case in the headlines nonstop for weeks after the slaughter took place. The press was all over the courtroom every day of the hearings and trial. There were sketch artists lined up all across the first rows of benches and there were police barricades outside the courtroom doors. The entire city was watching every mistake we made and every point we scored.

Michael Vernon's was not a straightforward murder case. His massacre was not motivated by drugs, love scorned, or money. Vernon was on his way to see his psychiatrist when he detoured into Little Chester's Shoe Store. He was a diagnosed paranoid schizophrenic and had been hospitalized in the past. Vernon had a history of auditory hallucinations and was supposed to be taking Haldol to suppress the symptoms. He was also supposed to be taking Cogentin to suppress the side effects of the Haldol: shaking, lethargy, and thirst. Like many schizophrenics, Vernon stopped taking his Haldol because he did not like the way it made him feel. He continued taking the Cogentin, not knowing that taken without the Haldol, it can exacerbate symptoms rather than suppress them. He was self-medicating with alcohol and marijuana. The prosecution would not have to prove that Vernon committed this mass murder: Vernon was going to admit to the shootings. What we had to prove was that Vernon understood what he was doing when he walked into Little Chester's that day and that he knew it was wrong. The defense, on the other hand, would seek to prove to the jury that, because of Vernon's mental illness, he was not responsible for his actions.

AFTER THE SHOOTING, Vernon and his victims were all brought to Jacobi Hospital. This never should have happened. Protocol is to take defendants who are injured to different hospitals than the victims to avoid any chance meetings. Nevertheless, due to the number of victims, dead and dying, and the fact that Jacobi is a Level I trauma center, all were brought to the same hospital. Important to our case and to introducing the statements that Vernon made at the hospital, the doctor who examined Vernon in the ER documented that Vernon was alert, oriented, and aware of what was going on around him when he was brought in. The doctor determined that Vernon was competent at the time of his admission to the hospital and had him sign a consent for surgery. In fact, the doctor's words at trial were that he found Vernon to "be very competent."

Vernon's injuries turned out to be little more than flesh wounds and he did not require much care beyond exploratory surgery and blood transfusions. While he was in the recovery room, Detective Kevin Tracy of the 49th Precinct detective squad took statements from Vernon. Detective Tracy is an imposing figure. He is a stocky, muscular man with a crew cut and barbed wire tattooed around his bicep. He is quiet and direct and his appearance belies his intelligence and crack detective work. I am certain that anyone who underestimated Tracy's intelligence based on his burliness regrets it.

At trial, Tracy was completely composed on the witness stand. He made constant eye contact with the jury and almost never referred to his notes. The courtroom sketch artist drew a picture of him the day he testified at the trial. It appeared on almost every news station that night—a stocky detective with massive forearms, the barbed wire literally projecting off his arm. Tracy told the jury that after being read his Miranda warnings and responding that he understood his rights, Vernon gave the following statement while he was at the hospital:

"Mr. Vernon, I'd like you to tell me about what happened today at the shoe store."

"I asked you have in my size, he say no. They only got it in twelve-and-a-half. Then I just like—just shot him in the head."

"And did you shoot anyone else?"

"Yes. I think like seven."

"And why did you shoot these other people?"

"They were witnesses."

"Had you ever been in the store before?"

"Yes. I think like five times. I wanted to buy my boots. I kept telling them, can you order them, could you order them."

"What did he say?"

"No, we can't order."

"Did you try another store?"

"I tried, you know. I have been trying mad stores, a lot of stores. I wasn't able to find them anywhere else. That's the only store."

"When he said he couldn't order them for you, did it make you angry?"
"Yeah."

"You went back there again today looking for the same boots?"
"Yes."

"And what happened when he told you he didn't have your size?"
"I shot him in the head."

"And why did you take the gun with you today?"

"I wanted my boots. I just wanted my boots."

"Today, when you left the house, did you take the nine-millimeter with you?"
"Yeah."

"Where did you get the gun?"

"Off the streets. I just got it like a week ago"

"And did you already have any other guns?"

"Yeah, another nine-millimeter."

"How come you just didn't bring that?"

"It could only take nine shots."

"How many shots did the new nine-millimeter take?"

"Sixteen."

"Did you load it?"

"Yes. Fifteen in the clip, one in the head."

"After you shot the 'like seven' people in the store, what did you do?"

"One got up and started running and I shot him. I ran out of the store then I started shooting outside because he was trying to run out of the store. Then I shot again. Then the police, they started shooting. I was running. I couldn't make it no more and I just dropped."

"Did any one of the people in the store have weapons at all that you saw?"

"I didn't give them a chance to. They probably did."

"But you didn't see anything and you didn't give anybody a chance to do anything. What did you do?"

"Started shooting."

"You opened fire on everybody in the store?"

"Yes."

"Did you notice if there were any kids in the store when you opened fire?"

"Yeh, it was one kid. He ran."

"When you ran out of the store, was there anybody in the store who had not been shot?"

"No. Everybody was on the floor. Nobody was standing anymore."

Tracy told the jury how later on that day, Vernon added that, "if he could do it all over again there was only one thing he would do differently, he would make sure he killed everybody." He was not even sure if he'd shot one or two kids.

The statements were key to the prosecution at trial because when Vernon was in the hospital, he did not blame the murder on hearing voices or any compulsion other than to get the sneakers he wanted. He said that he was feeling fine when the shooting occurred. It was not until the psychiatrists interviewed him several months later that he claimed that voices that sounded like "Alvin and the Chipmunks" were instructing him to "Shoot 'em. Shoot 'em" and that these voices were what compelled him to shoot and kill the victims of the Little Chester's Shoe Store Massacre.

THERE ARE TWO crucial steps to prosecuting a case with an insanity defense. The first is to prove that the defendant is fit to stand trial and the second is to prove that the defendant knew what he was doing at the time of the crime. If a defendant is claiming that he momentarily lost his sanity at the time of the crime only, then he will only be tested for mental fitness at the time of the crime since he is not claiming that he is not fit to stand trial. An example would be infanticide cases where women give birth alone in a room and then instantly kill their babies. They often claim not that they have a permanent mental disability or that they cannot assist in their own defense, but that they had a temporary illness or insanity just at the time the crime was committed.

In cases such as Vernon's, where the claim is ongoing impairment, the testing occurs in two phases. First, there is a test of current mental fitness to proceed to trial. This examination, called a "730.30 exam," seeks to determine if someone is able, at the time of the court case, to assist in his own defense. In the case of individuals with treatable mental illnesses, medication may make them cognizant and able to assist in their trial even if they were insane at the time of the crime. In situation's where someone will never obtain or regain competence, a different problem arises.

In my third year at the office, I inherited a case that was indicted some four years earlier. The defendant was a severely retarded adult male who was not able to function on his own and had lived in mental hospitals his entire life. He brutally raped one of his fellow consumers, as residents of mental facilities are sometimes called, who likewise was severely impaired. The defendant was indicted by the Grand Jury but, since he failed his 730.30 exam, the indictment remained in limbo until "such time as he became competent to assist in his own defense." This defendant never had been and never would be competent to stand trial so his indictment could have remained in perpetual limbo. In response to such circumstances, the United States Supreme Court, in a case called *Jackson v. Indiana*, said that such a circumstance violated due process and that if the defendant could never become competent, he must either be civilly committed or released from criminal custody. "Due process," they said, "requires that nature and duration of commitment bear some reasonable relation to the purpose of commitment."

In my case, the state, on behalf of the mental health facility, brought a *Jackson* hearing, as is their right, claiming that the defendant would never regain competence and should be "Jacksoned-out," or returned to civil commitment. This would give the mental health facility the ability to move the defendant to a facility outside the city or to put him in a lower-security facility. Jacksoning people out is a petrifying proposition in the case of someone who is mentally ill and dangerous. It leaves discretion to our overburdened mental health system to determine whether someone should remain in a mental health facility or what the level of security should be. The defendant in this rape case had been receiving counseling as a result of the rape and was able to parrot the phrase "no means no," but it was clear that it did not mean anything to him. When the judge questioned the defendant about the rape and what it means to have forcible versus consensual sex, the defendant could not comprehend what the judge was saying nor could he formulate an answer except to parrot "no means no" every time he heard the trigger word, "rape." Nevertheless, the judge held that this repetition of "no means no" was enough grounds to refuse to "Jackson the defendant out" and the defendant was kept in criminal custody. I do not for a second think that the judge really believed that this defendant would ever be competent but it was enough, at least, to give him an excuse to keep the defendant in a high-security criminal facility until the state's next opportunity for a *Jackson* hearing came up again in a couple of years and, by then, it would most likely be some other judge's decision.

In Vernon's case, if he was found not fit to proceed at the 730.30 exam, Vernon could potentially be on the streets again whenever the state saw fit. Although keeping someone institutionalized without a trial is fundamentally unfair, in cases like Vernon's, what else can be done? And while it was unlikely that Vernon would ever have been freed from the institution given the magnitude of his crimes, we have all heard the horror stories about the mentally ill pushing people onto subway tracks just a few weeks after being released from a facility. Vernon had been institutionalized and released at least twice before he committed this mass murder. He would decompensate, go to a facility, and as soon as the medications stabilized him, he would be released again. We also found out that Vernon had killed at least one other person before Little Chester's, possibly more. We just had not known it until he confessed to it this time around. My fears were allayed when Vernon passed the 730.30 exam and was deemed fit to proceed to trial.

Once someone is found fit to stand trial, the second phase of inquiry in New York State is to determine someone's mental state at the time that the crime was committed. This is called the "McNaughton Test." It asks if the defendant, at the time of the commission of the crime, understood the nature and consequences of his actions and knew that they were wrong. For example, if a defendant shoots someone to death and understands that guns can kill, then he understands the nature and consequences of his actions. If, however, he believes that the killing was commanded by God and was necessary to save the world, then he does not understand that his actions were wrong and is, therefore, not responsible for his actions under New York law.

The McNaughton rule developed when Englishman Daniel McNaughton killed the secretary to the British Prime Minister. He claimed to believe that the Prime Minister was conspiring against him and was acquitted "by reason of insanity." McNaughton's sentence to life in a mental institution led to a public outcry which prompted Queen Victoria to order the courts to develop a stricter test for insanity.

The McNaughton rule became the standard for insanity in the United States and the United Kingdom, and is still the standard for insanity in almost half of the states in the U.S. The rule states that there is a presumption of sanity unless the defense is able to prove that "at the time of committing the act, the accused was laboring under such a defect of reason, from disease of the mind, as not to know the nature and quality of the act he was doing or, if he did know it, that he did not know what he was doing was wrong.

In cases where there is a psychiatric defense, the general practice is that both the prosecution and the defense have doctors examine the defendant prior to trial. If doctors for both sides agree that the defendant is not responsible under either or both parts of the McNaughton Test, then the defendant cannot be prosecuted. However, if the parties do not agree, then the case proceeds to trail. This is what happened in Vernon's case. While the defense psychiatrist concluded that Vernon did not understand the nature and consequences of his actions, our psychiatrist said that he did. We took the case before the jury to decide. If we failed to prove at trial that Vernon knew what he was doing that day in Little Chester's, we would be right back where we started, leaving him to the discretion of the mental health system, which had already failed him and his many victims.

Michael Vernon's trial occurred in three basic steps. First, we had to prove a prima facie case against Vernon, i.e., we had to make out the elements of the crimes and establish his identity as the perpetrator of those crimes. You may have heard this referred to as "burden of proof." It is the prosecution's job to prove a case beyond a reasonable doubt no matter what the defense.

In a psychiatric defense case, such as Vernon's, after the people have presented the facts that they believe prove the case beyond a reasonable doubt, the defense can then put up an affirmative defense. In other words, the defense attorney can get up there and say, "Yes, my client did this but, under the law, he is not responsible due to a mental disease or defect." Finally, the prosecution rebuts this assertion of mental disease or defect with witnesses of their own.

THE VERNON TRIAL began with jury selection. There are two basic schools of thought about jury selection. One is that it's a science and that each juror must be carefully screened and spoken to in order to insure that he or she can be fair and impartial. The other school of thought is, "Hey, this is a crap shoot. Whatever is in the jury box is as good as what is in the audience. I'll ask a couple of questions, try to eliminate the total nut jobs, and spend my time trying to get them to like me." Bill was from this latter school of thought. As a matter of fact, he was so good at schmoozing juries that a few years before I met him, he married juror number twelve from one of his cases (months after the trial, of course).

Bill has a gift with juries. While the judge was doing his *voir dire* (or questioning of the jurors), Bill memorized the names of everyone in the jury box. He believed that it gave the jurors more confidence in his intelligence that he knew their names so quickly. It also gave him the ability to have a more natural and open rapport with them since he did not keep having to refer to his chart in order to call on people. Bill got up there to speak with the prospective jurors as if it were the most natural thing in the world to chat with twelve total strangers about their lives and experiences. He had the whole courtroom laughing and he was talking to them like they were old friends in no time.

After two days of Bill and the defense attorney questioning people, we had nine of the twelve jurors in the box and still needed to select the alternates. Bill let me do my first round of jury selection in the case. I had only voir dired once before on a misdemeanor case that pled after I put my first witness on. I was terrified. What did a white Jewish girl from the suburbs have in common with most of the people from The Bronx? How was I going to get these people to relate to me when I had hardly set foot in The Bronx until I started at the office? I heard Bill whisper in my ear as I got up, "Remember, it's your courtroom." I steeled my spine and approached the box.

There was a woman in the jury box who had told us during the judge's preliminary questioning that her son was a rap musician. As it turned out, the band was well-known and I had heard of them. I began here:

"Ms. Jones, ever heard of the Grammy Awards?"

"They're awards for records, for best records, best vocalist, groups, whatever."

"Right. So a bunch of so-called music experts, I don't know who they are, get together at the end of the year and they decide what we the people think is the best music from that year, right?"

"Uh-huh."

"Now, Mobb Deep has an album out, right?"

"Yes."

"At the end of 1997, these music experts are going to get together and they are going to vote on nominees for the best music of the year. So maybe they're going to nominate your son?"

"Yes," Ms. Jones was beaming, "He's in a very popular band."

"And very famous." I agreed, "A lot of people know who they are, lots of people think they're the greatest band in the world, probably. Well, these experts might decide at the end of 1997 that Mobb Deep does not deserve a Grammy, and we might not agree with that. We think Mobb Deep should win. But when it comes to deciding who is the best, and they say that Mobb Deep does not deserve to win, we don't have to agree with that, do we?"

"No, we don't."

"And applying that same reasoning to the experts that are going to testify in this case, you might not agree with what they say. They may be the experts on the subject, but you are the experts on the facts, right? And you can still use your common sense and the facts as you know them and agree or disagree with those experts, right?"

"I sure can."

"And just because more experts have one opinion than other experts have, that doesn't mean that the bigger group is right. Right? I mean three guys might say we don't give the award to Mobb Deep and one guy says we do. We go with the one guy who says give the award, right?"

"Sure do," she grinned.

And with that, I broke the ice. Suddenly it was like being on stage back in the high school musical. I was relating to these people. They liked me. They were laughing. I picked God knows how many juries over the next three years, but that was easily one of my finest moments at the office. By the end of day three, we had our jury.

ON SEPTEMBER 22, 1997, almost two years after Michael Vernon committed his mass murder, Bill opened the case by telling the jury that we would prove to them that on "December 19, 1995, at approximately 11:50 AM, at 2186 White Plains Road, Michael Vernon took the lives of five innocent people. He destroyed the lives of two others. He seriously injured a third, attempted to kill a police officer, and in the overall view of things, destroyed the heart of the city. This intentional act was done knowingly, was done deliberately, all with one aim: so that when he was done, there would not be one single living witness to his savagery."

Over the next several days we put on the surviving victims, the cops, the medical examiners and the ballistics experts. We rolled Mr. Dones out in his wheel chair to talk about the day he became blind, deaf, and paralyzed. Janet Ham got on the stand and was so terrified that she could not even look in Vernon's direction. We were unable to get her to identify him. Gonzalvo Saed Galvez described Vernon to the jury as a "killer without compassion." He told the jury how Vernon:

pointed the weapon at the head of the person that was in front of him. He shoots once. He shoots again twice fast. The mother of the children was screaming. He point the weapon and his eyes to the two children, he shoots twice, one to each one of them. They fell down on the floor. The mother is in total despair, screaming. Shoots as well to the mother twice. He looks at my cousin and shoots at him twice. I went behind the clothing that was hanging there to hide myself. He runs in front and he shot once to one of the salespersons who was a female. I stood up and I went towards the door. He pointed the weapon towards me, towards my head. While I was opening the door, two bullets went by my left arm. One bullet was in my lower part of the back. One in the colon. He continued shooting at me and I started to roll my body towards a car that was parked there. He shot me in the stomach. The police were surrounding him. They were telling him to drop the gun. I was in the hospital one month and fifteen days.

While each witness gave a slightly different account of how people were shot, or who was shot in what order, nobody was going to argue with them. No one tried to deny that regardless of the order, Michael Vernon killed those five people.

The testimony of the ballistics expert was a harrowing recitation of the deliberateness of the steps that Vernon had to go through that morning before his killing spree. To load the type of weapon that Vernon used, he had to remove the magazine from the firearm. He then took the live cartridges or bullets and, one at a time, stacked them on top of each other in the magazine. Even with a loaded magazine in the gun, still nothing would happen. The gun had to be "charged" to be ready to fire. Vernon charged the gun by grabbing hold of the top portion of the weapon and pulling it to the rear. This cocked the weapon, putting the hammer in firing position. It exposed the top cartridge in the magazine. At this point, he let the slide go forward. This stripped off the cartridge and put it into the chamber of the weapon. The gun was ready to go. He did all this before he even walked into Little Chester's that morning. When he pulled the trigger, he pulled it having prepared for a bullet to fire—with "malice aforethought." And Vernon's gun was different than a full automatic or machine gun. Each time he wanted to fire, he had to pull that trigger again. Sixteen pulls of the trigger that morning. Deliberate and premeditated. Not the actions of a crazy man reacting to voices but the actions of a calculating murderer.

Although, by law, we still had to prove our case, when all was said and done, the real question for the jury was going to be whether Vernon was responsible for any of it. Our direct case was just a warmup for the real act. After putting on the witness stand the cops, the medical examiners, the doctors, the victims, and the ballistics experts, we rested our case. Now, the burden was on the defense to prove that Vernon was not responsible for his crime.

Ira Brown, the portly gray-haired defense attorney, nervously shuffled back and forth in front of the jury box jingling his change and chain-smacking fruit-flavored Life Savers one after another. He had two psychiatrists and one psychologist who were going to testify that Vernon was not responsible for his actions. We only had one doctor. But, as I had told the jury in *voir dire*, sometimes less is more.

First, Brown put on a psychologist, Dr. Mercado, whose only contact with Vernon was to administer tests. His testimony seemed quite simple. Vernon took the tests, he got certain scores, and Mercado wrote down the scores and explained what they meant to the jury. What seemed simple, however, turned into a total fiasco for the defense.

In order for someone to testify as an expert witness, they must first be "qualified." In other words, the attorney has to demonstrate to the judge that based upon this individual's training and experience he or she is qualified to offer an expert opinion on a given matter. This is usually fairly routine and is rarely contested by the other side. In fact, sometimes the opposing counsel tries to stop the attorney from introducing information about someone's background and experience because they do not want the jury being overly impressed. Ira Brown began questioning Mercado about his background and experience. When Brown was done and offered Mercado as an expert witness, the judge, as is protocol, asked Bill if he had any questions for Mercado. Bill, of course, had done his homework.

Rising from his seat with a wink, Bill asked Mercado if he'd been demoted when he was employed by one of the mental health facilities listed on his resume. Mercado denied it, but Bill did not ask questions if he did not know their answers. In front of the jury and a courtroom full of newspaper reporters, Bill threatened to bring in the personnel director of the hospital to testify if Mercado did not admit that he'd been demoted. Finally, Mercado had to admit that he had lied and that he had indeed been demoted. He proceeded to explain that, at the time, he was going through depression due to problems with his oldest son. He started crying on the witness stand and explained to the jury that he wasn't sleeping and, "I just didn't care if I went to work. I didn't care. It reached a point where I didn't care what happened and in all honesty, there were a lot of absences, a lot of latenesses, there were unexcused absences and that's what happened."

You can imagine that having a psychologist on the witnesses stand crying and talking about his own severe depression did not instill too much confidence in his abilities to assess the mental health of another. I felt bad for Dr. Mercado. Had he just told the truth about his demotion, he never would have gone through this on the witness stand. But as heartless as it seems, it was a huge boon for our case. One down, two to go. Bill had what he wanted and, as an ultimate slap in the face, sarcastically stipulated to Mercado's expertise. Bill smirked at me as he sat down and whispered, "You learning anything yet?"

"Cruel, but masterful," I replied, burying my head in the evidence boxes so that the jury would not see me stifling a giggle.

"And work on the poker face, " Bill whispered.

The remainder of Mercado's testimony spun a tale of a profoundly disturbed young man. Mercado concluded that Vernon's IQ was somewhere around 67, which made him mild to borderline retarded. This finding was consistent with earlier testing done at Bellevue Hospital, where Vernon's IQ was placed at 72, and Our Lady of Mercy Hospital, where Vernon scored a verbal IQ of 63. Mercado also described a telephone interview that he conducted with the mother of Vernon's child, Maria Callas. She described a turbulent relationship with Vernon that was progressively marked by escalations of aggressive behavior and a deterioration of his mental functioning. She explained that over a period of time he was hearing voices, talking in quotes, and that he said that "Method Man" was out to get him. She said he believed that the TV and radio were somehow communicating with him and that the "fat guy from *The Honeymooners* was saying racial slurs to him." He thought that Snoop Doggie Dog was going to pick him up in a black limousine and take him to California so he could join a gang called the Crips.

Vernon also told Maria that he wanted to hurt himself because of the voices. He did not understand that she could not hear the voices as well, and sometimes this would frustrate him and he would hit her. In 1994, Vernon was first admitted to a psychiatric hospital. He was released after two weeks with medications in hand that he did not take. Maria learned from the hospital that Vernon was schizophrenic. In August of 1995, Vernon was again admitted to a hospital. He was discharged after 15 days, again with a diagnosis of schizophrenia and medications that he did not take.

Mercado also interviewed Vernon's mother. She described that starting at around six years of age, Michael was already having difficulties at school. He would come home crying that other children were teasing him. As he got older, he started to drink a lot. She confirmed that he heard voices and would not take his medication. She said that she was afraid of her son.

Mercado explained that Vernon suffered from "command auditory hallucinations," which refers to hearing voices that are in some way ordering you to do something. These voices ordered him to hurt himself and to hurt others. Vernon said that he "loved liquor," and drank steadily. He also admitted to smoking marijuana and occasionally using PCP. He dropped out of school in the tenth grade.

Mercado spoke with Vernon about the incident at Little Chester's. Vernon said that he had "lost control," and that he did not really recall much of what had happened on that day. He talked about hearing four voices and pointed to both his temples when he described this to Dr. Mercado. Vernon acknowledged that, at the time of the massacre, he was not taking his Haldol and that he had heard voices starting that morning. He said he had an "itch" to get the boots that he had seen with his mother. He had $200 with him that day to buy the boots.

Mercado diagnosed Vernon with schizophrenia, paranoid type. He described the condition to the jury as a serious form of psychosis where one is out of touch with reality. He said that the delusions are very real for the person experiencing them. He described that paranoid schizophrenics are very suspicious. They believe that someone is out to get them or to cause them harm or injury and these fears totally dominate them. Mercado concluded that at the time he committed mass murder at Little Chester's Shoe Store, Vernon was suffering from a mental disease that rendered him unable to appreciate the nature and consequences of his actions and that he did not understand that his actions were wrong.

Now it was our turn with Mercado.

Through Mercado, Bill brought out that Vernon would have had periods of remission where he would function normally. He elicited the fact that Vernon sold drugs and that this would imply that Vernon understood something about the quantity and value of those drugs—that he understood how to purchase them from one person and then to sell them to another person at a profit. He got Mercado to admit that Vernon probably got the money to buy the gun used in his murder from some of his drug sales. Bill went on to question Mercado about why Vernon had the gun in his pocket that day in the first place. Mercado replied that Vernon, "believed people were out to get him and that's in keeping with this paranoid delusional belief of his."

"Well, let me ask you something," Bill retorted. "Could it also be in dealing with his selling drugs that people *were* out to get him?"

One by one Bill went through the elements of Mercado's testimony and poked holes in his theories. His low verbal and math scores could have been affected by the fact that he did not attend school and that he abused alcohol and drugs. In spite of claiming that the voices also told Vernon to hurt himself, there was no record of his ever having done so. The records only showed that he hurt others. He also brought out the fact that, at some point, Vernon sprayed the store with lighter fluid and tried burning it down, a clear indication that he knew what he did was wrong and was trying to get rid of the evidence. Finally, he got Mercado to admit that it is possible for someone who is schizophrenic to know the nature and consequences of his actions and to know right from wrong.

Brown next called Dr. Abboud to testify. Abboud was one of the two psychiatrists who testified for the defense. Most of Dr. Abboud's testimony was a repeat of Dr. Mercado's. Important to our rebuttal, Dr. Abboud noted that when Vernon was experiencing his hallucinations, he would attempt to control the voices by isolating himself. He would lock himself in a room and "chill out in the dark." He also testified that after the shooting, Vernon expressed remorse, which indicated that he had at least some appreciation of the wrongfulness of his acts.

Abboud also described the meanings of malingering and confabulation and described Vernon's story as "confabulation." Malingering he simply described as faking symptoms of mental illness. Every doctor who examined Vernon agreed that his disease was real. He was never accused of malingering. Confabulation, on the other hand, is more complicated. Confabulation, Abboud explained, is "used when a person remembers point A in time and remembers point C in time, but cannot recall what happened in the interim period of time. In an attempt to logically make point A and point C seem coherent, that person would put in a statement, apparently a logical statement, which is not true, in order to make that sequence of events seem logical. In short, a person tries to fill in gaps in that person's memory by what he perceives might have happened." Brown attempted to use this phenomenon of confabulation to explain why Vernon told the doctors that he was planning on robbing the store. Not because he was but because, in retrospect, the course of events from that day did not make sense to him and he was filling in the blanks. Bill twisted it around:

"Now, Doctor, you reach a conclusion here in your report that it's unlikely that Mr. Vernon's intention was to rob the store, is that correct?"

"Yes, sir."

"And one of the reasons that you listed in your report that he couldn't have done the robbery is because people don't commit robberies early in the day, correct?"

"People do commit robberies early in the day. I listed a few reasons. That was one of my reasons."

"Okay, you also list as a reason that there is no prior history of robberies in the records, correct?"

"At the time I did not have that information. Now I understand that there is a history of robbery in the past."

"Oh, so we better knock that one out." Bill smirked at the jury. "In fact, your report listed that Mr. Vernon reported three prior arrests for assault, robbery, and selling drugs?"

"That's what he told me, but there was no evidence confirming that."

"Well, did you ask for his rap sheet?"

"No. I did not have his rap sheet."

"Didn't you also put the following information in your report? That

Mr. Galvez said that he observed the gunman going through the victim's pockets? Does that say to you that might be robbery there?"

"It tells me—it doesn't tell me that it might be a robbery. It might, possibly. But it doesn't tell me. The reason it doesn't tell me that is if you look at the picture, I had the occasion to see this unfortunate victim. Mr. Vernon chose to go through a pocket and as far as I know, this individual's purse was directly on top of her. Now, if it was a robbery for monetary reasons, one would look into the purse first rather than digging into a pocket."

Bill raised an eyebrow. "I just want to read this to you. I want to see if it changes your mind about evidence of robbery. It's a statement by a witness who testified. He's blind and in a wheelchair. 'I hear a gun and the guy, he goes "I'm here to hold up the store."' You think that's evidence of a robbery? Now, you also gave in your reasons for there not being a robbery he made no attempt to conceal his identity. What did you mean by that?"

"Mr. Vernon walked into a store where he had been many times before."

"Let me just throw this out at you, doctor. What if you know you've been there a number of times, what if you know you're recognizable, on the off chance you kill everybody. Would that be consistent, doctor, with concealing one's identity? By killing all the witnesses."

"I can't answer yes or no when you're taking it out of context with relation to his illness."

"I am saying, Doctor, isn't it conceivable that an individual could go into a store, commit a robbery and try to conceal it by killing the witnesses?"

"It's possible."

"And after he kills the witnesses, it's conceivable that an individual could try and cover up that deed by doing other things, for instance, burning the place down and getting rid of the evidence. Isn't that possible doctor?"

"That is possible."

"Is it possible, doctor, that a person seeing an individual who was escaping from the store, goes and chases that individual down, shoots them in the back, and then when they roll over, shoots them in the front so that he can eliminate another witness. Is that possible?"

"That is possible."

Bill also elicited from Abboud that Vernon said that he paid $1,000 for one of his guns and $750 for the other, and that he got some of the money by selling drugs and the remainder by "hustling."

On direct examination, Abboud also talked to the jury about the use of proverbs as a psychiatric tool to assess an individual's ability to think abstractly. He said that many people with schizophrenia cannot think abstractly. Their ability to interpret proverbs is therefore one of the tests used to make a diagnosis. He had asked Vernon what is meant by "Don't cry over spilled milk," and Vernon said, "It's too late." Abboud felt that Vernon's reply was not adequate and moved on to another proverb: "A stitch in time saves nine." Vernon said that he did not know what it meant. This indicated to Abboud that Vernon could not abstract, and that was a part of his psychosis. Bill tackled this one, grinning like the Cheshire Cat. He wiggled his eyebrows at me as he approached the stand. *Here we go*, I thought.

"Doctor, tell us what the statement 'he had a forty and the five-oh showed up' means?"

"I don't know."

"You don't know that a forty refers to a forty ounce bottle of beer and five-oh refers to the police?" Bill smiled conspiratorially at the jury, most of whom looked down to cover their smiles. They all knew what it meant.

"No."

"Some people know that. In fact, most people in The Bronx know that. Maybe Vernon's mom didn't stitch something, so he does not know what a stitch is. Is that possible?"

"Sure."

Bill leaned on the jury box. "So, as high as your level of education, a simple phrase that many people in The Bronx know, you don't know what it means, do you?"

"No."

"Does not make you a fool, does it?"

"No."

"Does not mean that you can't abstract, does it?"

"No."

Two down, one to go.

Dr. Horowitz was the third witness to testify for the defense. His testimony was intelligent and uneventful but, in the end, he too did more harm then good to the defense by contradicting some of Abboud's statements. In hindsight, Brown would have been best served by putting only Horowitz on the stand.

Now it was our turn.

Our sole witness on rebuttal was Dr. Robert Berger, director of forensic psychiatry at New York City's Bellevue Hospital, and sometimes a Hollywood consultant. Dr. Berger agreed with the defense witnesses that Vernon suffered from schizophrenia with paranoid features. He explained how the illness manifested itself in a history of hearing voices of different types, some telling Vernon to do things, others telling him to hurt himself or to hurt others. He explained that Vernon had "ideas of reference," meaning he believed that things in his environment referred especially to him. For instance, if he hears a song on the radio he might think that it referred to him or that a show he watched on television was giving him a special message. Having concluded that Vernon did, indeed, suffer from a mental disease or defect, the next question for Berger was whether at the time of the crime his illness manifested itself in such a way that it was interfering with his functions. It was Berger's opinion that it did not.

As Berger explained, "Mr. Vernon did not lack the substantial capacity to know or appreciate the nature and consequence or the wrongfulness of his conduct. He could appreciate those things. He had no symptoms that would have interfered with that in any substantial way and he is criminally responsible for his conduct." The basis for this opinion began with Vernon's personal history.

"If we look at Vernon's history," Berger began, "it starts out not particularly unusual for New York City. He is born in 1973 in The Bronx. He is raised almost entirely by his mother. His father died when he was three years old. His mother may have used alcohol excessively during certain points in his life and there is also a possibility that one of his brothers suffers from mental illness.

"He was educated in New York City public schools and was pretty much identified very early on as needing some kind of special education.

Gradually he begins to become truant in school. His grades, which had been fair to good with supervision, start to slip off. At around age thirteen, he started to smoke a lot of marijuana, up to thirty blunts a day. Around tenth grade he dropped out of school.

"There is some evidence of some violent conduct in school. In the eighth grade, he took a kid and smashed his head against a wall and was suspended for that. At that point, he had not manifested schizophrenia. He was not hearing voices or having paranoid delusions and it would be very unusual that they would occur at such a young age. We can see that this is a person who has somewhat low frustration tolerance. He doesn't handle stress. That stress gets him to feel irritable and angry and he acts out that feeling. Not in response to hearing voices, not in response to any kind of unusual belief or idea, but in response to that frustration."

Berger said that Vernon also admitted that he smoked PCP on occasion along with the marijuana. He stopped the drug use around 1994 or so because he was beginning to hear voices at that time and he thought that the marijuana use made it worse, but he continued to drink. Also, Vernon never worked. He was never employed gainfully and earned his money by selling drugs.

Berger emphasized the importance of some emerging patterns in Vernon's life story: Even before he had any manifestations of schizophrenia, he had certain kinds of social problems. He sold drugs, he took drugs, he drank, and he carried a weapon. Berger said that in his profession, doctors "generally don't see schizophrenics carrying weapons like guns. They don't have them." He said that they also don't see schizophrenics "shooting and killing people regularly. When a schizophrenic goes to hurt somebody, it's because they think that person's trying to hurt them and they're trying to protect themselves from that person. But it's usually an impulsive thing. It happens all of a sudden. The schizophrenic does not amass guns. The drug dealer does." And it was Michael Vernon the drug dealer, not Michael Vernon the schizophrenic, that bought the gun used at Little Chester's.

Dr. Berger then went into a little history of Vernon's life to paint a fuller picture of the man who stood accused. He had also interviewed the mother of Vernon's child. She told Dr. Berger that, at times, Vernon would become violent toward her and that he was hospitalized in 1994 as a result of his violent and erratic behavior. Berger said that a review of the medical records showed that Vernon was hearing voices and having experiences that upset him.

"He was stressed out by the experiences of hearing these voices and their not going away. And the record says that he started taking it out on his girlfriend." Berger concluded that it was not the voices that told Vernon "hit your girlfriend," and Vernon never claimed they were. Rather, it was "stress from the voices that made him consciously hit her."

"The hospital record says that when Mr. Vernon feels that someone is a threat to him, he hides at home. He avoids them. He withdraws when he feels he's in danger from these paranoid ideas. He doesn't go out seeking confrontation. He doesn't take a gun and charge into battle. He does what we'd expect if you're frightened, withdraw."

Berger explained that schizophrenics hear disorganized voices. Sometimes the voices will say bad things, but they do not give complicated directions. He said that when a clinician hears someone describe voices giving complicated directions, "it's often an indication of what the person himself is thinking and assigning to a voice. The voice is just a reflection of what the person is thinking about doing."

All four of the doctors that spoke to Vernon got a different account of voices that he heard. Berger speculated that this was because it is "hard to consistently recall that which did not happen." Berger's opinion was that Vernon did not in fact hear voices telling him to go into Little Chester's or to shoot people but rather, that these were feelings he had on his own. "Voices didn't tell him to buy the gun. When you buy a gun you are prepared for the possibility of using that gun. So the person who makes that decision to buy that gun doesn't need voices telling him to use it. He's already made the decision that he can use that gun when he bought it."

Berger broke down the day of the homicide one step at a time to demonstrate that Vernon committed murder with understanding and intent. "He put the gun in his pocket that day. He did not tell anyone that he heard voices saying to take the gun with him. He tells one doctor that he heard voices telling him to shoot these people before he even left the house and another doctor that he didn't hear voices until he got to the store. The depth of what he described to all of us is not the voices, but his anger toward the people in the store who weren't giving him the shoes."

Vernon had described to the police and to the doctors feeling frustrated over the course of weeks that he could not get the shoes he wanted. He told Berger that someone in the store was cursing at him. Vernon said, "Nobody is going to talk to me like that." Berger said that Vernon "felt dissed," and that the "diss factor here is the most prominent and consistent theme that is repeated over and over and over again and the diss factor accounts for more murders and deaths in this city and other major urban cities than anything else." Being dissed as a reason for committing homicide was not uncommon in The Bronx, and it did not take a schizophrenic to think it was happening to him.

"So, when he's telling me about these voices," Berger asked, "is he lying to me? I don't think so. I think that when you kill that many people, that's not something that you can accept for yourself. Especially an individual who has major mental illness. You don't have the resources in you to deal with that kind of feeling, that emotion. You externalize the blame. You blame something else. You blame voices."

What Berger said throughout his testimony made sense. He pointed out that, like anyone else, you had to look to Vernon's history to determine whether he was responsible for his crime. When Vernon the schizophrenic was decompensating, he hid in his room terrified. He avoided people, drank, and sat in the dark. There was also another Michael Vernon though, and that Michael Vernon sold drugs, carried a gun to protect himself, and sought trouble. The case ended with Berger's testimony explaining why Vernon was responsible for the murder. Now it was up to the jury to decide which doctor they believed.

THE JURY DELIBERATED for about two days while Bill and I joked around and chewed our nails. As we did throughout the trial, Bill and I entertained ourselves by making up various twisted versions of songs sung by Alvin and the Chipmunks (mostly to the tune of "The Chipmunk Song" from the "Alvin Show," like "Michael Vernon don't you see, you are just a travesty. . . ." It was all downhill from there). However, our humor belied our nervousness. We never thought that the jury would be out overnight. The first night they were out, we tried to stay calm by telling ourselves that the jury just wanted to milk a free night in a hotel, but the second night, we really started to worry.

Finally, after two days, the jury came back with a verdict. They found Vernon guilty on all counts, including five counts of first-degree murder and four counts of attempted murder. Several weeks later, Vernon received five life sentences without parole plus a few hundred years for good measure.

IMMEDIATELY AFTER THE verdict was announced, the jury was given the opportunity to speak with (or not to speak with) the attorneys in the case. Eleven of the 12 jurors stayed and spoke with Bill and me about the verdict. We took it that the one person who did not care to speak with us was the holdout in the case. It was encouraging to see the camaraderie that had developed among the jurors over the course of the trial. Where The Bronx is often divided by racial tension, these people of all different backgrounds, ethnicities, genders, and religions came together to speak as one and to render a verdict. They took their job very seriously and that moment made me proud of them, proud of our system, and proud of myself to be a part of it. I would not feel that way after every case during my career but that moment was a prime example of what the system is really supposed to be about. The jurors said their goodbyes, promising to invite Bill and me to a reunion/Tupperware party (one of the jurors sold Tupperware). I never saw any of them again.

The night of the verdict, for the first time, I had a feeling that became a familiar one to me. It was a feeling that I did not want to celebrate this verdict. It was a feeling of ambivalence toward taking away someone's freedom. It was recognition of this amazing amount of power over another human being that I had acquired rapidly at such a young age. In the end, I can sleep at night because I know that Michael Vernon will never be free and, in a way, that is all that matters. I helped to take away his ability to continue harming people. But I do not loathe Michael Vernon. I pity him. I pity the kind of torture that it must be to live with voices in your head and the guilt of taking innocent lives. If he stays on his medication, one day Vernon might have clarity about his actions and what a terrible sentence that will be for him—or, at least, I hope it will, because if he does not have remorse, he has no salvation. And what about Vernon's son, out there in the world with the worst kind of male role model and a good chance that he will inherit his father's mental illness. Will I see his name in the papers some day?

I started in the Domestic Violence and Sex Crimes Bureau of The Bronx District Attorney's Office the day after *People v. Michael Vernon* ended. I had finally gotten to the place I wanted to be for so many years. I had a second seat in one of the biggest press cases in the country under my belt and I was chomping at the bit for more. My start in DVS, however, was not glamorous. . . .

6

THE WANNABE WISEGUY
AND THE JUNKIE

I **CRY ALL** the time. I can't control it. I cry at weddings. I cry at funerals. I cry at tampon commercials when the sisters confide in each other over a fragrant flowered box. I sob hysterically during movies like *E. T.* or *Finding Nemo*. I even cried when in *South Park: Bigger Longer and Uncut*, Kenny earned his wings and flew from the pits of hell up toward the busty animated angels in heaven. My husband tells me that my emotions are too close to the surface, but I was not always like this. I used to need nary a tissue for the likes of such heart-wrenchers as *The Champ* or *Terms of Endearment*. Before this, before the army of damaged children began their parade through my life, before the constant deluge of uncontrollable tears, there was a little girl. She was a precocious and strong-willed child who walked through life with energy and purpose. She was brave and she was smart and, most of all, she was safe.

When my parents were young, children were sent out early in the morning to play and they were expected to entertain themselves until they were called in to eat or to do chores. When they were called, they were expected to come, but in the meanwhile, they rode their bikes up and down the streets or played stickball or handball at a nearby court. Or if there was no court, they played off the back wall of some local store. It was safe back then. Parents did not worry that if they left their child outside to play all day, someone would come and snatch him off the streets. There were no Amber Alerts or Meagan's Laws.

Things were still relatively safe when I was born in 1970. Even in the trashy neighborhood where I grew up in St. Louis, my brother Ari and I could let ourselves out of the house and play in the sandbox with our parents only having the usual parental fears, like that we would fall off the slide and break something. We moved a lot when I was a child and our changing neighborhoods provided me with neverending new places to explore. Often, my mother would wake up early in the morning to find me gone. I would creep out of my bed, pull on my jeans and hooded sweatshirt, and sneak out the door. When she would discover I was missing, she would take Ari with her in one car and my dad would go by foot with our German shepard, Dahlia, on her leash and they would scour the neighborhood looking for me. More often than not, they would find me sitting on some hill overlooking a construction site, just watching the workers. I was not afraid and, although my parents would have a little panic attack when I went missing, the fear was not who had taken me, but where I had gone and how easily they would find me. Once, when I was in pre-school, they found me a few blocks away in a laundromat.

When I was nine, my parents announced that we would be moving to New York. That night, my brother and I were watching our favorite show, *The Incredible Hulk*. We were in the den in the basement of our house in Boston with our feet up on the coffee table. My Mom had made the coffee table by gluing together coke cans for a base and you had to be careful not to kick too much when you got excited lest you dent the table. We had waited since the week before to see where Bill Bixby, who turned into the Hulk when angered, would end up and my legs could hardly contain themselves. Coincidentally, that day Bill found himself in New York. Ari and I were anxious to get a glimpse of our new home, which we knew little about other than what we gleaned from occasional visits to our grandmothers. In one scene, the Hulk was running down the streets of New York City in a green rage. Generally when the Hulk did this, people would jump out of the way or scream. But in New York, no one even seemed to notice the giant green man running barefoot down the street. They just ignored him and minded their own business. He had to run around some people who did not even bother to get out of his way. When he checked her in the shoulder, one old lady yelled at him to "Watch where you're going!" My brother and I knew right then and there that New York was going to be a very strange place and we did not like it.

Shortly before my family moved to New York that year, everything changed for us children. A little boy named Etan Patz disappeared one day on his way to school and was never seen again. Etan lived in an apartment building in Soho, a neighborhood in New York City, and while we would be moving to the suburbs and not to the City, there was little distinction in my young mind. The police realized rather quickly that this was not a typical missing child case and that Etan had not simply wandered off with a friend or gotten lost. By that evening, nearly a hundred officers were combing the area, knocking on doors, searching rooftops and basements. Over the next few days, the search area was expanded to encompass the entire lower end of Manhattan. Police searched with helicopters and scanned rooftops. Boats combed the waterways. The police appealed to the public for any information that could lead to the boy's whereabouts. Toll-free telephone numbers were set up and calls started pouring in with false reports of sightings. Etan's father, a professional photographer, disseminated photographs of Etan in an effort to find him. Neighborhood residents helped in the search, papering the city with color posters of the boy's face. I remember distinctly keeping vigil by the television as the days went by, hoping they would find the boy. He was six years old, just a couple of years younger than me. He was someone that I could have known. It could have been me. Etan was never found.

The massive search and media attention that followed Etan's disappearance focused the nation's attention on the problem of child abduction and the lack of plans to address it. Etan's disappearance remains an open case. He became the first missing child to be featured on a milk carton and, in the months and years that followed, became the symbol for lost children.

Then, for almost three years in Atlanta, Georgia, the bodies of young boys and girls began to turn up in lakes, marshes and ponds. By the time a suspect was arrested and identified in 1981, 29 bodies had been recovered. On July 27, 1981, six-year-old Adam Walsh disappeared from a Florida shopping mall. His parents, John and Revé Walsh, turned to law-enforcement agencies to help find their son, but there was no coordinated effort among law enforcement to search for Adam and no organization to help them in their moment of desperation. Two weeks later, Adam's severed head was found in a canal 120 miles away. His body was never recovered.

Everything changed. Child murder and abduction suddenly seemed to be an epidemic and cases emerged at the forefront of the news. Even in safe suburban neighborhoods like ours, parents kept a closer eye on their children. The parents of Etan and Adam launched personal campaigns to bring to light the danger to America's children and to try to save other children from the fate of their own sons. They continue to be active and influential voices in child protection and in politics to this day. Because of the parents of Adam and Etan, instead of playing games on the backs of our cereals boxes or trying to pronounce the names of the additives and ingredients, we look at missing children postings over breakfast. I do not think that it was unintentional that those missing children notices went on the backs of milk cartons. Children were meant to see them as much as parents, and we were meant to be afraid. As early as they could teach us, we started being warned not to talk to strangers. We memorized our addresses and telephone numbers. I still remember that my last address before we moved to New York was 296 Waban Ave, Waban Massachusetts, 02168. My number was 244-4558. I no longer went anywhere without, at the very least, my older brother by my side.

MY PARENTS MET at the Flatbush Yeshiva in Brooklyn, New York, when they were 13 years old. My mother was very religious and a model student. My father was a renegade with little prior Jewish education and a fairly socialist home. My mother's father died the year my parents met and in the tradition of very religious Jews, my Mom mourned his death for a year. She would not go out to movies or parties and would not even listen to music.

My Dad is ghostly pale with freckles and, as a child, he had impossibly red hair. It was almost orange. Like my Grandma, he feared the sun above almost all else. The sun's rays sent my father scampering for shelter like a sandcrab in high tide. My Mom, on the other hand, spent her entire summer on the beach. My Dad told me that the first time he saw my Mom, he "had never seen anyone who looked like that." He started in Yeshiva in the ninth grade and my mother was in his class. When he saw her that first day in school, he thought she was an Ethiopian Jew. Her hair was jet black and wildly curly and he had never seen such dark skin on a white person. Her aquamarine eyes stood out against her brown skin like a beacon and he thought she was beautiful.

When my Dad asked my Mom out on a date when they were 14, she turned him down. It took him three years to muster up the courage to ask her out again. He did not know that she turned him down because she would not date for the year after her father passed away and that it was not because she didn't like him. She was the goody-two-shoes and a favorite of all of her teachers. He was trouble, with the hair to prove it. They were perfect for each other.

On my parents' second date, when they were 17, my father told my mother that he was going to marry her. In 1959, my father told his parents that he would marry my mother. They forbid him to do so until he finished college so, in that same year, my dad left to study at Franklin and Marshall in Lancaster, Pennsylvania, while my mother stayed behind to study at Brooklyn College. My parents wrote to each other often and spoke on the phone occasionally, but phone calls were very expensive. My father was not able to visit often and, because she was so religious, my mother was not allowed to visit him. They missed each other. Both of my parents finished college in three years so that they could be together sooner, and in 1964, at the age of 21, they were married. My father started medical school at Downstate, in Brooklyn, just a few days after they married. My mother taught public school in the neighborhood, which was one of the worst in New York. Crime was so high that the school was built in a square with a windowed courtyard in the middle and no windows on the outside. After one of my father's classmates was murdered, my parents bought a German shepard. The dog, Dahlia, would not have hurt a fly, but she was huge and looked menacing. My mother took Dahlia to school with her every day so that she had some protection during her walk. In 1969, my parents left New York and swore they would never come back.

We lived many places during my childhood; Maryland, St. Louis, Maryland again and then Boston. In 1978, my father began looking to leave Boston for another job. That summer, we went to Israel for about three months. My father was to take a job in Haifa and we were considering life on a Moshav, which is something like a Kibbutz or collective, except that families live in their own homes rather than in communal ones. The job in Haifa fell through and, having run out of time and money, my parents bit the bullet and moved back to New York where a good job offer awaited my dad. How different my life would have been if we stayed in Israel. I would have been raised in a socialist environment and at 18, I would have gone to the army instead of to Barnard College, where my boyfriend broke up with me, which led me to Europe, which led me to my Grandma, which led me to the children.

TRY AS I might to get a trial to start in DVS, all my cases would plead out on the eve of jury selection. When I was a misdemeanor assistant, I had only two trials: a bench trial that resulted in an acquittal and a jury trial that pled out after I finished my direct case. After about a year as a felony assistant in DVS, I was anxious to finally do a felony trial and, on top of that, if you went too long without going to trial you started to get a reputation as someone who was afraid to try a case.

I will admit I was afraid, but not in the sense that I actually wanted to avoid a trial. It was more like a fear of skydiving or bungee-jumping; at the same time that you are dying to try it, you are totally terrified.

Some people at the DA's office were very picky about what they would take to trial, especially at the felony level. I was from the school that, at least at the beginning, you take anything you can get your hands on just to get the experience. I had no problem taking a case that was a "loser" as long as it would get me into the courtroom.

That was the case with the first trial I ever prosecuted while I was in Criminal Court. It was a misdemeanor bench trial and the charge was resisting arrest. The case came my way about eight months into the job when David Staton, who several years later would be the homicide ADA who went with me to the precinct on the Esmeralda DeJesus homicide, was out sick. He had a case scheduled for trial that could not be adjourned. He called our courtroom that morning to see if anyone wanted to try the case. I happened to answer the phone and jumped at the opportunity. I ran up to my desk, spent all of 20 minutes reviewing the file and interviewing the cops and, within an hour of taking the call,

I was arguing to the judge. Within two hours of that, I got my first acquittal. Not an auspicious beginning.

My first misdemeanor jury trial was a "menacing" case, where a tenant claimed that his landlord had threatened him with a gun. My complainant, the tenant, was a six-foot-five, rock-solid, 250-pound exterminator with a goatee. The defendant, the landlord, was about five-foot-two with spectacles and a British accent. Just about the only angle I could take in a case like that was to say that when you are the size of the landlord and you are picking a fight with someone the size of the tenant, you'd better bring a gun. The case started off badly with the judge introducing me as the "pretty little lady who should be out shopping instead of trying cases." It continued to go downhill when, after my direct examination, my witness, the tenant, got off the witness stand, leaned over and whispered, "Dick," as he passed by the defense attorney. The defense attorney whined about it to the judge who told him to "take it like a man." I pretty much just sat there with my head in my hands, trying to stifle a laugh. When the defense offered to take a plea before putting his witnesses on the stand, I jumped at the opportunity.

I don't mean to make it seem like the office generally handled cases so cavalierly or that acquittals were taken lightly. At the felony level it was rare that someone would be forced to pick up a trial on such short notice. However, at the misdemeanor level, the assistants and the courts were so overburdened that it was often impossible to avoid situations like my first trial. Often by the time a case went to trial, it would have gone through three or four assistants as people got promoted or left the office. The case would be delayed for various reasons, either because the court wasn't ready or the defense wasn't ready. It would not be unusual for a case to be 1-1/2 to 2 years old by the time it went to trial. And, while judges and defense attorneys could delay cases without consequence, every time the prosecution delayed, it used up speedy trial time. Running out of speedy trial time meant that the case would be dismissed. In the end, there was often no choice but to have to state "ready" on the case even if it meant that someone totally unfamiliar with the case would be trying it.

THE OPPORTUNITY TO try my first felony case and my first domestic violence case came through unfortunate circumstances. ADA Holdman, my mentor from the golden dildo case, was in a car accident and was out of work for several months. Since he was a senior assistant, most of his cases were more serious than what I was being assigned as a new felony assistant. There was one case, however, that was a low-level assault and was ready to go to trial. He asked me if I wanted the case with the caveat that the complainant, JoElle Martin, was "a little nutty." Well, I took the case, but "a little nutty" was the understatement of the century. I got sold a bill of goods. . . .

JoElle and the defendant, Sylvester "Sal" Cardillo, were live-in boyfriend and girlfriend. Sal was a wannabe gangster who was a union airport worker and JoElle was an unemployed junkie who was living off Sal and tolerating beatings in return for a decent lifestyle and enough money to support her habit.

Within days of having the case assigned to me, it was due to go to trial so I immediately had JoElle come to the office to prepare. And the first time that I saw JoElle, I knew that I was in for it. JoElle was about 55 years old and a good 40 or 50 pounds overweight. She looked like a ghoulish rendition of a teen at a fifties sock hop, with her hair pulled back in a tight ponytail on top of her head and a pastel scarf tied around it. Her hair color had grown out so that the top of her head was all gray but the ponytail was brown. She had frosty turquoise eye-shadow caked on her lids and was wearing black leggings with stiletto heels, bobby socks, and a tacky sweatshirt depicting something like glitter dolphins or sequined sailboats. I came to learn that this was her standard getup. During our interview, JoElle was jumpy and fidgety. She had trouble focusing on the questions and her answers tended to ramble. I took her behavior to be a result of nothing more sinister than nervousness but, boy, was I wrong.

JoElle proceeded to tell me her story. She and Sal had been living together for several years. She complained of on-and-off physical abuse by Sal but her primary complaints had to do with the way he treated her verbally. According to JoElle, Sal had never hurt her nearly as badly as the night of the arrest when Sal's punch to her eye had such force that it fractured the orbit, causing the eye to swell completely shut. Additionally, the fracture impinged upon the retina and could have caused blindness if the bone had not healed properly. At the time of the crime, there was little that the doctors could do but wait and see how the injury progressed.

Fortunately, JoElle healed fine and continued to see normally, but the injury had been severe and the prosecution proceeded.

After speaking with JoElle about the case for a while, I stepped out of my office for a moment. When I came back, JoElle was gone. I went down the hall to look for her but she was nowhere to be found. As I walked over to the women's bathroom, one of my colleagues was coming out. She looked a little pale.

"Was anyone else in there," I asked?

"Well, I didn't see anyone, but I heard someone smacking her arm"—(she demonstrated a motion of smacking her open palm against her inner arm)—"and saying, 'It's not woooorking.'"

Great. I only had a couple of hours to prepare the case and my witness was shooting up in the bathroom. I put on my most chipper, oblivious voice, popped my head in the door and told her to hurry up. When JoElle came into my office about ten minutes later, glassy-eyed but much less jumpy, I started preparing her for direct examination.

The first thing that she informed me, much to my chagrin, was that she was still living with Sal.

In 1974, Congress enacted the Section Eight program as part of a major restructuring of low-income housing programs funded by HUD. Section Eight was created to permit federal housing assistance to go for construction or rehabilitation of new low-income housing or to subsidize existing housing. As with any other government-subsidized program, demand for this subsidized housing greatly exceeds the supply. There is a long wait for Section Eight housing, but battered women often get priority due to the precarious situation they face if they cannot find housing separate from their batterer. Nonetheless, it takes a lot of finagling to get someone relocated quickly. When JoElle's case first came to our office, the crime victim advocates worked extremely hard to get JoElle an apartment quickly so she would be able to move out of Sal's place. I was livid when JoElle told me that, in spite of all our hard work, she was still with Sal. The apartment sat empty and unavailable to someone else who might need it and JoElle continued to expose herself to the danger of being beaten by Sal. When I asked JoElle why she hadn't moved out yet, she said that the new apartment was too small and didn't have any cabinets. "How can I live in a place without caaaaaabinets?" she whined.

In some ways, JoElle was typical of many battered women I met. She went from living off one man to another. She had no skills and was totally dependant on whatever boyfriend she had at the moment. While she wanted Sal prosecuted for beating her, she also refused to move out of the nice apartment that he owned and did not want him in jail because then he wouldn't be able to earn a living and support her. She was under the delusion that a court order of protection would stop the abuse but was unwilling or unable to do anything to help herself.

This is not to say that women of means and skills are not abused. I had a case my first year at the office with a female doctor from Pakistan. She was brilliant and beautiful and moved to the US to marry her husband. It was an arranged marriage and this man, who on paper was handsome and successful, was also a wife beater. It took three years of lying to co-workers at the hospital about where her bruises came from before she finally reported him on the threat from colleagues that if she didn't do something about it, they would. I had three more cases in my career involving spousal abuse in arranged marriages with women from the Far East, all of them beautiful, affluent, educated, and intelligent. I am sure that there were many other women of similar means and abilities who never reported abuse, maybe because they were too ashamed to come forward or did not want to lose face. With the women from the Far East, there were cultural issues that prevented many of them from reporting. Nonetheless, the bulk of the women I met were more like JoElle.

The People v. Cardillo was assigned to The Honorable Patricia Anne Williams who had recently transferred from Manhattan Supreme Court to The Bronx. When I was a law student, I had worked for Judge Williams as a law clerk in New York County. We remained friendly after I worked for her and I continue to speak to her occasionally and meet her for dinner. Since the judge and I knew each other, she recused herself from all of my cases to avoid any appearance of favoritism or conflict. I was hoping that she would do the same with this case. Having a trial in front of her would have been unneeded pressure on me. I would not only be nervous because this was my first felony case but I also knew that Judge Williams would hold me to a high standard since I knew how she operated her courtroom. I was afraid that I would let her down.

The defense attorney in the case was a man named Murray Richman.

Murray is a legend among prosecutors and defense attorneys in The Bronx. He generally dealt with drug defendants with big money or big connections and was rumored to frequently represent "wiseguys." He had also represented many high profile defendants such as Jamal "Shyne" Barrow, a co-defendant in the Sean "Puffy" Combs case, and the rapper DMX. His crack representation had earned him the nickname "Don't Worry Murray." His representation of Cardillo on a low-level domestic violence case was out of character. It made me seriously question who Cardillo knew to call in such a big favor. Regardless, Murray was a giant and that added even more pressure.

ON THE DAY the case went to trial, I waited in Judge Williams's courtroom until my case was called. I approached the prosecutor's table and the judge smiled at me. She was happy to see me, but clearly not happy about the news that she anticipated I brought. In her wry way, she said, "ADA Straus. You had better not be here to ask for an adjournment on this case." I explained to the judge that due to ADA Holdman's car accident, I would be taking over the case and that I was ready for trial. I got an approving nod and the judge turned toward the defense. Murray stated "ready" as well. The judge made a record about my relationship to her but, to my surprise, also made a record that her friendship with Murray went back at least two decades. She gave Murray the option of keeping the case in her courtroom or going in front of another judge.

Murray opted to stay with Williams. He waived his client's right to appeal for judicial indiscretion, meaning that should I get a conviction in the case, he would not appeal based on any impropriety by the judge due to my relationship with her. And with that, we were off.

I made it clear to both the Judge and to Murray that this was my first felony trial. I did this for two reasons. First, so that I would be somewhat forgiven if I screwed up and second, for strategy reasons. I was hoping that Murray would underestimate a young, inexperienced female. I would not know as much about the law in general than Murray, with his decades of experience, but I certainly did my damn best to know more than he could about this particular case.

I also learned rather quickly that Murray couldn't stand being disliked. Although he irritated me sometimes, I actually liked Murray very much.

After I pretended to dislike him for a while, Murray eased up significantly. The strategy worked like a charm, but the trial was far from smooth sailing.

Before I even put JoElle on the stand, Judge Williams asked me why I was wasting the court's precious resources trying this case. "She still lives with the guy. Why are you wasting my time? If she doesn't care, why should I?" I explained that sometimes in battered women's cases, it was the people's responsibility to do justice in spite of the victim. The judge did not seem overly impressed with my argument. But when I showed her the photographs of JoElle's injuries, it appeased her enough to allow the trial to commence. For whatever else I will say about JoElle and her antics, hers was the worst black eye I saw in my five years at the office. The hospital photographs were painful just to look at.

I was putting only three witnesses on the stand for the trial: the arresting officer, the treating physician and, of course, JoElle. The other witnesses were nice to have but, like any other case, the key to my success would be the victim. This worried me greatly in this case and my fears were justified the minute JoElle walked into my office on the day of trial in her usual gaudy getup, having completely disregarded or ignored my instructions regarding proper courtroom attire. I tried to get the case delayed another day so that JoElle could get some decent clothing. I was even willing to buy something for her, but Judge Williams would not hear about it and I was ordered to call JoElle to the stand in all of her sequined, frosted, spandexed, bobby-socked and high-heeled glory. To my pleasant surprise, however, aside from JoElle constantly interrupting my questions, the direct examination was relatively painless:

"Ms. Martin, who do you live with?"

"Sal Cardillo."

"What is the nature of your relationship with him"

"The last year, I've been more or less his live-in maid."

"Prior to that, what was your relationship with him?"

"We were lovers."

"Do you work, Miss Martin?"

"No."

"Is Mr. Cardillo supporting you?"

"No."

"Are you living with him?"

"Yes."

"Are you paying rent?"

"No. I clean his house. I have sleeping privileges and bathroom privileges, empty his cat box, you know. . . ."

"Ms. Martin, I'd like to draw your attention to June 29, 1997 at approximately 5:15 in the morning here in The Bronx. Were you present at that date, time, and location?"

"Yes, I was asleep."

"And was Mr. Cardillo home?"

"No. He walked in the room and I woke up. The TV was on. I have a little dog. The dog ran in with him because they're close and he said, 'I'm going to kill you tonight. Where is the bat?' And I said, 'What?' And I looked at him and his face was all distorted."

"Had you had an argument or a fight with him before he left that night?"

"Nothing, nothing."

"What's the first thing he said to you when he came into the room?"

"He said, 'I'm going to kill you tonight, you bitch. Where is the bat?' I started, you know, 'What's the matter? What happened?' 'Where is the bat that was by the bed?' I had put it in the closet. You know, usually people don't keep bats next to their bed."

Mr. Richman objected to JoElle's commentary and moved to strike. The judge overruled the objection as JoElle commented with unveiled sarcasm, "Why, Murray, you keep a bat by the bed, too?" The judge instructed JoElle not to comment on the defense objections and asked me to continue.

"Was there usually a bat by the bed?"

"Yeah. On his side. He wanted it there. It's the man's home, so I didn't ask him why, but I used to put it away."

"So, what happened that night when he asked you where the bat was?"

"He just took me and threw me off the bed on one side and there's like a glass top on the furniture and I says, 'The other night you did this and I had cut the bottom of my foot,' so he picked me up and he threw me on his side of the bed and there's this little corner. . . .I says, 'What's wrong,' and I was trying to like shake him and then he sat on my chest and my hands were down and everything."

"What were you wearing?"

"A nightgown."

"And where did he grab you?"

"He grabbed me—well, what was left of the nightgown, you know, it wasn't sexy. It was a nightgown and he threw me in this little corner and he sat like right here [indicating her chest]. My hands were down so that was the end of me talking because I couldn't even breathe."

"What happened at that point?"

"He just started punching me constantly. Wouldn't stop. I couldn't breathe. I couldn't move my feet. I couldn't use my hands. And he kept saying, 'I'm going to kill you tonight, bitch.' That's all he said."

"Do you know how long he was hitting you?"

"Until he got tired and then he told me, 'Don't move. I'm going to find the bat.' Until my eyes were closed bloody. My face was broken. He kept punching my face, my eyes, my head. I had stitches here and here."

"Were you bleeding?"

"Yeah. From everywhere. My mouth, my nose, my eyes. I couldn't see from either eye. They were totally closed."

"When he stopped punching you, what happened?"

"I got up and there's a long hallway. I don't know where he went. I couldn't see, and I ran down the hallway and I started banging on people's doors and screaming. We had a new neighbor, a young black girl. Everyone else on the floor knew him, they were tight with him so they made like they didn't hear. So this girl said, 'What's the matter?' I said, 'Help me. I can't see. I've been beaten up.' So she looked out the peephole and saw he was chasing me. She called 911, but she wouldn't open the door. She was petrified."

"Did you try to call 911 at any point?"

"Yeah, after that I ran back into the apartment, but he wouldn't let me into the bedroom to get to the phone. He kept throwing me and I was just trying not to hit the floor because once I hit the floor, that's it—I mean I get worked on."

"And then what happened?"

"He just turned. He went to the kitchen. He went and got a towel. You know, he was normal. He got the towels for me. He got the ice. That's when the police came."

"Did there come a time when the ambulance arrived?"

"Yeah. The ambulance worker said, 'You're face is broken.' I went to the hospital. I had an MRI, X-rays, stitches on my mouth, my eyes, my forehead."

"How long were you in the hospital?"

"Until about eleven that night. The plastic surgeon said my eye socket was broken. He was afraid my eye was going to . . . I said 'I got to go to court.' You know, I had to do something. 'I got to get an order of protection,' and they were arguing with me. I said, 'Let me get the order of protection. I'll come back.' So they let me go. I went home and he was sitting on the steps."

"Did you go back to the hospital?"

"No."

"Do you currently have any pain because of this injury?"

"My nose bleeds and my neck—"

At this point I put several photographs of JoElle into evidence including photographs of her within days of the incident and a photograph of bruises on her arm in the shape of a hand. I concluded my direct examination. Although JoElle's was not the most eloquent testimony, things did not go as poorly as I thought they would. I thought that I might actually have a chance to get a conviction on the case. That is, until Murray started his cross-examination:

"Good afternoon Ms. Martin. Do you go by any other names?"

"Like ex-husbands?"

"I don't know, how many ex-husbands do you have?"

"Two. One died. One was divorced. I was married a year and a half when I was twenty. I was married fifteen years after that."

"Are you also known as JoElle Matos?"

"That's my first husband."

"And JoElle Klein?"

"Thats my maiden name."

"And JoElle Martin?"

"That's my present name."

"Have you been convicted of a crime?"

"Yes."

"Could you tell us how many times you've been convicted of crimes?"

Murray let the rap sheet in his hand unravel and trail a few feet across the floor.

"No. I don't know."

"What types of crimes were you convicted of?"

"Drugs."

"All drugs?"

"Uh huh."

"And could you tell us from what period of time you were involved with drugs? Are you still involved with drugs?"

"I'm on methadone for twenty-seven years, before that I went to a live-in program, that was twenty-one to twenty-four years old. Then I got involved again, and then I went on a methadone program again."

Judge Williams gave me a wilting look and I forced a pained smile in return.

"And have you used heroin or cocaine in the last twenty-seven years?"

"Sure."

"And, in fact, you still use them periodically, do you not?"

"Yes."

Well, I thought, *at least she is being honest.*

"Have you ever worked since living with Mr. Cardillo?"

"He never supported me."

"He never supported you?"

"No. He never even bought me a pair of panties."

"You were living in his house, were you not?"

"Sleeping there."

"And would you go out during the day and do your thing?"

"No. Usually I was home. That's why he told me to go to college, you know, 'Do something. You can't stay home all day watching soaps.' "

"Ma'am, isn't it a fact that you had difficulty with Mr. Cardillo?"

"In the beginning, yes."

"In fact, he asked you to get out of his house, right?"

"Well, after my daughter ran away, yeah."

"In 1992 he asked you just to please leave and leave him alone; isn't that right?"

"Uh huh. Well, I had a sixteen-year-old daughter living there and she was getting nervous about seeing me get beat so much."

"Well, didn't he get an order of protection against you in 1992?"

"Uh huh."

"Didn't you abuse him?"

"No. What, am I just going to stand there while he hits me?"

"I'm not suggesting that. I'm not suggesting you stood there, but you did in fact strike back."

"Yeah. *Ohhhhh* yeah."

"Isn't it a fact that you would leave on occasion and not come back for months at a time?"

"I went to a shelter. You just told me he wanted me to leave. I went to a shelter and, you know, until they actually closed it and then I went and I rented a room for two years and then I came back to stay with him."

"And isn't it a fact that he told you on more than one occasion to please put your papers in for Section Eight or some other kind of housing and get out. Didn't he tell you that?"

"Yeah, when the development freeze was on."

"I'm sorry?"

"There was a development freeze in Section Eight for years."

"But, in fact, he pleaded with you to leave him?"

"Well, he didn't know the system."

"And Mr. Cardillo always worked, right?"

"You know, normal, unless he was sick or whatever."

"Did he ever say to you, 'Why don't you just get a job and clean out and make a life for yourself?' "

"No, what he said was, 'Go sell pussy. Go sell drugs. I don't care what you do. Just go make some money. He said, 'Go clean toilets.' So he would throw out my clothes, and that really helped." JoElle rolled her eyes and gave the judge a knowing look, which the judge did not return.

"Isn't it a fact that you sent a message through someone that you wanted $2,000 and that this would all go away?"

"Huh uh. $2,000? Yeah. No."

"You wanted more?"

"Oh, please Murray, no."

"You say in the last twenty-seven years you're in the methadone program, and you used other drugs. Heroin?"

"No."

"Never used heroin."

"No. I wasn't a heroin person."

"Cocaine?"

"Cocaine."

"So you're saying Methadone is a substitute for Cocaine?"

"No. For taking pills in The Bronx State Hospital for a breakdown."

"Have you ever received psychiatric help?"

"Uh huh."

"Can you tell us?"

"Attempted suicide, you know."

"How many times have you attempted suicide?"

"Four."

"Now, in 1970, you were convicted of possession of a dangerous drug. Do you know what that drug was?"

"Probably heroin."

"That was probably heroin, right? It's heroin, isn't it?"

"I don't know. You got the paper, why don't you tell me."

"You were arrested for obscene language and gestures. Do you remember that?"

"No."

"How about harassment?"

"To who?"

"I don't know to who. They don't say. How about petit larceny in 1971? Do you remember that?"

"No."

"You don't remember that either?"

"Evidently."

"Do you remember testifying before the Grand Jury?"

"I didn't know that was supposed to be a Grand Jury. They told me, 'We're going to put you in a room, ask you a couple of questions and then we'll let you go.' "

"And they put you in a room with a lot of people, right?"

"The ones that were awake."

From there on in, the dialogue continued to devolve and, by the time cross-examination was finished, it was more of an argument between two kids in a sandbox than it was an examination. Murray was yelling things at JoElle and she was telling him she didn't know or that she was drugged up at the time and couldn't remember. She was rooting through her purse while she answered questions and then asking the judge for some water to take her pills. The court officers were laughing out loud by the end and it was all I could do to keep a straight face. As sad as the facts of the case were, JoElle's total lack of deference was impressive. At one point when the judge told her to stop commenting back at Murray, JoElle leaned toward the judge and conspiratorially said, "I'm sorry, I thought this was caaaaasual."

The trial did not end well at all, but ultimately, no one could get around the fact that JoElle was terribly beaten. Regardless of her flaws or how much Cardillo really had a right to be angry with her, he had other ways to get her out of his house. The judge convicted Cardillo of the misdemeanor assault charge, but refused to issue an order of protection until JoElle moved out of his house. I was instructed to inform the judge as soon as JoElle moved into Section Eight housing and, at that point, she would issue the order of protection.

JoElle testified on November 23, 1998. In July of 2001, I ran into Murray on my way to the courthouse for a civil case after I had left the DA's office. As he told me every time we saw each other from the day of the trial on: "She still won't get out of his house!"

THERE ARE A million reasons to stay in abusive relationships—maybe more reasons than there are to get out of them, but the reasons are just not as good. JoElle's was a practical reason. She stayed for the money and for the better lifestyle. She was willing to suffer the blows in exchange for the perks and perhaps some money to feed her habit. The reasons that battered women stay in these abusive relationships are many and usually have deep psychological motivators. They have children together, they think the person will really change, they are afraid to be alone, they cannot take care of themselves or their children financially, they think that the problems can be fixed, or they want questions answered. They have been abused in the past or as a child and it satisfies some belief that they, and not their abusers, are at fault. Maybe, they stay because they love the person and it's human nature to want to believe that someone you love did not mean to harm you or that he will change. Perhaps, most of all, it's easier to believe that the abuse is your own fault somehow and not his because it allows you to forgive that person and go on.

The reasons that children will suffer abuse tend to be similar but can be distilled to more simplistic motivations. They are getting something that they want in return for tolerating the abuse or they are protecting someone they love, often the abuser. My first insights into the this world of child abuse and just how secretive and protective little children can be were learned from an eight-year-old boy named Juanito. His was my next case.

7

THE CASE OF THE PERJURING PASTOR

TWENTY-ONE-YEAR-OLD Luis Martinez looked barely fifteen. He was the youth group leader at a Pentecostal church located a few blocks from the DA's office on Gerard Avenue. Juanito was the eight-year-old son of an extremely devout parishioner named Maria. She had attended the church five times a week for the two years since she moved her family from the Dominican Republic to New York. Over time, Juanito and Luis developed a close relationship. Juanito regularly attended Luis's youth group classes and Luis often came to Juanito's house and played ball with him, bought him small gifts, or took him for hot dogs. Sometimes Maria even allowed Juanito to go to Luis's apartment in the basement below the church to play Nintendo or to watch television. Maria encouraged the friendship and regarded Luis as a caring role-model. Juanito's father was back in the Dominican Republic and Maria felt it was good for Juanito to have this "big brother" or father figure in his life. She also had an infant at home and she welcomed having Juanito out of her hair a few hours a day. She regarded the playtime as a reward for Juanito behaving in church and saying his prayers or doing his school work. Maria somewhat limited the duration of the visits during services, but as long as Juanito was back in his pew when she told him to be, there was no problem. Most important, Juanito seemed to enjoy going to Luis's place. He asked to go all of the time. And with so little to offer her son by way of time or gifts, Maria could hardly say no to allowing her son to spend time with this nice young man from the church.

AS TIME WENT on, Juanito began staying in Luis's apartment longer and longer—often longer than Maria had given him permission for. Juanito returned home from Luis's place progressively later and Maria became frustrated, especially when it started to lead to his absence from church. Maria warned Juanito several times that he was to spend more time in church and to return home when told or his privileges to visit Luis would be taken away. Juanito would beg that Maria not stop him from going to Luis's. They had the discussion several times, but Juanito continued to disobey his mother's orders. Finally, Maria told Juanito that he could not go to Luis's apartment anymore.

That night at church, Luis invited Juanito down to his apartment to play Nintendo. Juanito cried and pleaded with Maria to let him go and promised to be back when his mother told him to. Maria relented and decided to give Juanito one last chance. She told him that if he was not back in a half an hour, he would be cut off from playing with Luis during church time for good. Juanito promised his mother that he would not be late and excitedly ran down to Luis's. Forty-five minutes later, Juanito still had not returned. When he finally arrived, over an hour after promising he'd be back, Maria was livid. She dragged him into the hallway by the ear and began screaming at him and slapping him. Juanito broke down in tears, but the beating continued. Maria demanded over and over again to know why Juanito was late. Finally, Juanito couldn't take it any more. Before he knew what he'd done, he blurted out his confession that he was late because in return for allowing him to play Nintendo, Luis made him stay and "do bad things."

Maria was dumbstruck. She halted her beating and stood there mute, trying to absorb what her son had just told her. Juanito hung his head and sucked in desperate, sobbing breaths. At first, Maria didn't believe her son. In fact, she was furious that he would make up such a terrible lie just to get out of being punished. She waited a couple of days for her anger to subside. When the anger subsided, it was replaced by doubt: What if Juanito was telling the truth?

Maria spent days agonizing over what to do. Finally, she went to the church to seek the advice of her pastor. The pastor told Maria that he would handle the problem in the church and made her promise not go to the police. The same night, Luis's father and the pastor came to Juanito's house. Luis's father promised Maria that he would send Luis back to the Dominican Republic if she would keep her mouth shut. Maria promised to keep it between them, but she continued to mull over her decision. As promised, she did not go to the police. Part of the reason was that she was afraid of Luis's father, who was reputed to be a drug dealer and in some kind of Dominican mafia. But Maria continued to fear for her son's health and after another three days, she broke down and took her son to the emergency room for a check-up.

When Maria requested that the ER doctor examine her son's rectum, understandably it raised questions. Maria kept trying to come up with explanations for the doctors about why she wanted her son to have a rectal exam, but she was unable to give them a satisfactory reason and it was against her religious and personal principles to lie. Finally, she broke down into tears and confessed that her son said he'd been abused. The doctors reported the incident to the police.

ALTHOUGH JUANITO CLAIMED that Luis put his penis in his anus and that "it hurt," when the ER doctors examined Juanito, they did not find any evidence of rectal penetration. However, and importantly for my case, the ER doctor noted that there was "stool in the vault" at the time of the examination. Simply put, "stool in the vault" means that the person needs to go to the bathroom. This prevents proper performance of a sphincter "wink test," or a test of anal elasticity.

Two days later, the case was assigned to an ADA who immediately sent Juanito to see the specialists at Montefiore Child Protection Center. It was common for us to send child victims to Montefiore even when another doctor had examined the child. Doctors who are not trained to examine children for sexual abuse often do not know how to examine them or what to look for. The doctors and nurses at Montefiore Child Protection Center are specially trained to examine children for signs of sexual and physical abuse. When they examined Juanito, these doctors found evidence of decreased elasticity in the anus, which was consistent with penetration. That there was "stool in the vault" during Juanito's first exam was crucial in explaining the inconsistencies between the two examinations.

Based on this new medical evidence and Juanito's testimony in the Grand Jury, Luis was indicted for "Course of Sexual Conduct Against a Minor in the First Degree" and other related charges. Course of Sexual Conduct Against a Minor was a new law that raised the level of the crime when more than one act was committed against a child over a period of more than three months. It also allowed for the fact that children have difficulty remembering specific dates. Other sex crimes required that we narrow down the time frame to within a few weeks at the most, otherwise we couldn't prosecute the case. That requirement led to an inability of prosecutors to bring charges on many kid cases since children have difficulty with dates and times. Many serious crimes could not be prosecuted because of it. This new law allowed for a child to be able to tell us, for example, "it happened like five or six times, and it started in the winter and it ended in the summer."

Luis's family paid his bail and within days, he'd fled to the Dominican Republic. At the time, we had no extradition treaty with the DR and so, the case was doomed to rot in the endless stacks of warrant files until either Luis decided to come back to the US or until an extradition treaty was signed, which ultimately happened a couple of years later.

WHEN A DEFENDANT warrants or disappears on a case, the case goes into a holding pattern and is literally kept in separate archives until the defendant is rearrested. Sometimes an arrest is made within a short time of a warrant being issued. Other times, it could be years or never before a defendant is caught and the case is resurrected. Witnesses get older, move away, and disappear waiting for justice to be meted out and often, by the time the defendant turns up, the witness is nowhere to be found. Luis's case was sent to the warrant files with no one knowing when or if he'd be seen again. The ADA assigned to the case resigned shortly thereafter. With Luis gone, there was no reason to reassign the case and it sat in a drawer in storage waiting, perhaps forever, for Luis to return.

· · ·

DURING THE PERIOD of time that Luis was on the lam, his family was in constant contact with the pastor regarding his status. They adamantly denied that Luis had committed the crime and felt justified in helping him to flee the country. The pastor, also believing in Luis's innocence, convinced the family that Luis should come back to the US and surrender himself to the police so that his name could be cleared and they could go back to a normal life. After months of coaxing, the family finally agreed and Luis returned a few weeks later. A few days after his return to The Bronx, Luis, his father, and the priest called the police and informed them that Luis would surrender himself. On the way to the precinct, the priest was surprised to overhear Luis admit to his father that he had in fact abused Juanito. Luis surrendered himself. The case was pulled from the warrant files and assigned to me for trial.

Luis had been out of the country approximately five months. I had never met Juanito or Maria and I knew nothing about the case other than what was in the file. I had to appear in court on the case the morning after Luis surrendered himself to make a bail application. I had been assigned the case that same morning. I quickly read through the documents so that I would be somewhat prepared and then I ran to court. When I asked for bail, I reasoned with the judge that as a known flight risk with contacts outside the United States, Luis should be remanded (i.e., held without bail). I also explained to the judge that Luis's family had questionable resources and were believed to be involved in the drug trade. We thought they were able to make bail the first time using drug money. I told the judge that if bail was set, then at the very least, there should be an examination of surety. An examination of surety reviews the source of someone's bail money to try to make sure that it is legitimate. The defense argued that Luis should be released on his own recognizance, or freed without bail, since he had come back to court on his own. The judge split the baby. He set high bail and required the examination of surety that I requested. Luis's family was not able to make bail this second time and since the case was already quite old, it was scheduled for trial rather quickly.

My first order of business was to bring Juanito and Maria into my office so that I could meet them and begin preparing them for trial.

Juanito was a polite, quiet boy, but was extremely reluctant to talk about what had happened to him. In the six months since the incident, he'd matured significantly and had a much clearer understanding of what was going on. He also believed that the upheaval in his life was caused by his confession. He was embarrassed and guilt-ridden. He was upset that Luis was in jail and felt responsible.

Juanito was accompanied by his mother, Maria, who brought her 1-1/2-year-old baby as well. He was a fat, happy little boy with a dark, wide face and ready smile. He was covered from head to toe with glossy dark hair. Even his face was hairy and his arms and legs looked like a grown man's. The child had hypertrichosis, a disease in which a person has excessive hair covering his or her entire body. But I was so taken by the infant's charming personality and utter lack of knowledge about his strange condition, that I quickly stopped noticing it. I pitied him the cruelty he would face from other children as he got older. The disorder explained some of the disproportionate attention that Maria had paid to her younger child.

Maria was a small, nervous woman who constantly looked at the floor and chewed on her nails. I don't recall seeing her eyes until after the verdict. She had moved her family to the other side of The Bronx after the incident so that she could attend a different church. She detailed for me the constant threats and harassment from the defendant's father and from her pastor to drop the charges and to let the church handle the problem. Given the rumors in the community about the father's connections in drug trade, Maria was terrified. She also told me about a rumor in the parish that the pastor had overheard the defendant confessing to his father.

I sat down that same afternoon and started researching clergy privilege. Like statements to doctors, spouses, or attorneys, statements to clergy are carefully protected from disclosure unless the person making the statement consents to it being disclosed to others. The purpose behind such protections is to allow people to confide in certain others without fear of consequences. In this case, what the rule meant was that unless the statement by the defendant fell under some kind of exception to the rule, I would not be allowed to use it in court even if the pastor did admit that it was said. In reviewing the case law, however, it became clear that the privilege only applies to those statements made to clergy in a confidential setting and in their role as religious advisor. Statements made in passing to clergy outside of their capacity as religious advisors and things said to someone else in the presence of clergy members are not. As the scenario was explained to me, the defendant confessed to his father on a public street and the pastor overheard it. It seemed that we might have a shot at getting the statement into evidence at trial if the pastor would cooperate.

EMPLOYED BY THE DA's office are a group of detectives called "Detective Investigators," or the "DI Squad." They work with the DA's office and receive their assignments directly from the ADAs. Half of the fourth floor of my building was allocated to the DIs. Additionally, there were four DIs assigned specifically to DVS to investigate, assist with, and make arrests only on DVS cases. They were an invaluable resource for us.

When I started in the bureau, there were three male DIs and one female. We used to joke that ugly people weren't allowed to be DIs in DVS and this group looked like they fell right off a movie kiosk. But aside from being great looking, they were great people and excellent at what they did. They could be depended on to help out with just about anything. They were supposed to be reserved for work on internal office investigations only but we depended on them for everything. Our DIs frequently picked up the slack for their counterparts in the police department who handle sex crimes, domestic violence, and crimes against children. Called The Bronx Special Victims Squad ("BXSVS"), its members were often overworked and difficult to contact. Also, although BXSVS had some phenomenal detectives, as in any other job there were some that were pretty bad. Admittedly, I relied on the DIs frequently when I was dealing with a detective that I did not have confidence in. Detective Carlos Ortega of BXSVS, who I did trust, had originally been assigned the Martinez case. I had worked with him several times in the past and always had good experiences. But since making the arrest, Carlos had retired and moved to Florida, so I had to utilize the DIs.

The pastor did not speak English, so I approached a Spanish-speaking DI named Dave. Dave was about six feet tall with thick black hair and deep dimples that completely undid any attempt he made at being intimidating. He was bright, friendly, and reliable. I needed Dave to interpret for me and he agreed. I told him the situation and what I wanted from the pastor. Dave had been dealing with kid cases longer than I had and did not need me to explain to him that there were significant problems with the case. Even with the medical finding, the jury was going to be suspicious of the lack of findings on the first examination. A good defense attorney would know how to exploit that fact. Also, the abuse had gone on for quite some time before Juanito told his mother. It was always a challenge to make a jury understand that most kids don't tell right away. Dave understood immediately how important this confession could be to my case, especially in light of the automatic credibility that a jury would give the testimony of a pastor. Dave enlisted the support of John Hyland, another DI with the squad who was about six-foot-three and similarly muscular. Dave then called the pastor and made an appointment for the three of us to go to his home the following day.

The pastor lived inside the same housing project that his parish was in. As we entered the apartment building, I was glad to have Dave and John with me. The catacomb of buildings was your typical rundown city complex with high crime stats. I stuck out like a sore thumb with my white skin and in my suit and trench coat, but I was certainly not much of a target in the company of two huge guys with guns on their belts that they purposely left unconcealed.

We made our way up to the pastor's floor and rang the bell. The pastor's wife invited us into the apartment and sat us down in the living room. I could see immediately where a lot of the church money was going. The pastor's was not the first or last welfare-supported apartment that I saw where it was clear that the occupant, although getting a free ride from the city for his housing, was far from suffering. It was a decent-sized two bedroom loaded with new furniture, electronics, and appliances. There was a giant-screen TV in the living room that not one of my friends at the DA's office, with their government salaries and loans to pay off, could have afforded. The furniture looked like it was right off the showroom floor and was encapsulated in clear vinyl. A new computer sat on the desk in the corner. In the DA's office, no one had computers in their offices until the year I left because there wasn't enough funding for it. Every time I saw things like this, it infuriated me. Here were people who could do for themselves but, because of them, the people who really needed the help weren't getting it. My battered women were living in shelters because there was no public housing available and this pastor was on a shopping spree. I put my anger aside and glued a smile on my face as the pastor walked into the room. Dave introduced all of us and asked the pastor if he would mind if we tape-recorded the conversation. The pastor said that he didn't mind at all. Dave placed the tape recorder on the coffee table, hit the record button, and we began.

Through Dave, I explained to the pastor why I was there and what I wanted to know. The pastor was extremely cooperative and seemed nice enough. I knew better than to alienate him by confronting him with his constant harassment of Maria, which was so bad that instead of Luis being driven out of the church, she was. Whatever he did that I felt was wrong was pushed to the back of my head in hopes that he would give me what I needed. And he did. The pastor did make excuses for Luis, saying that he was sorry and that he was getting help from the church for his problems but he also admitted that he knew Luis committed the crime. I had what I needed. I told the pastor that the case was going to trial shortly and asked if he would testify to what he just told me. "Just tell the truth," I said. He agreed to cooperate. I walked out of his apartment feeling like I'd won the lottery. This testimony, combined with the medical evidence, was sure to seal a conviction.

SINCE THIS WAS my first jury trial, I was being second-seated by one of my supervisors, Larry Maloff. Maloff had resigned and was only going to be with the office another two weeks. We expected my trial to take about four days—two for jury selection and another two for the witnesses. It didn't appear that there would be a problem finishing the trial well before Maloff's last day. This was a concern for me as I was afraid that the jury might hold it against me if I switched second-seats mid-trial. We prosecutors were very superstitious about not changing anything mid-trial. If I wore my hair up the first day of trial, I had to wear my hair up for the entire trial. We did not want to do anything to distract the jury from its job.

The case was assigned to Judge Savitt. Although he had a reputation for being fairly pro-defendant, I wasn't too upset with the choice because he was a nice judge and ran his courtroom slowly. It was far better for my first trial to not be under the kind of pressure that other judges would have put on me to rush the trial. Also, the defendant did not waive a jury. Although a pro-defendant judge can certainly make decisions that are detrimental to the people's case or give more lenient sentences when there is a conviction, the decision about guilt or innocence was up to my jurors, not him.

The defense attorney in the case was David Goldenberg, another giant among defense attorneys with an impressive record of acquittals. However, Goldenberg, like Murray Richman who was my adversary in the Cardillo case, was known more as a drug attorney than anything else. In past cases with our bureau, he'd tended to alienate juries by coming down too hard on child victims—treating them the same way that he treated adult witnesses. This was not his area of expertise and I could only guess that he was representing Luis because the rumors about Luis's father being in the drug trade were true.

We began jury selection and things went slowly, albeit smoothly. I came to learn that it took much longer to pick a jury in a kid case than in just about any other. Often out of a pool of 70 jurors, three-quarters of them would have to be excused before we even began questioning them. Those that were excused claimed that they couldn't be fair because in the case either because the victim was a child or because they or their family members had been victimized in the past. We spent most of our first day just listening to people's reasons to be excused: "I was the victim of a crime." "My niece was a victim of rape as a child." "I have elderly parents at home and no one else can take care of them." "I am a single parent and no one else can watch my kids. . . ." The reasons went on and on and since there was no way to weed out the honest excuses from the ones that were simply made to get out of serving, generally everyone who asked to be let go, was. By the end of the first day, we still had no jurors selected.

The second and the third days of selection went equally slow. Unlike some judges who will seat between 16 and 20 people per round of *voir dire* knowing that a few will be lost along the way, Savitt only sat twelve at a time. Before we asked the jurors questions, Savitt went through a lengthy *voir dire* of his own. Then when it was our turn to question the jurors, Savitt set no time limits. I tended to keep it pretty short, not wanting to bore the jury, and my rounds of questions usually lasted under 20 minutes. Goldenberg, however, seized the opportunity to conduct what seemed like interminable rounds. His mode of operation was to schmooze the jurors and try to make them laugh and like him. He was much like my mentor, Bill Flack, in this respect. But Bill knew how to keep it short. Goldenberg went on and on. He ran around the courtroom cracking jokes and acting out various roles by sitting first in his seat, then in the witness box and sometimes on the railing of the jury box. He was congenial and likeable. But while he entertained the jury, I think they too were wishing he'd cut it out already after a long day. I knew I wasn't going to beat Goldenberg at his own game. He was comfortable and experienced and could laugh and chat with the jury with ease. I was nervous, uncomfortable, and inexperienced. So I countered Goldenberg's tactic by playing it straight. I got up and told the jury that this was not a popularity contest or night at the comedy club. I insinuated that Goldenberg's behavior was flat-out inappropriate. "This is serious," I instructed the jury. "This is either a boy who has been terribly abused or someone who has been wrongfully accused and, either way, you must take this seriously." I succeeded in taking a little bit of the advantage out of Goldenberg's court, and it certainly took some of the fun out of it for him.

After three days of jury selection, we'd gotten almost nowhere. Then, for the next four days, Goldenberg called in sick. I don't doubt that he was legitimately ill, as few attorneys would have the gumption to put a trial on hold unless they were seriously suffering. But I was irritated. The judge brought the jury back each day and instructed them to come in the following morning only to send them home again. By the second day, I started requesting that the judge excuse the jury permanently, declare a mistrial, and start fresh when Goldenberg got back. I didn't want an angry jury sitting on my case. We'd told them that the case would only last about a week and here they were, already in their second week, and they had not even heard opening statements. Also, it was getting closer and closer to Maloff's last day at work and at the rate we were going, I was certain that I'd have to switch second-seats mid-trial. Nonetheless, the judge refused to excuse the jurors that we'd already selected or those waiting to be questioned. By the time we finally had a jury, two weeks after having started jury selection, we were all tired and frustrated. And my second-seat was gone.

Maloff was replaced by Bernadette Perez. Bernadette was a tall brunette, a strikingly beautiful attorney with high cheekbones and sharp eyes. She looked more like she belonged on the cover of *Elle* than behind a prosecutor's table. She had a reputation among her colleagues as being somewhat unapproachable, but smart as a whip. The few people who made the mistake of underestimating Bernadette because she was good-looking did not make that mistake twice. Bern was a killer. She won her trials and was trusted with some of the most complex and highly publicized cases that came through the bureau. I had not had much contact with Bernadette prior to this case, and, at first, I was not too happy when I was told that she would be second-seating me. Although she had an excellent reputation as a trial attorney, she made no secret of her hatred for second-seating new people. She claimed to have no patience for teaching new attorneys the ropes and little tolerance for those who she perceived as lazy or who didn't follow her instructions.

In her first conversation with me, Bernadette reiterated the fact that she had no desire to second seat me or anyone else. In spite of her tough exterior and unfriendly introduction, however, Bernadette acted in direct contrast to her claim. She sat down and spent significant time reviewing the case with me, even going so far as to give me her home number in case I had to contact her at night or over the weekend. She went through my questions with a red pen, adding and deleting in a frenzy. She was truly excellent and by the end of the trial, I came to consider her a friend. Basically, Bernadette and I saw eye to eye on the case. She even admitted in the end that she didn't mind second-seating me since I worked with her and knew how to take criticism. I considered it a great compliment and one she did not give lightly.

The one strategy that Bernadette and I disagreed on, however, was whether or not to bring out the fact that the defendant fled the jurisdiction. I felt that it was persuasive evidence of the defendant's guilt that he fled from authority when he was accused. One of my mentors at the office, Dan McCarthy, was a huge fan of "flight as evidence of guilt." I couldn't wait to use his biblical quote on summation that "the guilty flee while no man pursueth while the righteous are steadfast like lions." Bernadette felt that the jury would sympathize with the defendant fleeing and would believe that any innocent man would do so rather than go to jail for being a pedophile. She emphasized that the jury instruction on flight was that it is the weakest evidence of guilt and that any reasonable explanation for running must be accepted. Ultimately we agreed to disagree and I went on to use the evidence. Finally, after almost three weeks, the trial started.

The first person I put on the stand was Juanito. His direct examination went terribly. I asked too few questions of him and failed to fully develop the nature of his relationship with the defendant on my first go around. I was also very concerned by the complete lack of emotion, or "flat affect," that Juanito displayed on the stand. He spoke about his abuse robotically, with no inflection in his voice and without once making eye contact with the jury. Although I understood that his reaction was a coping mechanism, I also understood that it would hurt my case. If I was bothered by it and I was sure of the defendant's guilt, how was a jury going to take it? I was terrified that they would perceive his lack of emotion to mean that nothing traumatic had really happened to him, rather than understanding that it is a natural and common way of dealing with incredible trauma. I always made sure to *voir dire* a jury on the fact that each person reacts differently to trauma—but saying it and not being bothered by it are two different things.

What would save the case was the detail that went into developing Juanito's relationship to Luis. The jury would not believe that this had happened unless they understood how important Luis was in Juanito's life. Without understanding that, they could not understand why the abuse went on for so long without Juanito telling anyone. Most people believe that a child will tell if he or she is being violated when, in reality, most don't tell. Parents want to believe that their children would tell them if they are being harmed. Time and time again, I heard parents tell me in disbelief, "But my children trusts me. I always told them to tell me if anyone touched them in a bad way." But children don't tell and it can be for the simplest reasons. They think they will get in trouble, or the defendant has threatened to hurt them or a parent or sibling. And most often, children don't tell because they love the person who abuses them and don't want to get that person in trouble. This was Juanito's situation and over the next hour that I kept Juanito on the stand, all I did was develop this relationship.

Juanito had no father. His mother was busy with church and with the baby. Juanito was not allowed out with friends. The family had no money, so he did not have things in his home like Nintendo or cable TV. Luis provided all these things for him. He was a father figure, a big brother, and a playmate. He took Juanito to baseball games. He let him play Nintendo and watch cable. Luis paid attention to Juanito. And Juanito loved Luis. He was willing to endure the abuse in exchange for all these things he lacked in his life. Luis told Juanito that if he ever told anyone what was happening, Luis would go to jail and they would never see each other again. Juanito did not want this to happen. The complexity of the relationship—and the odd way that it suddenly made sense that Juanito did not tell—rang of truth. Suddenly his flat affect was less important than the fact that he was describing such a complex and heartbreaking situation.

Over the next three years of trying cases, while I varied the formula and questions, I never varied my emphasis on the relationship between the defendant and the victim. Whether it was a relationship based on love, fear, or bribery, it was the understanding of that relationship that helped the jury understand the victims and their behavior.

I knew that by the time I was done questioning Juanito the trial was going better, but by no means had I won it. I still had a long battle ahead of me and anything could happen.

Maria testified second. Her testimony was brief and added little to the case outside of corroborating that Juanito was with Luis frequently and that he disclosed the abuse after he was yelled at for coming back to church late. After Maria testified, it was time for me to call the pastor.

Goldenberg and I argued back and forth during the recesses in testimony and between witnesses about the admissibility of the pastor's testimony. Ultimately, the judge agreed with me that if the statement was not made while the pastor was acting in his capacity as a religious advisor, it was admissible. However, winning this point of law would mean nothing if I could not get the pastor on the stand. For the last two days, I had attempted to contact the pastor to bring him to my office to prepare for trial, but he was not returning my calls. This first day of testimony, I sent the DIs, Dave and John, to the pastor's apartment to try and locate him. If he refused to come in, my next step would be a court order called a "Material Witness Order," forcing him, as a witness with information material or relevant to the case, to come into court or risk going to jail.

When I got back to my office after Maria's testimony, I was relieved to see Dave sitting there with the pastor, but Dave was shaking his head at me when I walked in, and he looked less than thrilled. Through Dave, the pastor told me that, first of all, I did not need to send detectives to his home threatening to arrest him, because he would always cooperate with the law. "Second," he lectured, "I don't know why you brought me here, because I know nothing about this case." I looked at him, puzzled, and reminded him that he was there to testify that he overheard Luis tell his father that he abused Juanito. "I don't know what you are talking about," he innocently replied, "I never heard such a thing." I couldn't believe my ears. While I was surprised that the pastor fessed-up in the first place, once he had, I thought he would continue to cooperate. On top of that, I had two witnesses and a tape recording of the conversation. I told Dave to get the tape, which he retrieved and brought back to my office. We played it for the pastor, who was non-plussed: "That is not my voice on that tape. I don't know who it is, but it's not me and you won't trick me into saying that it is." I was flabbergasted.

Next to the pastor's hand was a Bible that he'd brought with him to my office. It was in a black leather case with a small handle and a white dove stitched on the cover. I was infuriated. I grabbed the Bible and shoving it at him, grabbed his hand and slammed it on top. "Swear to God that you didn't say those things on that tape!" I ordered. The pastor, remaining totally composed, refused. "I don't have to swear to anything," he said, calmly removing his hand. "Go have a talk with him Dave. Get him out of here before I do something stupid." I was irate. Dave spoke with the pastor in a private interview room. I heard yelling back and forth in Spanish from both of them but, an hour later, Dave emerged shaking his head. "He won't budge."

I stormed down to my chief, Elisa's, office, grabbing Bernadette on the way. I inquired about the logistics of declaring my own witness a "hostile witness" so that I could impeach him. To simplify it, one cannot attack the credibility of one's own witness without declaring the witness hostile. There are very specific ways to do this and it's not easy. Only when a witness is declared hostile, can he be cross-examined by the party that called him. Elisa calmed me down and tried to talk sense and strategy to me.

"Do you really want to be attacking a pastor on the stand, Sarena? Do you really think that will sit well with a jury?"

"Well, maybe the jury will see him for the lying asshole that he is."

"Or maybe the jury will believe you are an asshole, that you brought two cops with you to threaten him and that you fabricated the tape. Either way, do you really think it's worth the risk to the case?"

Although I wanted more than anything to get that pastor up on the stand and show the jury what a liar he was, I knew Elisa was right. Odds were that rather than making him look bad, I would make myself look bad. I still had three more witnesses to go: the nurse practitioner who examined Juanito the second time around, Detective Carlos Ortega and the child psychologist. I would have to make my case without the help of the pastor.

THE NURSE'S JOB was fairly straightforward: to explain to the jury what the medical findings were during the second examination and to explain why those findings were not observed during the first examination. Leah Harrison, from the Montefiore Child Protection Center, was old hat at this. She'd testified dozens of times and, on the stand, was totally unfazed, by Goldenberg's implications that the findings during the second exam-ination were caused by the doctor who did the first examination. Her tes-timony was short, persuasive, and to the point. She explained that Juanito had medical findings consistent with penetration by a penis because his anus showed signs of decreased elasticity. She clarified that the ER doc-tor did not miss this finding, but was unable to perform a "wink test" because the child had stool in his bowels upon presentation to the emer-gency room. Goldenberg did a typical, noncontroversial cross-examina-tion by asking if a large bowel movement or penetration by something other than a penis could have caused the decreased elasticity. Harrison agreed that it could have been something else and emphasized that it was consistent and corroborating evidence, not conclusive. Nothing unex-pected took place, and within an hour, Harrison was off the stand.

Detective Carlos Ortega was one of the nicest, most even-tempered people I ever met. He came to my office from his retirement home in

Florida to testify about his investigation in the case. On the witness stand, he primarily spoke about his failed attempts to locate the defendant over the course of several months after the initial arrest. He explained that after he was unable to locate the defendant through the conventional means of hoofing-it door to door and asking family and neighbors about the defendant's whereabouts, wanted posters were generated and posted throughout the area. Within a few weeks of that, with no new leads, the case was closed pending further information. Ortega had nothing more to do with the case until several months later when he received a call from the defendant's father that the defendant was coming in to surrender himself. At that point, the arrest was made.

Ortega was a seasoned veteran. His testimony on direct examination was succinct and went very well. I sat down feeling quite pleased with our performance. I should not have tempted fate. Goldenberg, a seasoned veteran in his own right, starting nitpicking with Ortega about every detail of his investigation. He went over each and every report, pointing out every error and inconsistency and making any minor thing seem like a smoking gun. Ortega's testimony should have been unimpeachable. It was a routine investigation with a routine arrest where Ortega simply followed protocol. He had a defendant who surrendered himself without a fuss and made no admissions. There were no claims of coercion or police brutality. I thought that there was nothing to dispute. Yet, Goldenberg somehow managed to make Ortega lose his temper—a feat that I didn't think possible. Ortega was so angry that he was shaking and started yelling at Goldenberg and quibbling over issues that were totally inconsequential. Goldenberg played on Ortega's anger with childish glee for another 15 or 20 minutes and, having accomplished his goal of making the jury think this cop was a hothead who was out to make an arrest at any cost, he sat down. The jury silently filed out of the box for their lunch break. I was crushed. The Bronx is a borough with tremendous mistrust for the police department. Any time that a cop looked bad in one of our cases, it was bad for us. When the jury returned I would put on my final witness of the case. It was my last chance and I was not hopeful. I gathered my things together and glanced over at the defense table. Goldenberg turned to me and, grinning like the Cheshire Cat, shrugged his shoulders and said, "Oops!" I stormed out of the courtroom.

My final witness was a child psychologist, Dr. Anne Meltzer. Dr. Meltzer's job was to define child sexual abuse accommodation syndrome (CSAAS) to the jury. The syndrome would help explain Juanito's flat affect on the stand and his delayed disclosure. Meltzer first described that flat affect as a coping mechanism—that children, like adults, often mask their feelings about particularly traumatic events. She further went on to explain that it tends to be even more difficult for male children to disclose abuse by adult males because of the stigma that comes with same-sex abuse. She instructed the jury that disclosures fall into two basic categories, accidental and purposeful. Accidental disclosure occurs when someone interrupts the act and literally forces a disclosure by witnessing the crime. Purposeful disclosure is what it sounds like and may occur for many reasons. The victim may be afraid that the defendant will harm someone else and disclose to protect other potential victims. Sometimes the victim may even disclose because he is jealous or angry about attention his abuser is giving to another child. Juanito's situation fell somewhere in the middle: It was not quite purposeful disclosure because he did not want to tell. It wasn't accidental because the mother did not actually witness the act, but she did force the disclosure by confronting her son about his misbehavior. Basically, the pressure of Maria's questioning and screaming was too much for Juanito and, before he knew what he was doing, he blurted everything out.

The general practice in our bureau was to always have an expert testify on CSAAS when there was a delayed disclosure. However, I was ambivalent about testimony regarding the syndrome. On the one hand, I felt that it was necessary to help the jury understand behaviors that are contrary to what common sense would dictate. I did not want them to construe normal behavior under the circumstances to be evidence of lack of veracity. On the other hand, psychiatric expert testimony was like telling the jury to "ignore the white elephant." By bringing their attention to the issues, I may have been making them question what they would otherwise not be concerned with. Also, the population that generally sat on our juries in The Bronx might look skeptically upon psychiatric testimony. Particularly troubling in this case was that while Goldenberg did not have a great reputation regarding his ability to examine children, he had an outstanding reputation for his ability to make psychiatric testimony sound like hogwash, especially regarding CSAAS. The problem with defining syndromes like CSAAS is that part of what they convey is that any behavior is normal. For example, some children who are abused will improve in school because they bury themselves in their work to "escape" from the trauma. Other children will totally decompensate and their grades will plummet. Some children misbehave or act out in school, while others will be on their best behavior to avoid being "punished." An effective cross-examiner will successfully make it seem like the psychiatrist is saying that everything is consistent with abuse. In previous trials, Goldenberg was reputed to have made other experts basically agree that if it rains, it's consistent, and if it does not rain, that is consistent too.

I went over all of this with Dr. Meltzer and expressed my concerns to her. She seemed totally undisturbed. She explained to me that what defines CSAAS as a syndrome is the fact that there are readily discernable and consistent patterns of behavior among children who are victims of abuse. The key was not to focus on variations in behavior that will naturally occur from individual to individual, but rather to focus on the commonalities. She convinced me, and was equally persuasive under cross. Goldenberg made no headway with her. At the conclusion of her testimony I rested my case.

Goldenberg opted not to call any witnesses and the defendant did not testify. The trial concluded on a Friday and the judge decided not to instruct the jury until the following Monday so that they would not have to be sequestered over the weekend. For two days, I agonized over my every word and act. I berated myself for the things that I forgot to ask or those issues that I did not adequately prepare my witness for. I tormented myself about how the jury would interpret Ortega's angry outburst—if they would make some kind of crazy leap because they thought the cop was a hothead. Mostly, I beat myself up for every little error. I was new at this, but I could not use that as an excuse. This was too important. By the time I came in on Monday, I had myself totally convinced that Luis Martinez was about to be a free man.

Savitt charged, or instructed, the jury first thing that morning, which for him was about 11:00 AM. His charge lasted over an hour and the jury deliberated less than an hour before breaking for lunch. While the jury ate and deliberated, I sat by my phone in agony.

Everyone was telling me that the longer the jury was out, the better it was for my case. In the deliberation predication game, there were all kinds of superstitions and attempts at reading the minds of jurors. Long deliberations were thought to be a good sign for the prosecution as were requests to read back charges. When the jury requested read-back of certain testimony, we would try to guess why they were asking for it. If they were asking for a particular piece of testimony, like "the part where the doctor described the injuries on direct examination," we may read that as a good sign. When they requested "all of the testimony of the eyewitness," it was harder to guess. Attorneys on both sides would try to sway the results by interpreting the notes in their favor. For example, if the jury asked for the doctor's testimony on direct examination about the injuries, the defense might try to persuade the judge that what the jury really wanted was direct and crossexamination. Most judges would just give the jury exactly what they asked for and assume that if they really wanted something else, they would send another note. The worst was when the jury would ask for something really broad such as "all of the testimony of witness X." Usually, they only made that mistake once before realizing that it meant listening to the court reporter do a monotone rendition for six hours. After that, the requests were much narrower.

EVERYONE HAD THEIR crazy stories about things that happened while their juries were deliberating. My friend Asha had a juror inform the judge that another juror was refusing to deliberate. Another colleague had a juror report that a fellow juror told the rest of the panel that he made sure he was selected so that he could vote not guilty no matter what and that he refused to deliberate any other verdict.

My strangest jury experience involved the statutory rape and forcible rape of a 12-year-old by her cousin's 25-year-old boyfriend. The jury was sequestered for four days including a Saturday. As the deliberations went on, things got weirder and weirder. The first day, the jury started deliberating at about 5:00 in the afternoon. Within 10 minutes, they came back with a note asking for a read-back of my opening statement, which the judge informed them is not evidence and therefore could not be read back. Their next note, about 10 minutes later, said that the jury "is expired for the evening." After speaking with them, the judge elicited that they meant that they were tired or "retired" for the evening and wanted to quit for the night and start again the next morning.

In 2001, the law was changed to eliminate automatic sequestration of juries. Since then, sequestration is at the judge's discretions, but when I was an ADA, if a trial involved charges that were of a certain level, the jury was automatically sequestered. The forcible rape in my case was a "B Felony," which is the same level as an attempted murder and punishable by up to 25 years in jail for a first-time offender. It was an automatic sequestration case. Sometimes, when a jury would ask to go back to the hotel early and then came back with a quick verdict the next day, we assumed that they just wanted a couple of free meals and a hotel room courtesy of the taxpayer. Once they left the deliberation room, they were not allowed to discuss the case, so several court officers would be assigned to go with the jury to the hotel to make sure that no one discussed the case and that there were no shenanigans. The court officers also loved sequestration because it meant a significant chunk of overtime pay. They had stories about jurors trying to sneak down the halls to each other's room and trying to climb out windows.

We assumed, in my 12-year-old's case, that since the jury only deliberated for an hour and then went to the hotel, we were in for a quick verdict the next morning. So much for reading the minds of jurors. Over the next four days, the jury had the charges read back to them no less than 20 times. The first day, some of the women were coming out a little red-eyed. By the second day, they were openly sobbing. We were at a total loss as to what was going on in the deliberation room. Twice, the jury came back with a note that they could not reach a unanimous verdict. Finally, the last note on Saturday afternoon, after four days of deliberation, was "are these allegations or facts?" We were dumbfounded. The judge brought the jury out and with poorly masked sarcasm informed them, "If these were facts and not allegations, then we wouldn't need a jury now, would we?"

LUIS MARTINEZ, MY first jury trial, certainly did not give me a typical view of the jury deliberation experience that I came to understand over the years. As I said, they had hardly begun deliberations before they broke for lunch. I sat in my office simply trying to occupy myself, but I was totally unproductive. My colleagues poked their heads in occasionally to wish me luck. Some of the veterans sat with me telling me that I might as well relax and get some work done because I could be in for the long haul. I spent most of lunch going over the case with Elisa. I told her about all of the problems with the case, not wanting her to be surprised when I got the acquittal that I expected. I was still hoping that she would tell me, "Don't worry about it. You did great," but that was not Elisa's way. Instead of the pep talk I'd hoped for, I got, "There's always next time. We all lose a few. Hey, at least if they're out for a while, it will be a moral victory."

I went back to my office feeling even worse and tried playing solitaire. I wanted to call people, but I was afraid to tie up the phone. I stared at the wall, angry at nothing in particular, and waited. I was too nervous to eat. I was afraid that if I went to the bathroom, the phone would ring. I paced and doodled and tried to at least look busy.

About 45 minutes after leaving the courtroom, I got a call from the court clerk that he had a note from the jury and I should come over. He would not tell me what the note was. Although clerks were not allowed to tell what was written in the note until all parties were in the courtroom, they would usually say if it was a verdict or not. I was a bit miffed at him, but assumed that so early in the game, it was a read-back. I ran across the street to the court and then waited another half hour for the defense attorney, whose office was not as close as mine. I was a total wreck. I was also alone because Bernadette had gone on vacation. I had not brought a book or magazine, so I just stared at the table and kept trying to get some kind of clue from the clerk's demeanor about what the note was. He maintained a perfect poker face. I rapidly learned after that to befriend the court clerk at any cost so I would not run into this kind of torture again. It paid off eventually, but this time around I simply suffered.

After what seemed like eons, Goldenberg arrived. The judge waited for him to get his things together and then informed us that the jury had reached a verdict. I was devastated. Short deliberation equaled bad sign for the prosecutor. And Goldenberg, while he was telling me that it meant nothing, could not mask the relief on his face. We had to wait another 15 minutes while the court officers went to get the defendant. Goldenberg jovially bantered with the clerk and the judge. He tried to include me in the antics but I had no interest. I knew I was doomed. I sat there dreading having to tell my friends and family that I had lost my first felony jury trial and that I had freed my first pedophile— and also telling poor Juanito's mother, who had already been through so much.

As the jury filed in, I tried to stare and not stare at them at the same time. I didn't want to make them uncomfortable, but I was trying to read their expressions. They were quietly joking with each other. Another bad sign. Everyone told me that a jury is happy when they acquit because they don't shoulder the same emotional burden as when they convict. I started picking my nails and waited. The judge asked for the verdict sheet from the jury. He read it and handed it back to the foreperson, infuriatingly with no indication whatsoever on his face of what he'd read.

The court clerk stood and addressed the jury:

"Madame foreperson, has the jury reached a verdict?"

"We have."

"On the first count, course of sexual conduct against a minor in the first degree, how say you?"

"Guilty, your honor."

"On the second count, sodomy in the first degree, how say you?"

"Guilty, your honor."

"On the third count, sexual abuse in the first degree, how say you?"

"Guilty, your honor."

"And on the fourth count, endangering the welfare of a minor, how say you?"

"Guilty, your honor."

I bit my lip and tried my hardest not to smile and cry at the same time. My first felony conviction. And not only that, it was the first conviction in Bronx County under the new course of sexual conduct against a minor law. I felt proud, and my first reaction was to be overjoyed. I walked out of the courtroom and Juanito's mother hugged and kissed me, as did Juanito. They thanked me. I told the mother that I would not be contacting them anymore. The psychiatrists say that it's best for prosecutors to sever ties when a case is over because we just become part of a bad memory. I told them that it didn't mean that they shouldn't call me if they needed me, and they shouldn't think it meant that just because the trial was over, I didn't care anymore. I did care. I cared very much.

Luis was sentenced to consecutive terms of 8 to 16 years in prison on the sodomy and sexual conduct charges, 3-1/2 to 7 years on the sexual abuse charges, and 1 year on the endangerment charge. I never saw Juanito or his mother again. And I do still care. I still wonder what happened to Juanito. Is he okay? Has he learned to deal with this? Did his mother take him for help like she promised she would? As he grows up, how will he deal with what happened to him? How will he ever trust again?

After the verdict, I rushed back to my office to tell Elisa about my victory. I was elated. I smiled so much that, by the end of the day, my face hurt. I called everyone, friends and family, to tell them. I went out with some colleagues to The Yankee Tavern that night to celebrate over some beer. Anytime someone won a trial in the bureau, she had to bring in bagels the next day, so everyone put in their orders, telling me what to buy and where to buy it. They all bought me drinks and toasted my victory.

I took a cab home that night and walked into my dark, silent apartment just after 1:00 in the morning. I checked to see if my pets had enough food and water. My rabbit, Murphy, was 10 years old at the time. He hopped to the side of his cage in anticipation and started banging his bottle and thumping his hind legs. I opened his cage and picked him up. I buried my nose in his fur, which always smelled like fresh hay, and suddenly was overcome with such profound sadness. I realized that what I said to the jury in my *voir dire* was true. I had no right to be celebrating. I had just taken away someone's liberty and even if that was justice, I had no business enjoying the moment. I had no business enjoying this moment at the expense of Juanito's childhood and Luis's freedom. I sat down on the sofa, with Murphy tight under my chin, and cried.

It was a sadness that became familiar with every verdict that I took in a case, win or lose. It was a sadness that I thought would abate with time, but it only grew.

8

WINNING THE UNWINNABLE

THE COURT: "Miss Straus, you may make your final summation."

I stood up in front of the jury and, taking a deep breath, turned to face them. I had my summation written out on index cards which I held in my hand, but I never looked at them. I knew what I was going to say. I had known since a year before when the case started. I approached the railing of the jury box:

"Good afternoon, Ladies and Gentlemen. What you're sitting there thinking right now is, 'If Yohanna was my daughter, would I do anything differently than the defendant?' It's hard not to think that. It's hard not to feel terrible about this. This is a terrible situation and anybody who has children or nieces or sisters is sitting there thinking, 'Would I have done anything differently if this was my family—if my daughter came in looking the way Yohanna came into the defendant's apartment?'

"Ladies and Gentlemen, two wrongs do not make a right and what the defendant did is a crime. What he did was to take matters into his own hands and regardless of your personal feelings, regardless of how much you may hate the victim, David Otto, for what he did to his wife, Yohanna, you have to put those feelings aside. You have to judge this case coldly and objectively. And you will feel what you will feel, but you cannot use it in making your decisions in this case. Remember, Justice wears a blindfold. She doesn't see these things. Justice has to be blind because if there is no law for the defendant, Ramon Payton, there is no law for any of us.

"David Otto was prosecuted for what he did to his wife. He would have been prosecuted again if there were another charge brought forward. But that's not what happened. The defendant took matters into his own hands and you can't do that. There's a system of law enforcement in place to deal with situations just like this, to deal with wife beaters just like David Otto. And you have a very interesting job, Ladies and Gentlemen, because most of the time a jury has to sit up there and decide whether or not the person who's been victimized was injured by the person sitting in the seat over there. But you don't have to decide that. You know for a fact that Ramon Payton stabbed David Otto. The defendant himself testified that he stabbed David Otto. So what you need to determine is whether he was justified in doing that. What happened on July 28 of 1998?

"Well, David Otto got into a fight with his wife, Yohanna. He beat her up and she called the police. She was escorted by the police to her mother's house where her mother lives with the defendant, Ramon Payton. It's approximately two hours later that David Otto shows up at the door. He gets to the door, he knocks on the door, he asks to speak with his wife and he is denied access. So when they tell him he can't speak with his wife, he gets angry. But he was unarmed. All he had were his hands. Did he get angry? Yeah. Did he insult the defendant? Yes. And the defendant got furious. Furious. And Yohanna's mother was furious. We would all be furious. Her daughter had just got beaten up. Who could blame her? And, that's when the defendant, Ramon Payton, went and got a knife and started stabbing David Otto. That's what happened."

I walked across the courtroom to the judge's dais where I had a boombox set up to play the 911 tape. The jury's eyes followed me across the room. They had heard the whole tape three days earlier but I cued it to the spot I wanted them to hear. It was a neighbor screaming into the phone:

"There is a man getting stabbed! He's stabbing him! He's stabbing him! Oh, God! Hurry!"

I flicked off the tape and waited a moment. I turned back to the jury.

"Not two people having a fight. Not two men with knives, fighting. 'There's a man getting stabbed. He's stabbing him.' And the reason that's the call is because there was not a fight. There was a man getting stabbed."

I walked back to the box and put my hand on the railing.

"The defendant and his family had no less than three opportunities to call the police before this incident occurred. They knew David Otto was coming over. He called and he told them he was coming over. And the testimony from Yohanna's mother and from Yohanna and from the defendant is that they were all terrified when they heard he was coming over because he had just beaten Yohanna. Did they call the police? No. Would that have been the reasonable thing to do? Yes. Would that have been the right thing to do? Yes. So, if they're so scared of him, if he is so irate in that phone call, why aren't they calling the police?

"What was their next opportunity to call the police? Well, the next opportunity to call the police was when David Otto actually showed up at the door. Because if you're to believe that they didn't call the police because they didn't think he was actually going to come there, well, they had another chance when he showed up and he was banging on the door. They didn't have to open it, they could have called the police right then and there and he would have been arrested. Do they call 911? No. They open the door.

"What's the next chance to call 911? Well, the defendant testified that he was able to push Otto out the door and close the door. Did anybody call 911 at that point? No. Instead he went and got a knife.

"Three opportunities. They're so terrified of this guy, yet nobody called 911. Somebody explain that? The explanation is that the defendant wanted to take care of David Otto once and for all. He wanted to take matters into his own hands. That's why nobody called 911.

"The defense wants you to focus so much on how much you hate David Otto that you completely lose sight of the issue in this case. And you know what? It's not hard to do. Three-and-a-half hours of cross-examination of David Otto about what he did to his wife. Well, he's already been on trial for that. He's already been convicted of that. He's already admitted to it. But he's not being prosecuted here, the defendant is. For three-and-a-half hours to do what? To make you so angry that you can't see straight. Did it give the defendant a right to stab him? No. You have to use your judgment. You have to use your common sense. And you have to put aside your personal feelings about David Otto and decide whether the defendant committed a crime.

"The bottom line is that David Otto showed up at that apartment unarmed and he was stabbed. And even if you believe that he was initially trying to get into that apartment, he was pushed outside of that apartment and that's when the defendant went to get a knife. And even if you believe that he was trying to get into that apartment again, he turned and ran from the defendant after the defendant started stabbing him, and they can't get away from that."

I walked to my table and picked up several photographs that I had put into evidence. I held them up to the jury as I spoke. They were close-ups of gaping stab wounds taken at the hospital immediately after the incident, some showing glints of bone through the wounds. There were also photographs of those same injuries stapled together, and finally shots of the ropey scars that remained a year later.

"They cannot get away from those stab wounds in the back. You saw the scars. Two separate deep wounds in the back. The defendant claims they were tussling and rolling over and over and that when David Otto rolled over the knife, he was cut. If you're rolling over and over down the stairs, are you going to have scratches or slices or something that looks like you rolled across a knife or two deep stab wounds in the back?

"The defense has no obligation to put on any witnesses. It's the people's burden. And I submit to you that I met that burden of proof beyond a reasonable doubt. But the fact of the matter is that he did put on a case and those were his witnesses and what you choose to do with their testimony is up to you. So let's talk about the defense witness testimony.

"Now, first the defense put on Yohanna Reyes. And the judge is going to be instructing you on interested witnesses. I submit to you that Yohanna Reyes is an interested witness. What do I mean by that? The defendant is her stepfather. She loves him. And you know what? I feel very bad for the defendant, his wife, and his daughter because they're in a terrible position. But the sole purpose of Yohanna Reyes testimony was to prejudice you against David Otto. Why do I say that? Because the only thing that she could testify to you about was his assault of her. She couldn't tell you a single, solitary thing about what happened in the apartment when David Otto was stabbed, because she didn't see anything. She told you that she was in the bedroom the whole time, so the only purpose of her testimony is to make you feel bad for her and to make you angry at Otto. She didn't see anything. She adds nothing to the case.

"Consuela Payton. How did she feel when David Otto showed up at the door? Angry, irate, vengeful. Who could blame her? Yohanna is her daughter and she told you she adores her daughter. But what is the bottom line about her? Well, first of all, she's exaggerating. You heard what she said a year ago when she testified in the Grand Jury. You heard what she said in court now, a year later. Is she lying? No, she's not lying because the bottom line is she told you that she can't remember anything. She's an unreliable witness. She's an interested witness. She's looking out for the people she loves. She didn't see it happen. As soon as that knife came out, she closed the door because she 'just couldn't look.' She can't tell you what happened out there, either. So what does her testimony add except to prejudice you against David Otto and make sure that you can't see straight when you're deciding this case?

"And you heard the defendant testify in this case. And the judge is going to instruct you that he's an interested witness, too. He's minimizing what he did to David Otto. He's maximizing what Otto did. But what you can't get around is the knife. You can't get around that he could have called 911. When Otto showed up, Payton opened the door. When the defendant pushed Otto out the door, he grabbed a knife. The defense would have you believe that was the only way that he could handle Otto, that Otto is so much bigger than him that the only way that he could get this man out of his apartment, that he could protect his family, was to get out that knife. But you know what? It's a matter of inches, it's a matter of pounds, it's a matter of a few years—and the bottom line is that he was strong enough to push Otto out of the apartment before he got the knife, so what did he have to get the knife for?"

I held up a blown-up photograph of the defendant's mug shot. It was a full face shot of him immediately after he was arrested. I displayed it to the jury.

"Another really interesting piece of information is that the defendant didn't have any physical injuries. You're hearing all this information about David Otto swinging punches and David Otto jumping at him,

David Otto kicking him with those big black boots that you saw. But there are no bruises. It's an amazing coincidence, isn't it? And you can ask to see a picture that was taken of the defendant that day he was arrested and you can look at his face, where he was supposedly kicked in the face with that big black boot, and you can see there are no bruises. Why doesn't he have any bruises? Because David Otto didn't do anything to him. But you know who does have injuries? David Otto. And you know what David Otto's most important injuries are? The two stabs in the back that we talked about that you just can't get past. And defensive wounds: cuts on the arms, cuts on the hands. How do you explain those? He's getting stabbed. He's trying to defend himself.

"What else did you hear? Well, you heard that David Otto was stabbed sixteen times before collapsing from loss of blood and then the defendant ran out of the building. We know that David Otto was bleeding profusely. You saw the clothing. The defendant told you he was covered in blood. Otto told you how much he was bleeding and it certainly isn't a stretch to believe how much he was bleeding when you know what his injuries were and that he had a pumping wound in the arm when he arrived at the hospital. He collapsed on the stairs from loss of blood.

"When he saw Otto collapse, the defendant ran out of the building and started washing off the blood in the fire hydrant. When he saw the police, he threw the knife under the car. Why? Because he knows he's guilty and when he sees the cops coming, he has to hide the evidence of his crime. He's hiding the blood. He's hiding the knife because he knows he's guilty. And if he's not guilty why is he running?

"What makes sense, Ladies and Gentlemen? Well, you heard from David Otto. Like him or not, and I'm sure you don't, his story made sense. He admitted to you that he beat his wife. Heck, he even admitted to you that he put a knife to her throat and she didn't call the police for that. You don't gotta' like the guy. I'd be surprised if you did. But he got up there, he was frank and he was forthright about it.

"You heard from Doctor Anderson and I submit to you that she is the definition of a disinterested witness. She has no stake in this matter. She's a resident at the hospital. She's not even being paid to be here. She didn't give you expert opinions. All she did was read the medical records to you. She told you about all the stab wounds. She told you about the treatment that David Otto received and she told you how deep some of those wounds were. She even told you that one of those wounds threatened his limb. Those are some serious stab wounds. You draw your own conclusion. But how can you conclude that somebody was just trying to defend himself and keep somebody off and making such deep stab wounds that this person's limb was threatened and that some of the wounds were to the bone?

"Ladies and Gentlemen, if there's no law for Ramon Payton then there is no law for anybody. What the defendant told you that he did when he stabbed the complainant is that he was anticipating harm from this person. You can't stab somebody because of something they haven't done. You can't stab somebody because of something you anticipate and you cannot stab someone for a crime they did in the past—a threat that's already over. You heard his testimony. He took matters into his own hands. He stabbed an unarmed man for something that he thought that he *might* do—and that's a crime. And I would ask you to find him guilty for that."

I TURNED AROUND, walked back to my chair, and sat down. Now it was up to 12 strangers.

I was empathetic with the defendant in the case of the *People v. Ramon Payton*. It was a difficult case to try and, from the start, I was ambivalent about prosecuting the case myself. I have no doubt that Ramon Payton committed a crime, but sometimes you can sympathize with a defendant. And there are certain victims whose causes may not be the ones you want to take up what little time and resources you have. There were other victims that I would rather have devoted my time and energy to than a wife beater like David Otto. Nonetheless, the victory was a proud one for me. No one thought I'd win and we were all fairly sure that it was a textbook case for jury nullification.

When I was first assigned the case against Ramon Payton, I was immediately made aware that the complainant, David Otto, had a pending case for beating his wife. A misdemeanor assistant in DVS was handling the case against Otto and I kept close watch on it. When the victim on a case has a pending and related case as a defendant, the prosecutor is not allowed to speak to that victim without his or her counsel approving it first. It was a catch-22 for me. In order to keep Payton in jail for stabbing Otto, I had to have Otto testify within six days of Payton's arrest. But it was a problem to have Otto testify as a victim in the Grand Jury because he was also a defendant in a case with a related set of facts. His testimony could be self-incriminating.

When a defendant chooses to testify in the Grand Jury, he has to sign "waiver" papers. These are papers wherein the defendant basically agrees to waive his right against self-incrimination. In other words, by waiving his rights in the Grand Jury, the defendant or a witness makes anything he says before the Grand Jury the subject of investigation and prosecution. In exchange for being allowed to tell his side of the story, the defendant is required to answer all "legal and proper questions" put forth by the Grand Jury. On the rare occasion when a victim or witness is also a defendant in a related case, or when his testimony could be self-incriminating, that victim or witness also has to waive his right against self-incrimination in order to testify in the case. This was the case with Otto.

The first time I met with Otto he was with his attorney. He was sitting in the DVS waiting room among the toys and cartoon murals provided for the children who were frequent visitors to our bureau. Otto had just been released from the hospital and it looked like the hospital had literally stapled him together and sent him on his way. He looked like he still needed to be there. As the daughter of a doctor, the few times that I needed stitches, they were small and precise so as to cause minimal scarring. Otto was literally stapled up and down his legs and arms and the scars he bore a year later at trial were ropey and gnarled. One of his legs was blown up with an infection and I sent him back to the hospital to have it checked when we were done talking.

I was not allowed to speak with Otto alone until after his misdemeanor case against his wife was finished. So, in the presence of his attorney, I explained to David what would happen in the Grand Jury. He expressed unconvincing bewilderment at my accusations that he would harm his wife. By the time he testified at trial a year later, I had Otto convinced that his wide-eyed, innocent routine would not be persuasive to a jury and that the only way we stood a shot of convicting his wife's stepfather was if he hung his head and apologized sincerely for his own misdeeds. Although he never showed real remorse for beating his wife and definitely downplayed his responsibility, we had, nonetheless, come a long way by the time Otto took the stand as my witness. I had Otto sign the waiver paperwork and we went across the street to the building where the Grand Jury sat so that he could testify against Ramon and so that I could keep Ramon in jail.

I instantly disliked Otto. I had no sympathy toward him: Duty, not concern, caused me to prosecute his case. He was exactly the type of self-serving egotist I expected a wife beater to be. He smiled and tried to be charming at the same time he attempted to persuade me that his wife instigated all the fights they'd had. David was an average sized, well-muscled, handsome man. And as with most wife beaters, had I not known about his dark side, I might have found him charming. Many batterers are charming at first. It's how they get people attached to them and trusting them before the abuse begins.

IN 1973, IN response to the rising tide of drug crimes, then Governor of New York, Nelson Rockefeller, pushed through a set of severe anti-drug laws. The belief, at the time, was that rehabilitative efforts had failed and that the epidemic of drug abuse could only be quelled by totally unforgiving punishment for drug crimes. The purpose of these laws, which became known as the "Rockefeller Drug Laws," was to deter the sale and use of drugs. They established mandatory prison sentences for drug crimes which were related to the weight of the drug involved. However, while these laws were intended to target major dealers, most of the people incarcerated under these laws were convicted of low-level, nonviolent offenses, and many had no prior criminal records.

Enacted in the same year as the Rockefeller Laws, the Second Felony Offender laws mandated significantly increased sentences for second felony offenses. The severity of the punishment was regardless of whether both felonies were violent or nonviolent and without regard to any mitigating factors, such as whether the offender was a productive member of his or her community, or how many years had passed between convictions.

The combination of these two laws resulted in an exponential expansion of the prison population. In 1980, 11 percent of the prison population were drug felons. By 2003, 38 percent of the prison population in New York were drug offenders. Furthermore, under the Rockefeller Laws, judges had no discretion over sentencing. People convicted of drug offenses under the Rockefeller Laws served a mandatory minimum sentence based solely on the quantity of a drug involved in the offense. These sentences were mandatory regardless of the individual's background, his or her role in the crime, or the circumstances of the crime.

Finally, in 2004, the Rockefeller Drug Laws were somewhat modified, but this did not help Ramon Payton in my assault case against Otto. In 1988, Ramon Payton had been convicted for criminal possession of a quantity of cocaine. He was sentenced under the Rockefeller Drug Laws to the absurd term of three years to life. He was released early for good behavior in 1990. It was eight years between his release for this drug crime and his stabbing of David Otto. If Ramon Payton was convicted for stabbing David Otto, he would be subject to the Second Felony Offender laws and would be going to jail for a long time.

Payton seemed to have genuinely rehabilitated himself and was a far more sympathetic character in many ways than David Otto. He was a soft-spoken, gentle-looking man with dark curly hair. Payton had held down the same decent job for eight years. He was well liked by his bosses and co-workers and he reportedly treated his family well. When I presented Payton's case to the Grand Jury, I was certain that they would sympathize with him. I thought that they might sympathize with his attack on Otto for beating Yohanna. I would not have been at all surprised if the Grand Jury had nullified the case by voting no true bill. Although I knew that Payton was guilty, I would not have lost sleep if the case had been dismissed then and there. Maybe I would have even slept better.

First, I put David Otto before the Grand Jury to testify. As much as I disliked him, his testimony made sense and he was consistent in his rendition of events from start to finish. He explained that he and his wife got into a fight and, although he claimed that she instigated it, Otto did admit to punching her. After the fight, Otto went to a friend's house to cool off. He knew that Yohanna had called the police, so once he calmed down, he called his mother-in-law's house to find out from Yohanna where she reported him so that he could turn himself in. He was afraid that if he did not report to the precinct, the cops would show up at his job the next day to arrest him. His mother-in-law kept hanging up on him and refusing to let him speak to Yohanna, so he went over to the apartment. When he got to the apartment and they continued to refuse to allow him to speak to Yohanna, Otto got angry and starting yelling insults at Payton and at his mother-in-law. He and Payton were yelling through a crack in the door with the chain on. At some point, Payton slammed the door shut, and when he opened it again a few seconds later, he had a knife in his hand. He started swinging and Otto blocked the blows with his arms and then turned to run down the stairs. Payton chased him down the stairs, stabbing him in the back with the knife. When Otto fell on the steps, Payton stabbed him in the legs. Otto then recalled starting to lose consciousness. He saw Payton run down the stairs and he dragged himself out of the building and passed out. The next thing he recalled was waking up in the hospital.

Payton also testified before the Grand Jury and his version of events was fairly consistent from start to finish as well. He testified to much the same as Otto up until the point where Otto got to the apartment. Payton claimed that Otto was trying to force his way into the apartment.

The Grand Jury indicted Payton and, about a year later, the case went to trial. My feelings about the case today and when I tried it are pretty much exactly what I said to the jury in my summation. I cooperated extensively in the Grand Jury and throughout the life of the case with the defense attorney, Steven Caeser. I was very much on the fence about the case emotionally and felt that the best thing to do would be to put everything in front of the jury and let them decide whether the prosecution would continue. My goal was to let the jury know everything that I knew so that they could make a fully informed decision. I think, however, that Caeser mistook my obvious misgivings about the case with my thinking that a conviction was not justified or that I would not prosecute the case to the best of my ability. My desire to handle the case fairly did not mean that I would not try to litigate it well. Ultimately, when the jury convicted, I think Caeser felt that I had violated some kind of unspoken agreement to make sure that Payton was acquitted. I certainly never intended to convey that I did not want justice in the case or that I did not think that a crime was committed.

On November 5, 1999, Payton was convicted of assault in the second degree. He was not released until July 1, 2004. Justice was done, even if that justice was not so easy to accept. The Payton case had another effect on my reputation in DVS that I did not foresee, and that was as someone who was not afraid to take a tough case and who could win it. In some ways this was true. I was willing to try just about anything, but that does not mean that I wasn't scared of it or afraid of losing.

9

THE PEOPLE V. DARNELL THOMAS

RANDOLPH H. PLOPNICK WAS somewhat of a legend in The Bronx, and not for good reasons. He died shortly after my only trial with him, so I feel that I must temper my comments, but I never heard anyone speak of a positive experience with him. I first encountered Plopnick as a new assistant when he appeared frequently in the misdemeanor parts. Initially, I felt bad for him. He was a morbidly obese man with thinning hair, missing teeth and a terrible case of psoriasis. He dressed poorly, in ill-fitting maroon or pink polyester pants with plaid jackets. And he spit when he talked. Trying to ignore the warnings of my colleagues, I attempted to judge Plopnick for myself. I rapidly discovered that compared to his personality, his appearance was almost pleasant. He was a nasty, abrupt human being and a poor excuse for an attorney. I especially felt sorry for his clients, who did not stand a snowball's chance in hell with Plopnick as their "advocate." There had even been rumors that Plopnick accepted sexual favors from his clients in lieu of payment, and these allegations had been investigated by DVS on occasion. Within a short time of my victory in the Payton case, I had more than adequate opportunity to see Plopnick perform.

One of my fellow DVS assistants, Roberta Baldini, resigned. I inherited one of her cases, *People v. Darnell Thomas*, which, she told me up front, was a loser. Roberta had inherited the case from an assistant who went on maternity leave just a short time earlier. The folder was in disarray, having been through two assistants who were on their way out the door when they handled it. To top it off, Roberta had no contact with victim, Sheryl, for quite some time. For the few weeks that Roberta had the case, Sheryl had refused to come to the office to discuss the case or even to answer Roberta's phone calls. It seemed that Sheryl wanted to drop the case.

The gist of the case was that Darnell shot Sheryl, his common-law wife and the mother of his child, in the head. She survived her wounds and although she initially cooperated with us in the prosecution of the case, she now wanted to drop the charges and get back together with Darnell. We refused to let her do so and she subsequently stopped answering our calls. Obviously, it's hard to prosecute a case without a witness.

The only charge on the indictment was reckless assault, and my first order of business was to find out why we had not indicted the defendant for attempted murder. Elisa informed me that since the victim was facing away from the defendant when she was shot and he claimed that the gun was triggered accidentally, we could not prove intent in the case, and therefore, had only indicted for the assault. I disagreed with her, drawing attention to the fact that when the victim first came to our office, she told us that earlier that morning, the defendant had attempted to electrocute her in the bathtub by sticking radio wires in the water while she was bathing. I thought that gave us pretty good reason to believe that he was trying to kill her. Regardless, it was too late in the game to do anything about it, and I was stuck with the one charge on the indictment.

Just a couple of days after the case was assigned to me, it was scheduled for trial. I made several efforts to contact Sheryl before my court appearance but, like Roberta, I had no luck. I made my way to the court having had no success in contacting my witness. To add insult to injury, the case was in front of Judge Aaron Hogan (who for reasons unknown to me we all called "Skippy"), a notoriously pro-defendant judge who had a tendency to fly off the handle on occasion. I stood before him explaining that ADA Baldini had just resigned and I was requesting two weeks to familiarize myself with the case and to attempt to locate Sheryl. Generally speaking, my request was a reasonable one and few judges would have denied it, especially in a situation such as this where there was plenty of speedy trial time left on the case and all prior delays were due to defense requests. Plopnick, smelling an opportunity, made an extensive record regarding his conversations with Sheryl wherein she indicated to him that she would not cooperate in the case. He said that it was unfair to keep his client in jail since I could not prove the case without Sheryl's testimony. Skippy agreed. He gave me two days to get ready for trial and said that if I was not ready by that time, he would release the defendant.

I ran back to my office and prepared a material witness order for the judge to sign and for the detectives to attempt to deliver that night. The problem, of course, was that the witness had to be given the order to know that she was required to appear. The detectives could not find Sheryl anywhere.

I HAD RECENTLY attended a conference on prosecuting "victimless" domestic violence cases. Since it was common for DV victims to refuse to press charges and they often even testified on behalf of the defendant, there was a huge push to try to prove cases without the victim's cooperation. The conference covered the types of evidence needed to prove a case without a victim's testimony and various methods of meeting the burden of proof "beyond a reasonable doubt" without the cooperation of the victim.

Misdemeanor assistants in DVS had been prosecuting such cases for a while with mixed success. But as far as I knew, there had been no victimless prosecutions at the felony level in DVS. Since it appeared that my victim was not going to be located by the next day when my trial was to begin, it was either try to prove the case without her or let the judge release the defendant and continue to try to locate her and obtain her cooperation. Darnell's was a very serious crime and I was loath to allow the judge to release him from prison. Especially if Sheryl intended to go back to him, it was only a matter of time before he did succeed in killing her. I had to find a way to prove this case without Sheryl.

I reviewed the file to see what proof I had. The results were dismal. The most powerful piece of evidence when there was no victim—or often even when their was—was the voice on a 911 tape. I heard 911 tapes over the years that made my hair stand on end. They are usually expressions of someone's fear at the time the incident is occurring, and the impact of that cannot be duplicated even by a cooperative victim. In this case, there was no 911 call by the victim, since she had been shot.

What I did have, however, was the videotaped "confession" by the defendant. On the tape, the defendant claimed that he was looking at his gun. He had removed the clip from the gun and the clip was empty. He said that he did not know that there could be a round in the chamber of the gun with the clip empty. Darnell said that he went to put the empty clip back in the gun and that the clip jammed. He slammed the clip into the gun with the heel of his hand and this caused the gun to fire. Sheryl was sitting on the bed and he shot her. He claimed to be totally shocked that there was a bullet in the gun and said that the shooting was accidental. Having this statement was a start. At least I had a statement from the defendant admitting to shooting the victim, even if he claimed that it was an accident. But the law in New York does not allow a defendant to be convicted on his statement alone. I needed corroboration.

My only corroboration was Sheryl's medical records, which confirmed that Sheryl was shot in the head. I was going to be hard-pressed to prove the case with such scant evidence. It was not enough for me to prove that the defendant shot Sheryl. I had to prove that he was reckless in doing so. With nothing more than his claim that it was an accident and medical records confirming the gunshot wound, I did not see how I was going to prove my case. The only angle that I saw was that the defendant claimed that he had no knowledge of the use of guns. However, several years earlier, the defendant had been convicted of gun possession. If I could show, based on this prior gun conviction, that the defendant had knowledge of weapons and should have known that there could be a round in the chamber even if the clip was empty, I might be able to prove my case.

I brainstormed the case with Elisa who agreed that I didn't have much of an angle, "But waddaya' got to lose?" We discussed the fact that my only chance of proving that the defendant was reckless in firing the gun was to get the judge to consider evidence of the defendant's prior gun conviction. Although, under New York law, evidence of prior convictions is normally inadmissible, I hoped to get the prior conviction into evidence under an exception that I was using it solely to demonstrate the defen-dant's knowledge of guns and not for the fact of the prior conviction. It was how I intended to prove that the defendant did know, or should have known, that there could be a bullet in the chamber when the clip was empty. I stayed up late that night preparing my case and preparing an argument for the admissibility of the defendant's prior gun conviction. The next morning, I walked into the court room in my black trial suit and stated, "Ready." Plopnick blanched.

Apparently, Plopnick never actually expected me to call his bluff and actually go to trial without the victim. He made a lengthy record about how he had spoken with Sheryl and she had told him that she wasn't coming in and that I, therefore, could not really be ready for trial. I responded by telling the judge that, indeed, I was not able to locate the victim but that I intended to prove the case without her through use of the videotape, the medical records, and the prior conviction. I made my legal argument for admissibility of the gun conviction and the judge, although still skeptical that I could win the case, agreed that for the pur-poses that I sought to use it, the conviction was admissible.

Plopnick was beside himself. He began to sputter and started claim-ing not to be ready because I had refused to turn over the file. I had antic-ipated that Plopnick would do this. I reminded the judge of a statement that I had made, on the record, two days earlier indicating that if there was any documentation that Plopnick did not have in the case, I would make it available immediately. The judge agreed that I had made this record and that Plopnick had said that he had everything he needed in the case. The judge ordered us to commence the trial with the proviso that if, after reviewing the records, Plopnick needed to recall any of my witnesses, he could. Banking on the skepticism that the judge had expressed earlier about my ability to prove the case, Plopnick waived a jury. Our trial would only be heard by this pro-defendant judge that had already told me that he did not think I could prove my case. I was in for a good fight.

First, I put the doctor on the stand to testify about the injuries, and the detective to get the defendant's video statement in. I put in a certi-fied copy of the defendant's gun possession conviction so that I could argue on summation that the defendant had knowledge of guns, and I rested my case. My entire case presentation took less than a day. Although I felt that I did the best I could with what I had, it was highly unlikely to result in conviction. I chalked it up to experience and assumed that Plopnick would do the smart thing and not present a case. I should have known better. I should have known that Plopknick's ego would get the best of him. When the judge asked Plopnick if he wished to call any witnesses, Plopnick put the defendant on the stand.

CROSS-EXAMINATION IS an art that prosecutors get to practice far less frequently than defense attorneys. One cannot cross-examine one's own witness, so only in the rare case that a defense attorney puts witnesses on the stand does a prosecutor get the chance. It's not easy to know how to lead a witness into saying what you want him to say and at the same time, steer him away from saying what you don't. The hardest part is knowing when *not* to ask the next question—and when it's time to sit down. In my career, I had some successful cross-examinations and some disastrous ones but, without question, my cross of Darnell Thomas was the most skillful and artfully prepared of my career. It went exactly how I was taught that it should. I started broad and then I narrowed and narrowed until he was boxed in with nowhere to go. It may have been the most fun I had in all five years I spent in a courtroom because when I was done, I knew I'd won.

I didn't know much about guns when I started at the DA's office, and I still don't. It took lectures to teach me the difference between revolvers, semis, and automatics, bullet calibers, cop killers, full-metal jackets—it was a foreign language to me. I have only fired a gun on one occasion, when I went to the shooting range with a friend of mine. Aside from that one day, I have never held a gun other than as evidence in a case. I was one of those people who thought that if she touched a gun, it was going to jump up and bite her. So, the day before the trial of Darnell Thomas, I got on the phone with a cop I was friendly with and, for about two hours, he taught me everything he could about the .380 caliber pistol that Sheryl was shot with. I cross-examined my friend for practice, asking him all of the what-ifs and hows and whys so that when I did the actual cross, I would understand the weapon, how it worked and, most important, how there could be a bullet in the chamber when the clip was empty.

I started my cross-examination with the premise that Darnell Thomas would not have bought the gun without first making sure that it worked. I asked him where he bought it, how much he bought it for, where he stored it, whether he stored the bullets with it or separately, how often he'd carried it, whether he'd ever fired it, and so on. Thomas claimed that he'd never loaded or fired the pistol and always stored the shells separately from the gun. He claimed that, being such a good father, the only time that he even took the gun out of the closet was to leave it with a friend when his older son came to visit so that the boy wouldn't hurt himself. "My friend must have loaded it," he claimed. I asked him whether he fired the gun before he bought it.

"No."

"How about the guy that you bought the gun from, did he fire it?"

"No."

"So you mean to tell me that you paid five hundred dollars for a gun and you didn't even know if it worked?"

"Yeh."

"Well, you said that you didn't know anything about guns, how were you going to use it?"

"The guy showed me how to load it."

"Well, did you watch him load it?"

"Yeh."

"How did he load it?"

"He put the bullets in the clip, he put the clip in the gun, and then he pulled back on the slide."

"And what happened after he pulled back the slide?"

"He said that's what got the round in the chamber so that the gun would be ready to fire."

"So you did know that there could be a bullet in the chamber even if the clip was empty."

"No."

"So what happened at that point?"

"That was it."

"Well you said before that you never had the gun loaded. Did you bring it home loaded that day?"

"No."

"Who unloaded it?"

"He did."

"And did you watch him unload it?"

"Yeh."

"How'd he unload it?"

"He took the clip out of the gun."

"And what about the bullet that was in the chamber?"

"Huh?"

"The bullet that was in the chamber. The one that you said went into the chamber when he pulled back the slide so that the gun was ready to fire?"

"He emptied that out too."

"And how did he empty that out?"

"He pulled back the slide and emptied it out the top of the gun."

"Before or after he took out the clip?"

"After."

"Just so I'm clear, he took the clip out, so there was no clip in the gun, and then he emptied the bullet out of the chamber?"

"Yeah."

"So you did know that there could be a bullet in the chamber when the clip was not in the gun?"

And that's when I knew that I had him. I addressed my summations to the judge's power in a bench trial:

"Your honor, if Sheryl were willing to testify on her own behalf, her voice would be the voice of the people. If there were twelve jurors here, theirs would be the voice of the people but, here and now, there is only one voice, your honor, and that is yours. It is easy in a case like this to cloud issues and to believe that a case is less important when the victim is not interested. Don't let that happen here. This is not Sheryl Anderson against Darnell Thomas, this is the People of the State of New York against Darnell Thomas and you are the voice of the people. Let the defendant hear that voice.

"In order for you to convict the defendant, the people must have proven, beyond a reasonable doubt, that the defendant recklessly caused serious physical injury to another person by means of a dangerous instrument or a deadly weapon. I submit that we have proven all of these elements beyond a reasonable doubt.

"You heard the credible testimony of Dr. Gail Weinberg, a chief surgical resident at Jacobi Hospital, which is a level one trauma center. She testified about her extensive experience in trauma medicine with head injuries and gunshot wounds."

I approached a large black-outlined diagram of a human body that the doctor had marked up with a red pen. Using a laser pointer, I went through the injuries with the judge while following along with the pointer:

"Dr. Weinberg told you that Sheryl suffered a gunshot wound with an entrance behind the left ear, which continued through the esophagus, split her palate, knocked out several teeth, and exited through the right side of her mandible.

"She testified that Sheryl was intubated to prevent her from choking to death on her own blood, that one of the arteries to her brain is permanently embolized, and that a plate had to be placed in her jaw to repair the palate and secure new teeth. She sustained a vertebral fracture and will have permanent facial scars to her right upper lip. She will be at increased risk for seizures and arthritis to her fractured vertebrae. Because of Darnell Thomas's recklessness, Sheryl will suffer the rest of her life. There is no question here as to serious physical injury."

I walked over to the witness table and picked up the .380 caliber pistol in the unsealed evidence bag. I took it out of the bag and held it up in front of the judge:

"The defendant admitted that he had a gun. He admitted that there was a bullet in the chamber and that the gun fired due to his recklessness. Beyond a doubt, he possessed a deadly weapon. And he possessed that loaded gun in the house with Sheryl, his ten-month-old and four-year-old sons living there. He admitted in his written statement to the police that he 'pushed' the trigger. In his videotaped statement he said that his 'finger was through the loop when he slammed the clip in the gun, and that the gun was pointed in Sheryl's direction. That is reckless behavior. Darnell Thomas also had a gun conviction ten years ago. This shows that he has knowledge of guns and shows absence of mistake or accident in this case."

I put the gun down, and waited a moment before looking up at the judge. I walked out from behind the table and stood in front of him, looking up to him where he sat. Behind him in large silver metal letters mounted on the wall it said, "In God We Trust." Below that, the judge had scotch-taped a picture onto the wood. It was a Christmas tree made of green-painted elbow macaroni pasted on to a piece of construction paper. He had proudly pointed it out to me earlier that day, telling me that it was the first picture that his child had brought home for him from school. In crayon in the upper right hand corner were big block letters that said, "For Dad." I looked at the person in front of me and decided to appeal for a moment not to the judge, but to the father:

"Your honor, it was once said that if you leave it up to the woman to decide whether to prosecute and the defendant controls the woman, then the defendant controls the prosecution. Don't let Darnell Thomas control this prosecution. Don't let Sheryl's absence confuse this issue. This is not about if Darnell Thomas is a good guy. It's not about whether or not he feels badly about what happened. It's about having a gun and the responsibility that comes with that. Sheryl's absence has no bearing on that responsibility. Anyone could have been shot with that gun: one of the children, a neighbor, someone walking on the street. Is it okay just because she's not here? When the defendant chose to buy that .380 caliber pistol to keep in his house he took on a huge responsibility. He had a responsibility to make it safe for everyone around him. He told you in his own words that he was shown how to load the gun and that he saw how the bullet leaves the clip and enters the chamber. Blaming the fact of the gun being loaded on someone else does not negate his responsibility to check that it's empty. Mr. Plopnick called this stupidity. Stupidity can be reckless. Carelessness with a gun is reckless. The defendant was reckless. Your honor, don't send the message here today that if you blame it on someone else it's okay. You see that here every day. It's always someone else's fault. No! It was his fault. His gun. His obligation to make it safe. And disregard of these obligations was reckless."

That same day, the judge came back with a guilty verdict. I enjoyed the challenge of the case so much that after that, I wanted to take other cases where the victims refused to cooperate. I took a case where the victim was going to testify for the defendant, her ex-boyfriend. I was going to impeach her with her own hysterical 911 tape in which she called the police from a laundromat. The defendant held her hostage in the apartment and repeatedly raped her for two days. When he left the apartment for a few minutes, she chewed through the plastic bags that he'd used to tie her hands and feet to the bedposts and ran to the corner. It was the middle of January and when the cops picked her up, she was wearing a bathrobe and nothing else. Her entire face was black and blue and swollen. She had hand-shaped bruises on her inner thighs. When I interviewed her, she was wearing pajamas that she'd borrowed from the hospital. A year later, when the case was going to trial, she was going to testify for the defendant, whom she had forgiven because she wanted to get back together with him. I had pages and pages of visitation records showing that she was visiting the defendant in prison at Riker's Island, in spite of the order of protection she had so pitifully begged me for a few months earlier. I had no intention whatsoever of allowing his crime to go unpunished just because she did not have the strength to protect herself. Ultimately, he pled guilty in exchange for a significantly reduced sentence, but I wonder what would have happened if I had another chance to try to protect a battered woman in spite of herself.

Shortly after the Darnell Thomas trial, Plopnick died. A couple of years later, after I had started my position at a civil firm, I got a call from an attorney in the appeals bureau. He told me that Darnell Thomas was appealing the verdict based on the judge allowing in evidence of his prior gun conviction. I laughed to myself, thinking, "Right idea, wrong claim." My consolation, regardless of what happens with the appeal, is that he was still in jail for shooting Sheryl when I got the call.

I was moving up: It was time for me to go from attempted homicides to successful ones.

10

HOMICIDE DUTY

Ghost in the Graveyard ★

A ghost stands in the shadows of the bodega.
She is shielded by a door-frame,
head down, lighting a cigarette
and watching as you whisper into your collar.
You disappear around the corner.
She hears: "Five on the D'"
then the radio dies
as you enter the vestibule of the projects.

She slips around the corner,
bandana-hooded-eyes,
pop-walking like a crackhead
and praying the white boy sent to buy drugs in the South Bronx,
doesn't get whacked.
The radio: "Give me five," Still alive, she sighs,

★"Ghost": slang for an undercover police officer who shadows another undercover
who is making a drug buy.

"Three months to go, never lost one before.
Don't intend to blow my gold shield on you."

She tries to see you through the double glass doors,
but you're hidden in the shadows behind the stairwell.
"Cocky boys die," she thinks, then you are there.
She gets the signal to move to the next set,
slipping into a heroin shuffle. I went to a fundraiser

for the family of a ghost named Sean
who died in plain clothes:
not even a photo inside his hat, yet
his daughter's picture was plastered all over the papers,
and he was a hero. Who was the first cop
to put a picture of his child in a police cap? Someone hopeful of living,

or someone afraid of dying?
Sean now lives only in his daughter's mind,
and is memorialized on T-shirts emblazoned with his shield
that I wear to the gym and sweat in
on the treadmill.
Tell your ghost I'm not interested in heroes.

IT WAS SATURDAY morning and the alarm went off at 8:50 AM. I fumbled for the off button and, keeping my eyes closed, groped around on the floor for my pager. I flicked it on and rolled over to go back to sleep. At 9:10 AM, I sat bolt upright when the pager shrieked. "You've got to be fucking kidding me," I mumbled. I shuffled into the living room, grabbed a pen, paper, and the phone, and crawled back into bed. I dialed the front desk of the DA's office: "Homicide assistant. You paged me?"

"Yeah. We got a body."

"You're fucking kidding me," out loud this time. "Is this the first call you got on this? Because I'll kill Simon if he dumped this shit on me," I ranted, thinking that my friend Simon, who was on duty the night before, had deferred this case so that I would have to take it.

"Nope, first call." I jotted down the information to contact the detective who had called the case in. I then called the detective. He gave me the location of the crime scene, directions, and a brief explanation of what had happened. Within 10 minutes, I was on my way to my first homicide scene.

I had to call Simon first. The night before, we had arranged for me to come to his apartment at around 11:00 that morning to pick up the homicide car, thinking that the odds of my getting called out before then were nil and that it would give both of us some time to sleep. I called four times before I was able to rouse him from his deep slumber. "Yoon. Waddaya' want," he mumbled sleepily.

"I got a body. I need the car."

"You're fuckin' kidding me."

"Nope. Thought you told them to sit on it for a while so you didn't have to take it."

"Naw. I had three bodies last night. Didn't sleep a wink. C'mon over. You may have to ring the buzzer a couple of times to wake me up."

I headed over to the East Side in a taxi thinking about how, three years earlier, Simon and I had started at the DA's office together in the smallest class they'd hired in years. We were a close-knit group and all knew each other well. Simon had since been assigned to the Investigations Bureau and we did not see each other often. Simon is a Korean guy whose parents worked hard so that he could live the American dream. I'm sure that vision included him perhaps becoming an attorney but, probably, they had pictured him behind a desk, on Park Avenue, in a fine suit and tie. Like my parents, I can't imagine that they envisioned "lawyer" meaning scratching to earn a living and driving a shitty car into The Bronx's worst neighborhoods to see dead bodies at all hours of the night. Simon had grown up in Philadelphia, and the story of his interview to get the job at the BXDA was legendary.

Simon is a deceptively soft-spoken, low-key guy. He is quick to laugh and I had never seen him lose his temper or heard him raise his voice. Early in our careers at the office, most of our class had been out drinking and having a good time one night. We had been talking about the interview process to get our jobs and what each of us had gone through. Simon told us that at the second of what would be three interviews for the job, he was questioned by a panel of three senior members of the office. He was being challenged by one of the executives, Richard Mangum, about whether he had the stuff that it takes to be a prosecutor in The Bronx. Mangum was an intimidating guy when he wanted to be. He was well over six feet, with deep black skin and a snow-white beard. He had a booming voice and a presence as towering as his stature. Most people flinched when Mangum challenged them. Not Simon. When questioned on how a "pipsqueak from the burbs of Philadelphia" was going to even survive in The Bronx, Simon said, "Let me tell you a story."

"When I was growing up, I was a pretty small guy. My parents owned a market and I used to work there every day after school. There were some kids from my school who used to come in and pick on me and steal stuff. I generally let it go but, one day, I had enough of it. See, what they didn't know is that I was taking karate from the time I was a little kid. So, this day, they came in and these guys were busting my chops. They tried walking out of the store with a couple of things in their pockets. So I walked up behind one of the guys and tapped him on the shoulder. I told him he'd better give back the stuff 'or else.' 'Or else what,' he said, and when he turned around . . . "

Jumping out of his seat, Mangum yelled, "TELL ME THAT YOU KICKED HIS ASS!"

"I KICKED HIS AAAAAASS." Simon yelled, jumping up too, and throwing a right hook in mid-air.

Needless to say, he was hired. The guy standing in front of a building on the East Side with car keys in hand, in sweatpants, with his eyes swollen half shut and his hair sticking up in more directions than I knew were possible, looked nothing like this legendary warrior of Bronx fable. He mumbled something incoherent to me, handed me the car keys, pointed across the street to where the car was parked, and shuffled back inside. I got into the car and took off.

BY AROUND THE third year at The Bronx DA's office, assistants begin what is called "homicide" duty. Approximately once a month, for 24 hours, I was on beeper duty and had to respond in the event of any homicide or statement on a homicide. When there was a body at a crime scene, part of my obligation was to respond to the location. The basic purpose of this was to make sure there were no O. J. Simpson-like incidents where evidence was tampered with or cops tracked blood up and down the halls on the soles of their shoes.

Just before I left the office, with DNA testing becoming more and more common and valuable, a protocol was established that any ADAs going into a crime scene had to wear white paper jumpsuits with hoods and booties to avoid any contamination of the scene. Fresh suits were kept in sealed bags in the trunk of the homicide car. Although I never had the honor of wearing this Stay-Puff Marshmallow Man costume, I have two visuals in my mind associated with that horrible white outfit. The first is my friend, Asha, who is five feet tall and 87 pounds soaking wet, trudging around in the one-size-fits-all spacesuit. The second is of ADAs showing up at the scene in those get-ups while 24 uniformed cops, who've been dropping their own DNA samples all over the place for the past two hours, look at them as though they're from Mars.

In reality, at homicide scenes, ADAs are pretty much just in the way, especially when there is no one to interview. Our job is to guard the scene and make sure protocol is followed but by the time a cop called the case in and the homicide assistant actually arrived, there would have been people all over the scene for at least two hours. Often the medical examiner had already come and gone and everyone was pretty much just waiting for us to get out of the way so they could get on with their jobs. If there was an arrest or witnesses, we were more useful and would do interviews at the scene or back at the precinct. But when it was just a body, we simply held up the works. In that case, we would just look at the body, ask the detectives a few questions, and then go home.

WHEN I ARRIVED at the crime scene that morning, there were several police cars in front of the building. Bleary-eyed cops milled around sipping coffee. The people sitting on the stoop took no more notice of our presence than they would a fly. I identified myself to one of the cops standing out front and he directed me to the fifth floor.

I walked through the vestibule of the pre-war apartment building. The dull beige paint in the hall was an inch thick and pitted like at my Grandma's apartment in Flatbush, Brooklyn, where I used to visit her when I was growing up. The building had that same smell of age, moth-balls, and something like chicken soup. I got into one of those old ele-vators with an outer door and a diamond shaped reinforced window. The door slammed shut and the elevator groaned and creaked upward.

I had gotten away with being on beeper duty about three times before having to respond to my first homicide, and I dreaded and looked forward to it in equal measure. In the elevator on the way up to the crime scene, I thought of a story I had heard about a transvestite who had been missing for several weeks. The cops suspected the boyfriend, but after combing through the building five or six times, came up with nothing. They thought it was just going to be another unsolved murder in The Bronx until tenants started complaining about a smell in the elevator shaft and something oozing through the ceiling of the elevator car. Apparently after stabbing his lover, the boyfriend had dropped the body on top of the elevator car. Fluid from the decomposing body started seeping through the roof after two weeks.

I looked up at the ceiling of this elevator and shuddered, steeling myself for what I was about to see.

I watched the floor numbers float by the window in succession until moving slightly past, and then thumping back down, at five. Two tired-looking guys from the Crime Scene Unit started schlepping their equip-ment into the elevator just as I was getting out. "I'm just happy that there's a working elevator in this Godforsaken place so we don't have to haul this crap down the stairs," one was mumbling to the other. I momentar-ily waylaid them to get their names, shield numbers, the crime scene run number, and other identifying information before I walked down the dim hall to the apartment.

I didn't have to ask where the crime scene was. A detective stood guard out front and the apartment door was ajar. Lights sporadically lit the dim hallway as the lamps mounted on video equipment passed back and forth across the crack in the door. Inside, The Bronx Video Unit was filming the scene. I waited for the lights to pass by and slipped into the apartment.

The front door opened directly into the living room, where a porn tape was blaring on the giant screen television. Lines of cocaine on the coffee table stood in stark contrast to the black fingerprint powder adhering to every available wall, magazine, videotape, and piece of furniture. The apartment was small, cluttered, and hot. It smelled like rust. Gay pride and Puerto Rican flags flapped back and forth in the open window. I scanned the scene: half-empty highball glasses, an open bottle of rum, cigarette butts—no lipstick on the filter. I walked down a narrow hall to where the detective indicated they had found the body in the bedroom and stopped before the door. I inched my head around the opening, afraid of what I was about to see.

I WAS PREPARED for the tricks that cops played on rookie ADAs. A favorite was asking the rookie if he had brought a pencil when he got to the scene. "Not a pen, a pencil." When the rookie, invariably, said, "no," because who the heck carries pencils? The cops handed the rookie rubber gloves and told him to stick a finger in the bullet hole to see how deep the wound was. "Normally, you use the pencil, but since ya' didn't bring one . . ." Legend had it that one young female ADA actually fell for the trick and was about to stick her finger in the hole when the cop grabbed her and said, "Sheesh. I can't believe you actually got through law school."

But here, at my first homicide scene, I was not sure what to be prepared for. I had seen many crime scene photos of dead bodies but the only dead body I had seen in person was my grandmother's. She died of cancer in a hospital on clean white sheets and surrounded by the people who loved her. So, as I inched my head around the door to Hector Rivera's bedroom, I had no idea how I'd handle it.

The first thing I saw was bloody feathers everywhere: on the floor, the dresser, floating into the hall. My eyes followed the trail of feathers to the source, a bloody pillow on the floor, and then up to the bed where the murder victim, Hector, was bound, gagged, and hogtied. His rear faced toward the door and his head pointed away from me, downward and toward the floor. At about 300 pounds, Hector looked like he would have been a formidable opponent had there been a fight. But the medical examiner confirmed that there were no signs of a struggle. Neighbors said that Hector often brought home strange men that he met at local gay bars. Our assumption was that this was a bias crime. The killer probably met Hector at the club. They came back to the apartment, drank some rum, and snorted some coke. They then proceeded into the bedroom where Hector was willingly tied up as part of some kinky sex but, instead of what Hector expected, the killer put a pillow over the back of his head and shot him. The killer then went back out to the living room, put on "straight" porn, had another drink, smoked a few cigarettes, did a few lines, and left. Several hours later, Cecilia, Hector's neighbor and friend, heard the loud video blaring from inside the apartment. She walked into the hallway to take a peek and noticed the door was ajar. She knocked a few times and called for Hector. When he did not answer, she walked into the apartment and found the body. Hector had only been dead about four hours. Cecilia said that he was a nice man and that he was good to his neighbors, "Always helping people out."

The body on the bed was not Hector anymore. The pants and underwear were around his ankles. I knew that the police couldn't do anything about Hector's position or the fact that he was naked until the investigation was complete, but I felt sad that someone would have to be seen in such an undignified way by so many people. I tried to review the scene quickly and get out of there, expecting an emotional response from myself. But I felt none of the things that I thought I would. I thought that I would get sick or cry. I was worried about looking "girlie" in front of the cops. Instead, I felt nothing. The thing in front of me seemed as artificial as a mannequin: an empty shell that used to be a human being but was not any more. I did my job. I did not rush out or try not to look. I scrutinized the crime scene, carefully moving around the room so as not to disturb anything and taking note of as many details as I could. I noted the swelling around the wrists and ankles from the ropes, which seemed to have sunken into the skin where they were tied. I did not see any abrasions. I moved around to the side and then to the front of the body so that I could see Hector's head, which had been hidden by the rise of his large back. I bent over to get a better look.

Hector had been shot in the back of the head with a small-caliber gun. He had a sock shoved in his mouth and a gag tied around it. A noose went around his neck, and the tail end of the rope was used to tie his hands behind his back and then to his ankles. Since his bald scalp was angled downward when he was shot, rivulets of blood dripped down his face. His head was such an unnatural shade of deep purple that I could barely discern the blood against the skin. The medical examiner could not find an exit wound for the bullet. (This is a common issue with injuries from small caliber bullets, which have the force to enter through bone but often do not have the force to exit. Especially with a shot to the head, the bullet can bounce around inside the skull looking for an exit while turning the brain into swiss cheese.) The medical examiner had poured a solution into the bullet hole to try to track an exit wound. The solution caused fluid and brain matter to percolate out of the bullet hole in the back of Hector's head. The bubbling movement contrasted against the utter stillness of the body suddenly jarred me out of my analytical trance. I gagged and quickly walked out of the room.

On my way out of the apartment, I stopped at the bookcase where Hector had framed photographs of himself with friends and family lined up on the shelf. I leaned forward and took a good look at one picture. Hector had his arm around a friend and the two of them were laughing. He was wearing a sombrero and held some kind of fruity frozen drink with an umbrella in it. It looked like Cancun or Tijuana, and they looked so happy. In a totally emotionally masochistic act, I forced myself to remember Hector's face. I forced myself to think about the time I was in Tijuana with my friends, Jenn and Alex, doing the same thing. Then and there, I promised never to let myself be the kind of person who would just look at a victim, dead or alive, and ignore the fact that he was a human being. Ultimately, that was my salvation as much as it was my undoing. Hector's killer was never found; as far as I know, the crime remains unsolved.

MY NEXT HOMICIDE call was not quite so macabre. It was not a body, but a statement, which came to me in a most bizarre fashion. I was called to the four-six precinct to speak with a 19-year-old who said he had information on a homicide. When I got to the precinct, a female narcotics detective met me at the door. She told me that she had locked up the informant and his girlfriend for smoking a joint on a stoop. Neither of them had any prior arrests. The detective told me that when she brought the couple back to the precinct for what she thought would be a routine and uneventful processing, the informant broke down into tears: "He begged me to let his girlfriend go. Told me she's a good girl and just got into college. Then he told me he had info on a homicide and he'd give it all up if we would let the girl go, so I called you."

I went into an office and introduced myself to the bleary-eyed teen. He was a tall, handsome kid, nicely dressed, polite and well spoken. He didn't look at all like the type of kid who would get tangled up in a homicide. Then again, in The Bronx, some of these kids can't avoid seeing what they see. He first asked about his girlfriend. Was she okay? Had we released her yet? He asked what I could do for her if he gave me good information. I told him that I could get her an "ACD," meaning that she would have no criminal record and that as long as she stayed out of trouble for six months, it would be as if nothing ever happened. Normally, I would not be allowed to make a "deal" under any circumstance without approval from higher up. However, what I was promising to do for his girlfriend was what the law required. Under New York State Law, a first arrest for marijuana possession in small amounts gets you an automatic "ACD," or "adjournment in contemplation of dismissal."

There is a difference, especially in law enforcement, between lying and failing to mention. Cops were allowed, and in fact encouraged, to lie to get confessions, such as in the case of the cop who put the fingerprint on the condom wrapper. In the police department, it was an accepted method of getting someone who did not deserve any better to give you what you wanted. ADAs, on the other hand, were expected to take the high road. We were not expected to lie—but that certainly did not mean that we could not refrain from mentioning.

So, I refrained from mentioning to this kid that I was not promising him anything more than the law already required and, honestly, it did not hurt my conscience. I did not have a problem with getting information from him in exchange for nothing. He supposed that I was doing him a favor, I did not enlighten him and, in return, he gave me something. The kid became an "informant," and the informant proceeded to tell me about a crime that was about to be committed. He stated that about a week earlier his friend, "Flaco," contacted him about going fifty-fifty on a hit. A guy from the post office had found out his ex-wife "had a new man." The postal worker had offered Flaco $5,000 to take the guy out.

In order to have a conspiracy charge, there needs to be some act in furtherance of the crime. The informant told me that he and "Flaco" (which was as likely to be the nickname for a skinny guy as it was for an incredibly fat one in The Bronx) bought a loaded gun for $200 and went out looking for the intended victim for two nights in a row. These were my acts in furtherance of the crime. Fortunately for the intended victim, he was out sick from work for two days so the informant and Flaco were not able to locate him. The night before the informant's arrest, Flaco checked at the victim's workplace again and found out that he was back. Flaco and my informant had agreed to go back the next morning and finish the job. Flaco gave my informant the gun to hold until they met up the next morning to finish the job.

That night, the informant's girlfriend saw the gun and asked what was going on. The informant told her everything. According to him, the girlfriend talked him out of doing the hit. He told me that he had hidden the gun in a garbage can in an alleyway and that when his friend came the next morning, he was going to give him the money back and tell him where the gun was. They were supposed to meet at 5:00 AM, about an hour before the victim got off work. It was 3:00 AM just then. I had to act fast.

I paged the homicide supervisor and gave her the details of the story. I got her permission to allow the cops to put a wire on the informant and send him back out. The detectives moved into action. By 5:00 AM, the kid was wired and home, waiting to meet with Flaco. The cops followed the two as they retrieved the gun from exactly the location that the informant had described and drove to the victims' place of work. In the interim, another team had gone to the victim's workplace and taken him back to the precinct where he'd be safe. Once the two arrived at the victim's job, the cops arrested both of them so that Flaco would not suspect our informant. Ultimately, Flaco gave up the name of the guy who put out the hit, gave us copies of bank records to prove that money had been handed over, and even gave up the guy who sold him the gun. It was truly crack detective work. And our informant's girlfriend got her ACD, as promised.

ALTHOUGH I TOOK many statements while on homicide duty, in five years of work with the BXDA, I saw only five homicide victims. The first was Hector. The second was some poor guy who was dying of AIDs and barely weighed 90 pounds when his lover bashed his head into the floor, killing him. After killing him, the boyfriend covered the body with laundry and left the apartment. When I came to view the crime scene, the victim was so tiny that the laundry completely concealed him except for one foot that was sticking out. I almost stepped right on him passing through the room, when a cop grabbed my arm and pointed silently to the foot. The last two bodies I saw were in my last week at the office, both on the same night. And, then, there were the children.

I AM LOOKING at the X-ray of the skull of a dead 13-year-old boy. The X-ray looks normal until you get down to the throat, which is surreally clogged with small stones. I do not know how to explain it. It does not look comical, but it looks so improbable as to be almost cartoonish. Nearby are crime scene photos of the same boy. He is half-covered in leaves and, in the faraway shots, it almost looks as if he was playing and perhaps jumped into the pile of leaves. A close-up shot shows a handsome young boy with straight hair. You can tell this in spite of the swelling in his lips and the broken tooth. The X ray and crime-scene photos are from 1979 and the boy is named John Pius. I recall seeing the photo almost like a timewarp, recognizing the boy's shirt not for what it was, but for *when* it was. Perhaps a bright horizontal striped "Hang-Ten" shirt like they wore on the Brady Bunch. It is the first crime-scene photo that I have ever seen. And I am not a prosecutor. In fact I am not even a lawyer. It is 1993 and I am a law student. And I am not trying to put one of John's four accused killers away. I am trying to free one. The man I am trying to free is named Michael Quartararo.

When we moved to New York, we were not just in danger from depraved adults or people who snatched the likes of Etan Patz. We were in danger from each other—from other kids. Before Columbine and other such press-grabbing murders of children by children, there was this case that most people outside of New York never even heard of. But it was as heinous and vicious and depraved a murder as I have ever seen— and from it I learned early on that children can be just as cruel, if not more so, as adults.

In 1979, in a middle class neighborhood on Long Island, four white boys from seemingly decent and normal families were said to have beaten John Pius and suffocated him to death by forcing rocks down his throat. The motive was, supposedly, to silence the boy, because he had seen one of the four steal a mini-bike. A Suffolk County Grand Jury indicted the four young men: Robert Brensic, Thomas Ryan, Peter Quartararo and his brother, our client, Michael Quartararo. They were all charged with complicity in the crime of murder in the second degree under penal law section 125.25. The charge against Michael was that he was, "acting in concert with and aided by the [other three defendants] with intent to cause the death of John Pius, caused his death by beating, kicking, and shoving rocks in his mouth and throat." John Pius was just 13 years old when he was murdered. He was 5 feet 4 inches tall and weighed only 116 pounds. At the time of the murder, Ryan and Brensic were 17, Peter was 15, and Michael was only 14 years old.

Fordham Law School, like many law schools, has clinical programs where law students, with the oversight of professors, are allowed to assist real people with real cases. Often, clients of the clinical program get some of the best representation out there from the zealous and thorough work of law students. Fordham had been representing Michael Quartararo for many years and on many different issues when I joined the clinic. In 1993, when I was a law student, 14 years after the murder of John Pius, Michael continued to seek our assistance in the fight for his freedom.

Michael had been primarily convicted on the basis of his own brother's confession to the murder. According to the Second Circuit Court of Appeals in the case of *Ryan v. Miller*, after initially denying involvement in or knowledge of the murder, Peter first told the police officer interrogating him that Ryan and Brensic killed John because they thought John had seen the four boys with a stolen minibike. Peter initially denied any involvement by himself or Michael. Later, Peter told his interrogator that he and his brother had observed the attack but had not participated in it. Finally, Peter offered a third version in which all four boys had participated.

Ultimately, the courts held that Peter's confession was improperly obtained and therefore inadmissible as evidence of guilt. The court said that, "Given this substantial evidence that the confession was but one of several, each containing material differences, that it was obtained from a juvenile after lengthy custodial questioning, and that it was given under circumstances which suggest that it was induced by the hope of leniency, the confession should not have been placed before this jury as evidence of defendant's guilt."The police were found to have employed illegal and coercive methods to induce Peter, an "unrepresented, inexperienced, and confused juvenile, to give numerous inconsistent and unreliable confessions."

All four of John's accused killers claimed they were innocent. Ultimately, it was the unreliable confession of Peter, with its varying accusations against the other three boys, and the prosecutor's insistence on trying to introduce it in some form, that caused many reversals, mistrials, and retrials in the cases against the four boys accused of killing John. At one point, after all four young men had served eight years in prison, the convictions were set aside for "ineffective assistance of counsel," or incompetence of the defense attorneys. Rather than go back to jail, Thomas Ryan pleaded guilty to manslaughter in exchange for time served. Peter's murder conviction was thrown out in 1989 and he was never retried. Robert Brensic, after numerous appeals, was released in April 1993. And Michael Quartararo, the youngest of the accused, was released last, in February 2004. The case is replete with examples of wrongdoing by law enforcement.

In 1981, following a joint trial of Michael and Peter, a jury found both boys guilty of murder. In 1988, the court granted Michael and Peter's petitions for a writ of *habeas corpus* on grounds of ineffective assistance of counsel based, in part, on counsel's failure to object to highly prejudicial evidence, i.e., Peter's confession. Inexplicably, while they did not retry his brother, the prosecution did retry Michael in 1990. At this second trial, a jury again convicted Michael of second degree murder. When Michael was convicted, he was about 16 years old. When he was paroled, he was about 39 years old.

I spoke with Michael on the phone several times during the course of my year working in the clinical program. He was patient, polite, and well spoken. He maintains his innocence. I did not form an opinion as to whether Michael, or any of the other young men he was with, were innocent or guilty. It was not what I was there to do. I did form an opinion that the system had terribly failed John Pius by failing to properly handle his case from start to finish. The evidence was improperly preserved and analyzed. The suspects were improperly treated. And the jury was improperly persuaded they were guilty, by the media, even before hearing the evidence in court. It seemed impossible that with the string of errors, incompetence, and corruption in the case, Michael could still be in jail whether he committed the crime or not. What we sought to prove—and did prove—was that Michael could not get a fair hearing by the parole board because, in spite of a court order to the contrary, it kept considering his brother's coerced confession.

Six years later, when I visited my third homicide scene, it would be to see another dead child, killed by a child. He lay in much the same position as John Pius, on his stomach with his head turned to the side. Like John, he had been beaten and asphyxiated. And, also as with John, I can still see his face.

I RECEIVED THE call about a half hour after I picked up the homicide car from the assistant on duty the night before. Once again, it was a weekend. I was in the process of driving the car back to the city when my pager went off. I pulled over, called back the desk sergeant, and then called the precinct. The detective at the crime scene did not have a cell phone so I got what little information I could from the desk sergeant at the precinct, which amounted to the location and directions. I turned the homicide car around and headed right to The Bronx. It was July and one of those days where you can see the heat waves rising off the asphalt. In an unpleasant case of déjà vu, I was once again headed for an un-air-conditioned Bronx apartment in the middle of the summer to go look at a dead body. The desk sergeant knew nothing about the case so I was just hoping that the body hadn't been there too long.

When I was fairly new to homicide duty, I was told that they never leave kids at the crime scene—that it's too hard for the cops to just let a kid lie there and that, except on very rare occasions, the body will be taken right to the hospital. No one I knew had seen a dead kid at a scene except for the occasional infant discarded in an alleyway. I heard stories all the time about cops paying for funerals and baptisms for these unnamed kids because no one else would. "No one can handle the kids," they said. So the last thing I expected on that hot July was 10-year-old Julian.

The apartment building where the crime scene was located was amazingly quiet when I arrived. It was too hot for people to be sitting outside. In stark contrast to the fleet of squad cars outside at my first crime scene, one lone marked patrol car sat outside this building. I made my way up the stairs to the apartment and knocked on the closed door. A yawning cop answered and his partner sat snoozing on the sofa, arms folded over his stomach and head nuzzled into his Kevlar vest. He barely cracked open one eye to see who I was and then went right back to sleep. Both of these guys were fairly new to the job, and thus given the unenviable task of babysitting the apartment while they waited for the "bus," or ambulance, to come take the body. After only a couple months on the job, they had already acquired a cop's skill at sleeping wherever and whenever possible. I'd seen cops sleep in unimaginable places and positions. Once I came into my office and the cop I was about to put on the witness stand was curled up under my desk using his arm as a pillow and snoring away.

"Where is everyone?" I asked.

"They're all done. We were just waiting for you and then they'll take the body. Anyhow, the bus is backed up with two bodies in Queens."

"What happened?"

"Some twelve-year-old killed his ten-year old retarded brotha.'"

I stopped in my tracks. The apartment was stifling. I could hardly breath. I wasn't expecting to see a dead 10-year-old. I stalled, not wanting to see the body but the cops were, understandably, anxious to get out of the apartment and gave me a quick rundown of what had happened. Julian's older brother, Jose, was a problem child. A couple of weeks earlier, he had tried to poison his mother by putting dishwashing detergent in her wine. When Jose was 11, he had tried to kill himself. He had classic symptoms of a child prone to violence, including cruelty to animals. His mother tried to have him institutionalized several times, but the hospitals kept releasing him after a week or two. The mother and father were legally married but separated. The night of the murder, the mother was going out and the father came over to spend the night and babysit. The 14-year-old sister was also there. The apartment had two bedrooms. The father and sister were asleep in one bedroom. Jose was to sleep on the top bunk in the second bedroom and Julian on the bottom bunk.

Julian was autistic. A couple of hours before the murder, his sister had changed his diaper, given him a cup of orange juice, and put him to bed. Jose had stayed up to watch his favorite TV personality, "The Rock." After a little while, he went into the bedroom to play a little WWF with his brother. It was not uncommon for him to do this and sometimes get a little rough with his brother, who was pretty much incapable of defending himself. Jose had persuaded Julian to play with him on the top bunk. In the course of wrestling, he pushed Julian off the top bunk. When Julian fell to the floor, he started to cry. Jose was not supposed to be awake and tried to quiet his brother so that his father and sister would not hear them. He lifted Julian onto the bottom bunk and tried to get him to stop crying by giving him orange juice. When that didn't work, Jose pushed Julian's face into the pillow and held it there until he stopped moving. Later on, at the precinct, when I took Jose's statement, he told me that he knew he had killed his brother. When I asked him what he did at that point, he said, "I went back to watch the end of the wrestling match."

I walked into the bedroom expecting to see Julian, dead on the bed and in his pampers. Instead, I found him naked and face down on the floor. The medical examiner had removed the diaper as part of his examination. (By the end of my tenure, I came to believe that the first thing the ME did upon arrival at a crime scene was pull down the victim's pants). Julian was placed face down on the floor when Crime Scene needed to remove the bedding for evidence. Apparently, they just left him there.

When you see a homicide or deal with trauma, you latch onto the oddest things. I could go for months speaking to children who had been terribly abused and keep my cool, and then something small would happen and I would have a meltdown. I remember one five-year-old girl who was abused by her babysitter's father. Her mother had come here from Uruguay to give her child a better life. She worked two jobs a day trying to get her child a decent education and future, only to have this horrific act occur. I explained to the mother, through an interpreter, what had happened to her child. She covered her mouth and was utterly silent as the tears leaked out of her eyes. The daughter stood soberly behind her mother, smoothing her hair. "You see," she told me in crystal clear English, "this is why I told you I don't want to talk about this. It makes my mommy cry."

I still can't get that moment out of my head. Just as I can't erase the picture of Julian, lying face down on the floor. I didn't wonder why he was dead. Or how a 10-year-old ends up being murdered by his 12-year-old brother. I just kept wondering why they couldn't have picked him up and put him back on the bed.

11

JOLANDA BURMUDEZ'S EAR*

The Ear, (well, really a small
but clearly identifiable bit of it)
began its journey
when Hector Burmudez, repeatedly
smashed his mother's head against a wall,
then bit it off and spat it
onto the floor next to the bed.

Police Officer Luis Perez
(a mere rookie: one week out of the academy)
found it
peeking out from under the front paw
of Oscar De La Hoya!
(the family Pekinese).

Seeing it was fairly intact,
Perez lifted it with a gloved hand, placed it

★ The names of all characters have been altered to protect their identities. This account is—in all other respects—non-fictitious.

in a Ziplock, centering it
on Jolanda's chest, so that
when EMS carried her out on the stretcher
an EMT would place it on ice
hopefully for reattachment.

Declaring her brain-dead at the hospital,
a surgeon concerned it would be misplaced
fastidiously sewed it on, nonetheless,
where with her it died two days later.

The Medical Examiner
ignored it
until an over-eager forensic dental student
noticing the scalloped edges
that locked together perfectly
with the protuberances of skin
on the side of her head
removed it meticulously

placing it in cold storage
until an order from the District Attorney
for an imprint of Hector's teeth
matched it like a fingerprint
uniquely to his mouth.

The Amputated Bit,
its amputee having been interred,
earless and partially cheekless,
(never found, the cheek is believed digested)
shortly following autopsy
languishes in storage
neither mourned nor eulogized
awaiting the possibility
of Hector's successful appeal.

IT WAS OSHA'S wet dream. My first office was affectionately known as "The Barn" due to the unpleasant smell caused by the closeness of bodies in the summer—and the way we were herded in there like cattle. It was a large room with numerous dilapidated, maroon fabric-covered cubicles. The cubicle walls were covered with cigarette burns, and constantly toppled over. We sat at broken-down desks with no locks. Asbestos ceiling tiles shed fibers over our heads. We were hermetically sealed in the windowless room where we re-breathed stale air that had circulated throughout the entire building, including through the prisoner holding cells. Every time there was a T.B. scare with a prisoner, I was afraid to inhale. Every time someone had a cough or a cold, the whole room caught it.

At any given time, there were upward of 70 people crammed in there sharing about 15 desks. I was assigned to my first desk with five other people. Eight people shared the same phone line. It was impossible to find time with our busy schedules to contact witnesses and cops. And on the rare occasion that we did have an hour to catch up, there were so many people vying for the phone that contacting witnesses was impossible. If you actually did get hold of a witness to bring in for trial prep, there was no privacy and the din made it nearly impossible to speak.

By my fourth year at the DA's office, I had my private office in the new building with a pristine wood desk and a huge window. My case-load was down to about 24, which was usually manageable. I had my own telephone with only my name on the voicemail. And the desk and door both locked.

But it was not the office or the desk or even having my own phone line that signaled that I had finally made the big time. It was a homicide. I was finally assigned my first murder case. I was lucky, if that's an appropriate word to use for it. Many people went six or seven years before being assigned a homicide. Much of the reason that I was assigned one so early was a matter of need. The job market was good and people were leaving the office in droves for higher paying jobs in the private sector. DVS was pretty lean at the top because it had lost many of its senior assistants and, at four years, I was already one of the more senior assistants. I had already been trusted to second-seat newer felony assistants on their first trials. Hopefully, most of the reason I got this rapid assignment of a homicide was also that I had proven myself and that the office felt I was up the task. Within the next few months, I was handling not just one, but four homicide cases.

I inherited my first homicide case from someone who was leaving the office. Within two weeks, the defendant pled guilty to manslaughter. So much for my first homicide trial. Within a couple of weeks, I saw a murder case reported on NY1, a local television station that I watched every morning for the crime reports. When I got to work that same morning, Elisa asked me if I wanted the case and I jumped at the opportunity.

Hector Burmudez was 19 years old. He lived in a small apartment with his mother, his 18-year-old sister, Nina, and their small dog. The father had been missing in action since they were children but there was an older brother, Diego, who lived in Maryland, had a successful business, and was fairly wealthy.

In the few weeks before he beat his mother to death, Hector had been under serious stress. Against his wishes, his ex-girlfriend moved to Virginia with their two children, thereby effectively cutting off his visitation. He had just taken a job working nights in the stock-room at a 24-hour Home Depot in Brooklyn in order to pay child support. His current girlfriend, Marcia, who also worked at Home Depot, was switched to the day shift, so he was hardly able to see her.

In the weeks leading up to the murder, the family observed Hector exhibiting what they thought were normal symptoms of stress due to his surrounding circumstances. He was extremely upset about not being able to see his kids and was having difficulty sleeping as a result. He became paranoid that his girlfriend was cheating on him with a guy from the day shift. In order to relax, Hector took to smoking marijuana with some frequency, but it only seemed to make things worse. The few hours per day that he was home and should have been sleeping, Hector was sitting in family court trying to get the judge to either force his ex to move back with the kids or to grant him custody. The process was moving slowly and the judge was not leaning toward a favorable ruling, since Hector's job did not pay well and he had no one to take care of the kids while he was at work.

The day before the murder, his sister said that Hector's anxiety escalated. He was pacing the house, mumbling, and confided to his sister that he believed Marcia was cheating on him. Hector called Marcia at work a couple of hours before he left for his own midnight shift and was told that she wasn't in. He began to rant to Nina that he knew Marcia was with the other guy. He paged Marcia repeatedly and when she called back, he started screaming at her. Marcia later explained to us that she tried to tell Hector that it was her day off and she was at home with her mother but he wouldn't believe her. Marcia explained, "He kept saying, 'What did you say?' when I wasn't saying anything. He kept saying that he heard me whispering into the phone that he was a fool and a sucker but I wasn't saying anything. We fought for about two hours before he slammed the phone down, saying he had to go to work before he lost his kids, too. I'd never heard him like that. Hector was a calm guy. He never lost his temper. He was really scaring me."

Hector went to work that night and although colleagues said that he seemed a little tired and irritable, they did not notice anything too unusual. When Hector got home from work early that morning, he curled up on the couch to go to sleep. Nina was asleep in one bedroom with her boyfriend, Jose, who had been staying there for the last few weeks. Hector's mother, Jolanda, was asleep in the other bedroom.

Hector was his mother's pet and she babied him. Most of the time, she slept on the pull-out sofa in the living room and let Hector sleep in the bedroom. It was rare that she would take the bed for herself as she did the night of the murder. The apartment that Jolanda shared with two of her three children was small but tidy. The two bedrooms were clean and sparsely decorated. There were bright floral sheets on the beds. The living room contained little more than the sofa, a television, and a small, plain kitchen table with four chairs.

Jolanda went to sleep that night concerned about the tremendous stress that Hector had been under. When she heard him climb into bed early that morning, she came out and kissed him, tucked the blankets under his chin, and went back to sleep. A short time later, Hector awoke and walked into the bedroom. Without a word, he grabbed his mother and started frantically squeezing and biting her cheeks. He bit off a piece of her cheek and part of her ear and then repeatedly beat her head against the wall until she stopped moving and he thought she was dead. He called 911 and then ran into his sister's room, shaking her awake. He was covered in blood and Nina started screaming hysterically. He kept telling her that there was an imposter in the apartment and to "hush up" because the place was bugged by the mafia. He was hugging Nina and telling her that he thought they had already killed her. When Hector ran out, Jose, trying to calm her down, told Nina to go check on her mother to see if she was okay. Nina went into her mother's bedroom and starting yelling, "She's alive! She's alive." Jose instructed her to keep talking to her mother, to tell her to hang on and to stay alive. The police arrived and started banging on the door. Jose ran out to try to open it, but the door was stuck. He kept yelling to the police that he was trying to open the door and that he was not armed, "Don't shoot! I'm going to open the door. Don't shoot!" He was pushing on the door as the police pulled, and when the door flew open, the police grabbed and handcuffed Jose. The police looked over Jose's shoulder and saw Hector standing in the living room covered in blood. He kept muttering about the mafia and imposters and admonishing everyone to keep quiet so they wouldn't be heard. The police immediately realized that Jose was not involved, released him, and took Hector into custody. Hector surrendered calmly, continuing to mutter the same things over and over again. He did not fight them or put up any kind of resistance. Nina, meanwhile, was in the bedroom begging her mother to stay alive. Jolanda was struggling for breath. The doctors later said that they were amazed that she lived as long as she did, given the amount of brain damage she had sustained. EMS arrived and rushed her to the hospital. The police took Hector directly to Bellevue.

SOMETIMES, THE CIRCUMSTANCES of a crime were so unusual that, once assigned to the case, one would become an expert in the field or area relevant to those circumstances. I was somewhat familiar with psychiatric cases from my work on the Vernon case. That one psychiatric defense case was one case more than anyone else in the bureau had handled. I had also handled a case shortly after my assignment to DVS that involved the alleged rape of a young woman who was institutionalized for schizophrenia. She claimed to have been raped by one of her caregivers. It turned out that she fabricated the story. So, with two schizophrenic defendants under my belt, I seemed to be the bureau "expert" on psychiatric defense cases and Hector's case was right up my alley.

For the next few weeks after I was assigned the case, I interviewed Hector's family and girlfriend extensively. I viewed crime scene photographs, reviewed hospital records, and listened to the 911 call that Hector had made immediately after the murder. It was clear, early on, that the question, ultimately to be determined far more by the psychiatrists than by me, was whether Hector had a psychotic episode or not.

I began, as in all cases, by interviewing the witnesses. The first person that I interviewed was Hector's sister, Nina. She'd been living with her brother and mother her entire life and was very close with Hector. Nina was a sweet, soft-spoken girl and was in an extreme state of shock when I met her for the first time, two days after the murder. Her recollection of the events of that evening was clouded because she could not absorb what had just happened. Nina and her boyfriend were sound asleep in their bed when Hector burst through the door, literally shaking her awake. He was covered in blood and yelling nonsensically.

"He kept saying that there were imposters in the apartment pretending to be Mama and that he thought they'd already killed me. He kept telling me to be quiet and not say anything because the apartment was bugged. I wanted to call the police but he told me I couldn't because the phones were tapped. We heard the police banging on the door and Hector was crying and begging me not to answer it. My boyfriend, Jose, told me to go check on my mother while he let the police in." Nina could not remember anything after being told to go check on her mother. It was impossible for me or for her to tell what were her actual recollections and what she now believed to be the truth based on what her boyfriend, the media, and the police were saying. Also, it was impossible for Nina to view any of the events objectively. In her mind, it was impossible that her brother did any of this intentionally. She was completely willing to accept the possibility that her brother was mentally ill. In fact, for her, that was the only explanation. Throughout the course of the investigation, Nina begged for us to let Hector out of prison. She kept promising to take care of Hector and make sure that he took his medication if we would let him out.

Jose described the events similarly up to the point when Nina walked into the bedroom to check on her mother. "When Nina went into the bedroom she started screaming hysterically. The room was covered with blood, on the walls, on the sheets, tracked across the floor. Her mother was beyond recognition, but Nina was screaming 'She's breathing! She's breathing.' I told her to stay with her mother and keep talking to her. Keep her alive. I heard her sobbing and whispering, 'Don't die, momma, don't die.' I was trying to open the door and I kept telling the cops to 'Don't shoot!' because I was standing right there trying to get the door open. They were pushing and I was pulling, and I kept telling them 'don't shoot!' and that I wasn't the killer."

Both Jose and Nina described to me a loving relationship between Hector and his mother. They said that he adored his mother and that she babied him. They agreed that there were no problems between them beyond what was normal for a parent and child and, if anything, their relationship was better than most.

The police told me that when they arrived at the apartment it was chaos. There was screaming inside and Jose yelling that the door was stuck and "Don't shoot!" They pushed against the door as Jose pulled and as soon as the door flew open, they grabbed Jose and cuffed him for safety reasons. They saw Hector standing behind him wearing a T-shirt and boxers and covered in blood. They cuffed Hector, whom they described as "cooperative," and let Jose go. The police said that Hector was telling them that he killed the imposter in the bedroom and he wanted to know what they did with his mother. He was telling them that they killed his sister, too. The first officer on the scene told me, "He was mumbling about the mafia spying on his family and that we shouldn't talk because the phones were tapped and the apartment was bugged. He said he knew it was an imposter and not his mother because his mother's cheeks were soft and when he squeezed the imposter's cheeks, they were hard. He said he bit it to see if it was soft and it was hard, so he had to kill the imposter."

When EMS arrived, Jolanda was barely breathing. Her small dog was running in circles and barking hysterically. Nina was crying and holding her mother, begging her not to die. EMS pried Nina off of her mother. They were amazed that Jolanda was alive at all. They heard her raspy breathing but her face was completely pulverized and a portion of her cheek and ear were missing. There was blood everywhere. The crime scene photos looked like something from *The Shining*.

Yolanda lived for three more days on life support in the hospital, but there was never much hope that she would survive and, if she did, it would have been in a vegetative state. The doctors said that her brain was severely damaged from the repeated blows. For some reason, someone at the hospital reattached the bit of Yolanda's ear that Hector bit off, but the gesture was futile. The medical examiner described the cause of death as "blunt force trauma," and I started to prepare my first homicide case for the Grand Jury.

The Grand Jury presentation went smoothly and they voted a true bill with little deliberation. The only difficulty was persuading Nina, who wanted her brother out of jail, to testify. I explained to Nina that her job in the Grand Jury was just to say what happened and that she was not going to be asked to make any statements about guilt or innocence. Hector, who remained in Bellevue from the time of his arrest on, did not testify before the Grand Jury.

One of the requirements for proving a homicide in the Grand Jury is that someone has to testify to the body identification. Normally, we have a family member do this if at all possible. But Nina was in no condition to talk about what she saw at the morgue. Instead, I had the first officer on the scene go to the morgue to make an ID. He testified that the person that he saw in the morgue was the same person that he saw in the apartment when he responded to the crime scene. The Grand Jury indicted the case with little ceremony and it was sent "Across the Street" to Supreme Court, Part 36, Justice Ira Globerman presiding.

JUDGE GLOBERMAN RAN the recently created felony domestic violence part. As such, DVS assistants were in front of him far more often than they were before any other judge. I knew him quite well and although we did not always see eye to eye, we got along. I had spent a significant amount of time before Judge Globerman over the course of the previous year, fighting with him about a defendant named Kelvin Wayne. Wayne, at only 16 years of age, was already a serial pedophile. He was caught fondling several kindergartners in a schoolyard the year before I started in DVS. I took over the case from an assistant who left the office and, shortly thereafter, Wayne pled guilty to the top count on the indictment.

Globerman gave him straight probation with the condition that he attend sexual offender treatment. Wayne reported to court once a month with updates from the program. For the first few months, he was apparently doing well but then his attendance started to slip off. About six months after pleading guilty, Wayne was riding a schoolbus with much younger kids, which he was explicitly prohibited from doing. The bus driver intercepted a note from Wayne to a 10-year-old boy that contained extremely sexually explicit solicitations wherein Wayne told the boy that, among other things, he wanted to put him in a bath full of chocolate and lick it off. I will give Wayne credit for the fact that his requests were creative. I demanded that Globerman at least place Wayne in residential treatment at that point, since he obviously could not be trusted to stay away from kids on his own. At first, Globerman agreed and kept Wayne in prison pending placement. However, Wayne's attorney was unable to locate a program that would accept him. It seemed that Wayne did not quite meet the criteria for any of the programs. They required that he be older or younger, that he have committed a violent act, and so forth. Each time the case was in court, Wayne's older sister, who was also his guardian, was there promising to supervise him more carefully. She was a nice, intelligent young woman with a good job and the best of intentions. After several months of going back and forth, Globerman started indicating that his inclination was to give Wayne another chance. I protested vehemently, asserting that no matter how good his sister's intentions, she could not supervise her brother every minute of the day. I firmly believed that Wayne was beyond help and that the safest thing to do was take him out of circulation. "If he's already violating little kids at sixteen, don't you think it's only going to get worse!" Globerman, over my strenuous objections, ultimately decided to give Wayne that chance.

In spite of my aggressive admonitions and protestations, Judge Globerman and I maintained a friendly relationship. Hector's case was the next major case that I had before him.

At the Supreme Court arraignment, the defense attorney, predictably, requested a 730.30 exam of the defendant. As with Michael Vernon, Hector's case was put on hold while an examination was done to see if he was fit to stand trial. At first, the doctors at Bellevue found that Hector was not able to assist in his own defense. But after a few weeks on medication, Hector stabilized and was deemed fit to proceed. He was transferred out of Bellevue and into Riker's Island. Just as with Michael Vernon, the next question would be whether Hector was responsible for the crime committed under the McNaughton Test.

Hector's case was not a simple one. The psychiatrists would have to determine if he had really experienced a psychotic episode or if he was malingering or faking. It's never an easy determination to make. There is no blood test or brain scan that gives you an answer. The diagnosis is based on interviews of the defendant and his family and friends. Prior to the day he killed his mother, Hector's family saw no signs that he was a paranoid schizophrenic. They were aware that he was under tremendous stress but did not think it was unusual given the circumstances in his life in the weeks leading up to the killing. From my work on the Michael Vernon case, I had some knowledge of schizophrenia, but I was far from qualified to make a diagnosis. What I did know, however, is that schizophrenia usually rears its ugly head in the late teens or early twenties and that stress can precipitate an episode. I also thought that some of the behaviors that the family described in the weeks leading up to the killing may have been precursors of the disease rather than normal symptomology of stress. For example, as Dr. Berger taught us, paranoid schizophrenics often turn to drugs and, specifically, to marijuana, to try to alleviate the symptoms of schizophrenia. The family thought that Hector was using marijuana more often than usual due to the stress he was under with his children. But it could have been more than that. Also, it seemed from my conversations with Hector's girlfriend that he was hearing voices the night he committed the crime. She said that Hector kept telling her that he was hearing her say things that she wasn't saying. Hector could have been hearing these things for weeks or even months but been able to ignore them or at least not talk back to them until that night.

When I finally received the 911 tape, it was further confirmation that Hector had a genuine psychotic episode. His discussions with the 911 operator were totally disorganized. While he was the person who called 911, he refused to tell her where he was located since the "phones were tapped." He was ranting to the 911 operator and saying the same things that he later said to the cops and to his sister. While he could have been faking, it would have been an impressive acting job.

In fact, of all of the interviews that I conducted, including those of the cops, the only person who absolutely thought that Hector was faking was his older brother, Diego. Diego was definitely the family success story. He had a different father from Hector and Nina and lived in Maryland with his wife, where he ran a successful business. They had a nice car and a nice home in a good neighborhood. Diego had succeeded in escaping from The Bronx and from poverty. He was an intelligent man and a hard worker, but it was clear that he thought little of his siblings. He felt that they were lazy and that they took advantage of his mother. Diego and his wife described to me a summer that Hector came to live with them where he did nothing but "get in the way and sit around." Diego's perception of the whole crime was that Hector intentionally killed his mother for her money and that he was faking the whole "crazy thing." Diego told me that he'd asked his mother to move in with him and his wife numerous times, but that she refused to leave Hector.

It was nearly impossible to get facts from Diego that would be useful in figuring out what had happened to Hector. Like his sister, Diego's mind was already made up; he just came to the opposite conclusion. He could not be unbiased with details because he already believed that Hector was malingering and nothing was going to change his mind. Diego's wife, on the other hand, like Jose, was slightly removed from the situation. She was willing to accept the possibility that Hector really had a breakdown, but agreed with me that her husband was not ready to hear it. So, on the one hand, I had the sister who wanted her brother home with her and promised to take care of Hector and make sure that he took his medication. On the other hand, I had his brother who wanted him to get the chair and would accept nothing less. To add to the bizarre comedy of it all, Hector thought that if we let him out of jail, he could go live with Diego and that Diego would take care of him and make sure that he took his pills.

The defense attorney's psychiatrist interviewed Hector and his family extensively. He returned with the conclusion that at the time Hector killed his mother, he was not able to understand the nature of his actions since he thought that he was killing an imposter who was intruding in his home to murder his family. He was able to understand the consequences of his actions, i.e., that beating someone's head repeatedly against a wall could kill her, but as explained earlier in the Vernon case, only one prong of the McNaughton Test needs to be met in order to show that a person is not responsible. Hector could not understand that he had killed his mother. He thought that he killed someone else, in self-defense, who was trying to harm his family. This was enough to indicate that he might not be responsible for his actions under the McNaughton Test. At this point, our office hired yet another psychiatrist to do an independent review of Hector so that we had a determination from an expert who was not on the defense payroll. Shortly after I left the office, our psychiatrist came back with the same conclusion; that Hector was not responsible for his actions. Hector was remanded to civil custody. While he will never stand trial for his mother's murder, he could have received a life sentence, nonetheless.

In a way, Nina got what she wanted: a doctor's confirmation that her brother did not intentionally kill her mother. But really, what kind of consolation prize is that? She no longer has her mother or her brother, and Diego will never be there for her in the way that the rest of her family was. When I last spoke to her, Section Eight was trying to evict her from the apartment. (Since the apartment was not in her name, and she lived alone, they were insisting that she was not entitled to live there.) I tried calling Section Eight numerous times and asking them to back off, at least until she had some time to deal with the trauma in her life, but to no avail. I do not know how Diego reacted. I am sure that he was irate and I wouldn't be surprised if he went straight to the top to try to get the doctor's decision reconsidered or overturned. I hope that, in time, he will accept the fact that his brother did not intentionally do this. I hope it will give him some measure of peace.

And what of Hector? With consistent use of his medication would come clarity about what he had done. I cannot imagine his own horror at discovering that he killed the person he loved most in the world while he was trying to protect her.

I HAD NOW been groomed by the office for over four years. I went from child abuse to child sexual abuse to murder. It was the pinnacle of success for a prosecutor. And the only place left for me to go? Television.

12

THE DOCUMENTARY DID NOT TELL
THE WHOLE STORY

The last woman to die by hanging in the State of New York

In 1884, Roxalana "Roxie" Druse,
of Warren, Herkimer County, New York,
got into an early morning "argument" with her husband.
Enlisting the support of her retarded daughter Mary,
she put a rope around his neck and fired two shots into him.
The bastard wouldn't die, so she shot him again.
The bastard wouldn't die, so she wielded an axe
and as he pleaded "Oh, Roxie, don't!"
chopped off his head, then spent the next day
chopping him to bits while her nephew and her son
played checkers. She then burned the chunks
in the kitchen stove, and poured his ashes into the pig sty.

Newspaper accounts report that Roxie killed her husband
because he made her work too hard.
But Roxie was a frail, shivering woman.
In 1887, she stood on the scaffold in the jail yard
wearing a pretty rose patterned dress

as State Militia in high bearskin hats
kept back the crowd while her execution took place.
It wasn't a clean death.
She dangled and writhed, for fifteen minutes
at the end of her rope: a slow strangulation.

LINDA FAIRSTEIN may be the most famous prosecutor in the country. She is the notorious buxom blonde former head of the Manhattan DA's office sex crimes unit turned crime writer extraordinaire. She has published numerous novels and a nonfiction book. She does talk shows and lectures all over the country. In direct contrast is Elisa Koenderman, head of DVS during my tenure, and now head of the Child Abuse and Sex Crimes Unit. Elisa is, on the one hand, a hard-as-nails Queens womyn (with a "y" because there ain't no "men" in womyn), smart, aggressive, and perceptive. On the other hand, she is a girl who kicks her feet up and giggles and can't figure out how the hell she ended up as head of what may be the largest sex crimes unit in the country. Elisa is better than anything you'll see on TV. A striking, high-cheekboned brunette with a sharp chin and a quick tongue, she is brilliant on the law and rapid to the draw. It was an honor to work for Elisa for three years.

I used to love to sit with Elisa and talk to her about trial strategy. That is when she was in her element. Although the initial response was usually something to the tune of, "Ah you seeereeyus? Ah you fuckin' kiddin' me?" once she was on a roll, she was brilliant and innovative.

In my final year at the office, the Discovery Channel did a documentary on justice in The Bronx. The producers of the show went to the heads of The Bronx DA's Office and The Legal Aid Society and asked for permission to follow cases that would be of interest to the public. The Legal Aid Society suggested that the Discovery Channel follow a case with a unique slant. The angle was that the evil Bronx DA's Office was prosecuting a battered woman who cut her husband's arm in self-defense. Elisa and I turned that case on its head.

LIKE THE CASES of many battered women, the case of Roxalana Druse in the late 1800s was not so straightforward. Roxalana was hung from the second floor, in the back of the Herkimer County jail, for murdering her husband. If you visited the old courthouse today, you would still see the boarded-up door that Roxie walked out of at the time of the hanging. Over the door, the hook from which the rope was attached for her hanging is still mounted.

It took 15 minutes for Roxie to strangle to death. But the gruesome execution did not spark an inquiry into whether she had had a real case for self-defense. Rather, it fueled investigations into alternate means of execution. Thanks to Roxalana, New York instituted death by electric chair rather than by hanging. But nothing was done to further the cause of the battered woman in response to her hanging.

Roxalana was found guilty of killing her husband with an axe. Although accounts of spousal abuse were not well kept at the time, some newspaper reports imply that Roxie was a battered woman. At the time, however, such crimes were considered personal matters and not matters for the courts or for the police. There was no such thing as self-defense for battered women and "Battered Woman's Syndrome" was a century away from being a concept, let alone an accepted theory.

Western history is replete with laws authorizing men's use of violence against women in order to punish or control them. In ancient Rome, men were allowed to use physical force to discipline their wives. Coverture, a law that stated that a married woman's existence was incorporated into her husband's, was part of the Common Law of England and the United States throughout most of the 1800s. A wife had no existence of her own and no individual rights. She could not own property, vote, get an education, or even enter into a contract. If a wife was permitted to work, she was required to relinquish her wages to her husband. English rape laws considered rape a crime against the husband, father, or fiancé of the victim, but not as a crime against the victim herself. Rape cases were settled when the injured male was compensated for the damage to his "property." And of course, there was no such thing as marital rape since wives could not legally refuse their husbands.

By 1910, 25 years after Roxie killed her husband, only 35 out of 46 states classified wife-beating as assault. Even now, many people, especially some of the older male judges that I dealt with as an assistant, feel that what happens between a man and a woman behind closed doors is a family matter—a matter that does not belong in the courts. These beliefs are ingrained in our society and change is coming about slowly.

It is only recently that "Battered Woman's Syndrome," traditionally used to explain why women stay with abusive husbands, has morphed into a "Battered Woman's Defense." The defense, simply put, allows a woman to claim that her acts were in self-defense against the continued abuse. But, like any other defense, sometimes it is hard to tell when it is being used and when it is being abused.

I remember going to a conference on domestic violence during my second year in DVS. The entire conference was about prosecuting domestic violence cases. Almost without exception, this meant prosecuting men for beating women. The conference was cutting-edge and many of the discussions were about prosecuting cases where the victim would not cooperate. There was an entire half-day devoted to prosecuting attempted strangulation cases as though they were attempted murder cases, even if there was no more evidence of strangulation than a hand put to a throat for a second. Most people who choose to prosecute domestic violence cases are on a mission, and there is little room for debate in such cases about who is guilty. The prosecutors attending this lecture tended to see the whole thing in black and white. The man was guilty and the woman was an innocent victim.

The one exception during the entire two days of seminars was a lecture given by my chief, Elisa, on prosecuting a case where the defense is battered woman's syndrome. I remember her being booed as she went on stage and booed against after her lecture ended. But the point of Elisa's lecture was important. Not all battered women who defend themselves are justified in their use of force. Like other self-defense cases, like my case against Ramon Payton, things are not always so clear-cut and you have to know everything before you can make a decision. In my case that was going to be aired on national television, it turned out that we agreed with the defense.

BARBARA DIAZ MADE the grave error of falling in love with a batterer. Barbara was a lovely, smart, and extremely affectionate person. She had a pretty heart-shaped face and thick jet-black hair. When Barbara first met Jesus Silva, he seemed like a dream come true. According to Barbara, Silva was kind to her, treated her well, and often would tell her that she was beautiful. He had a steady job and was good to her daughter, whose own father was in jail. Incrementally, however, Silva grew violent. It started with verbal abuse and, then, like most batterers, the hitting was followed by lavish apologies, gifts, and promises that it would never happen again. Over time, the apologies and gifts decreased as the violence increased. He beat her numerous times, choked her to unconsciousness, and punched her in the stomach while she was pregnant with his child.

At the point in their relationship when Barbara became pregnant with Silva's child and the abuse did not stop, Barbara attempted to break off the relationship for the sake of her unborn child. One afternoon, shortly after Barbara told him that she did not want to see him any more, Silva called her from the subway platform and told her to come meet him to get her keys. Barbara was about four months pregnant at the time and had a high-risk pregnancy due to a compromised uterus. She walked the five blocks to the train station slowly. In her hands, she carried a glass of ice and a glass of lemon slices. She alternately sucked on the lemons and the ice cubes because it helped with her nausea.

When Barbara climbed up the stairs to the platform, she was confronted by an irate Silva. He threw her, glasses and all, against the wall. One glass smashed on the stairs while the other glass broke in Barbara's hand. When Silva went to swing at her, Barbara lifted her hand to protect her face from the blow. A shard of glass cut Silva's elbow, severing one of the tendons. When Barbara saw Silva bleeding, she panicked. She ran down the steps screaming for help. At the platform base was a squad car. Barbara hailed the RMP and told the police what happened. Silva was rushed to the hospital.

The police spoke to Silva about the incident but he refused to press charges. Subsequently, Silva continued to harass Barbara and to threaten her. Barbara obtained an order of protection against Silva that he repeatedly violated by coming to her job to threaten her and by showing up at her apartment.

In the interim, Silva got a new girlfriend, Brianna, who was extremely jealous of Barbara, and conflicts developed between the two of them, as well. To add to the drama of it all, Brianna was Barbara's cousin and was also carrying Silva's child. At some point shortly after I took the case, Silva and Brianna got married.

On the day that Silva was supposed to appear in Criminal Court on an assault case, Barbara was sitting in Victims' Services. She was attempting to have Silva rearrested for several violations of her order of protection. Brianna saw Barbara sitting in Victims' Services and told Silva. Silva was still in a cast after having undergone extensive surgery to repair his tendon. Showing his arm to a court officer, he informed him that the woman who "stabbed him" was sitting downstairs and that he wanted her arrested. The police walked into Victims' Services and, without even asking anyone why she was there, arrested Barbara and charged her with felony assault.

Barbara's case went on for several months after that. She went into labor in her fifth month and gave birth to a child that was smaller than a hand. The baby was placed on life support, but had no chance of surviving at such an undeveloped stage. Barbara and Silva came together briefly to agree to detach the child from life support and to say goodbye to him. After that, things were worse than ever. Silva started stalking Barbara and threatening her at her house, her job, and her friends' houses. Silva was so disruptive at Barbara's office that they told her if he did not stop, they would have to fire her. Silva even came to her office one day with a knife hidden in his cast. He force-marched her down the block and past her apartment where she saw her little daughter waving to her out the window. She smiled and waved back, trying not to scare the child. Barbara was endlessly back and forth to court filing new complaints against Silva but, with an open case against her and his severe injuries, she made little headway.

CLAUDIA MONTOYA WAS a defense attorney with the Legal Aid Society for as long as I was a prosecutor. I worked with her briefly several times over my years as a prosecutor, but had no extensive contact with her until Barbara came into my life. In my prior dealings with Claudia, I found her to be a compassionate person with the utmost integrity. If anything, her flaw was having too kind a heart. She wanted to believe that her clients were either innocent or, if not innocent, savable. She is the type of person who will go to the ends of the earth to help someone in need. In a way, this could work to her disadvantage with the DA's office since we felt that she would go to bat for anyone whether they deserved it or not. But she was pleasant to deal with, honest, and a good lawyer.

Barbara's case was initially considered a cross-complaint. In other words, both victims brought charges against each other. As in Ramon Payton's case, this meant that we could not speak to either victim, Silva or Barbara, without their counsel present. Sometimes in cases of cross complaints it was clear that there was one true victim and that the other complaint was a retaliation. In such instances, we might dismiss one of the cases and just pursue the other. In many cases, cross-complaints were vicious cycles. Frequently, such cases involved two people who would constantly harass and report each other. Unless one or both of them was seriously injured, the cases that resulted were often handled as misdemeanors and were considered impossible nuisances. It was not unusual for a misdemeanor assistant to have 10 "white folders" (our term for misdemeanor and unindicted cases) that represented complaints back and forth between the same two people. The ideal in such cases would be to get both sides to agree to drop their charges, often in exchange for nothing more than mutual orders of protection. Usually, unless one side relocated, these people just kept coming back. There were cross-complainants who were notorious in the office, with years of cases assigned to numerous ADAs and bureaus depending upon what accusations they would make against each other.

As with other cross-complainants, Barbara and Silva's cases were resulting in numerous white folders on the desk of one misdemeanor assistant named David Eisenreich. Although the case against Barbara for cutting Silva's arm was a felony, it was unlikely to be indicted since Barbara had numerous complaints against Silva. Barbara's case would have suffered a similar fate to that of all other cross-complaints were it not for Claudia's dedication and the fact that Eisenreich took the time to really hear her out.

It is unusual in a cross-complaint for either side to really care about the outcome of the case. Usually, everyone just wants it all to go away. The cases often amount to a "he said she said," with no evidence to support either side more or less than the other. Barbara's case made it less likely that she would walk away with no punishment and more likely that Silva would walk away with just a slap on the wrist, since Barbara's complaints against Silva all amounted to misdemeanors, while Silva was genuinely badly injured. He had multiple surgeries on his dominant arm (and may never regain full use of it).

In the interim, the Discovery Channel had approached the DA's office and the Legal Aid Society for some interesting cases to follow for a documentary called *Crime and Justice: The Bronx*. The Bronx DA's office put forth a huge press case against a woman named Tabitha Walrond who was accused of starving her baby to death. The Legal Aid Society offered up Barbara's case.

The Discovery Channel adopted an angle for its story about how we were prosecuting Barbara, who was the real victim in the case and was just defending herself against Silva. But then, when they found out that our office believed Barbara, the channel opted to change the slant of their story to make it appear that we were persecuting Silva.

The documentary had already been filming for several months when Claudia took a chance and showed Eisenreich her cards. She came into our office with hospital records, police reports (or "61s"), and audiotapes evidencing Silva's stalking and abuse. Claudia was brilliant in her presentation and her defense. She went out on a limb on Barbara's case and took a huge risk doing it. I give her tremendous credit for that. Showing a prosecutor all of your evidence can help or it can backfire. I used to tell defense attorneys that if they had exculpatory evidence, they should tell me about it and I would investigate their leads to the best of my ability. If the outcome was favorable to their client, I would use this information in evaluating my case and making recommendations about its disposition to my chief. On the other hand, if the information didn't pan out, the defense attorney would have lost the advantage of surprising me with the information at trial.

Eisenreich brought the information to Elisa. Ever the skeptic, Elisa did not think she'd be impressed, but she humored Eisenreich by listening to an excerpt of a tape:

"You stayed at Marco's house last night, didn't you?"

"That's none of your business."

"Answer my question, you stayed at Marco's house last night."

"You don't know what you're talking about."

"Yeah, because you know what? Because yesterday when we were on the phone you said you had to go because you told me, 'Oh, someone is beeping me,' and you left. Then I went to the house and you were not there. And you weren't at your father's house. So where did you stay."

"You went to my house looking for me?"

"Did you fuck him last night?"

"No."

"Where did you stay, Barbara?"

"What are you planning on doing to me? You sound like you're going to kill me."

"Barbara, where did you sleep last night?"

"It doesn't matter."

"It matters to me! Answer me!"

"In my house."

"You fucking little liar. Your tongue is going to fall off, you offspring of a bitch. Let me tell you something. You stabbed me. You made me bleed. You lied to me. You have gone out with someone that I know. That's two strikes. Barbara, if you know me you know that I will kill you, you damn bitch. I will kill you. And no one will ever find you. You are making me lose my patience. I will stab you in your face a hundred times. I'm going to rip your face open. You believe I'm playing with you, but when it happens Barbara, you are going to see that this is no joke. You are going to see the 'G-Nice' that you didn't think existed. I don't do things out of craziness, Barbara, so tell me, where did you sleep last night?"

"I told you, it doesn't matter."

"Barbara, wherever you go, I will find you, because remember that I know your name. I know your social security number. I have ways of finding out where you are. And I'm telling you, if you don't tell me where you stayed, honestly, honestly, last night, I am going to lose my patience with you. And I'm telling you. Record it. No matter where you go, no matter what you do. In Puerto Rico, I will find you. In Florida, I will find you. In Ohio, and wherever you go I will find you."

"But G, you said that you love me."

"Yes, I love you. Just the way you did it to me. I will kill you, cocksucker. I will kill you because I love you and you are going to be with me and with no one else."

"You know what G, I don't care anymore. I've had enough. Either let me live my life, or if you want to kill me, kill me. Just don't do it in front of my daughter. Just leave her alone."

"Look, you can tell me you don't care, but let me tell you something.

What you want is to live your life. Well right now, this is just you and me talking. There is no one else here. There is nobody else alive right now in the world but me and you. That's it. You started this, and I am going to finish it. Now where did you stay?"

"It doesn't matter."

"It matters to me. Damn it! I am going to kill you, Barbara. I am going to kill you. Don't make me get a taxi and go over there right now, right now, right now!!!"

The transcript cannot fully convey how terrifying the tape was. The conversation ended with Silva screaming and repeatedly slamming the phone. Barbara grabbed the tape, ran out of the house and went straight to Claudia with it. She was afraid that if she stayed in her apartment, she would be killed. Even Elisa was impressed. Elisa brought Claudia into the office with Barbara and she and Eisenreich heard Claudia out. They gave Barbara "Queen for a Day," like I had done with little Quanie's mother, and listened to her story—a typical one of battery and abuse.

TO SAY THAT after 15 years in the business Elisa was not easily convinced is the understatement of the century. She looked at cases through the skeptical prism that all prosecutors must adopt. She'd heard every sob story in the book and, as deputy chief of DVS and then chief, she'd seen it all. It was highly unusual for her to be involved in an interview. Frankly, it would not be humanly possible for her to hear out each and every assistant about even a tenth of their cases. She also rarely got involved in misdemeanor assistants' cases. There was simply not enough time. Furthermore, Elisa was not aware at this initial interview that the Discovery Channel was following Barbara. Her interest in the case had nothing to do with the press involvement, it was simply because of how terrible that tape was.

I was lucky enough in my five years to not have a complainant killed by a defendant during the pendency of a case, but that was very lucky. It was not unusual for a misdemeanor or felony case, sometimes a case as simple as a harassing phone call, to become a homicide case. When I was a misdemeanor assistant, a friend of mine in Criminal Court had two victims killed on him within the span of a month. Both of his cases were harassment cases, which were not even crimes but merely violations—

something akin to a traffic summons. Yet, these simple cases of verbal abuse had turned into murders. There was no way to tell whether a person would act on his threats. You relied on your instinct in trying to figure it out. Elisa truly believed that Barbara was going to be another statistic if we didn't act immediately. I don't know why she selected me to become part of Barbara's case, but she walked down the hall that day and brought me into the meeting with Barbara and Claudia.

I was immediately taken by Barbara. She was a bright young woman who seemed oddly in touch with her errors and emotions for someone who had stayed with an abuser for so long. She was kind, gentle, and affectionate and wore her heart on her sleeve. It was easy to see why Claudia was going to such lengths to help her. Barbara seemed like the type of woman who had a chance to make something of herself in spite of the mistakes of her past.

Barbara spoke to me about the first day she realized that she was a battered woman. She was sitting at a seminar and the speaker was talking about abuse. She started describing the cycle that a battered woman finds herself in. At first, the batterer is the kindest person she's ever met. He gives her affection, buys her gifts, hangs on her every word. The speaker also described how a major factor in an abusive relationship is dependence—for example, a woman who does not have the means to support herself and is afraid that if she leaves her batterer, she will have nowhere to live or no way to feed her children. When the abuse starts, it starts small, usually with verbal abuse. The woman is demeaned and told that she's worthless. The batterer will then apologize and bring gifts, saying it will never happen again. The abuse then escalates, slowly, with pushing or hitting so that an attachment is developed along with a belief that it will get better. Often there are also elements of sexual abuse. Barbara's eyes welled up as she spoke about the lecture and how sitting there she started to think to herself, "Maybe that's me?" Barbara went up to the speaker afterward and told her, "I think that I'm one of those people you are talking about." The speaker gave her the resources to help herself. She talked to Barbara about Victims' Services and how to get into shelters and have her locks changed free of charge. This, Barbara explained, started her on the road to helping herself.

Claudia showed us everything she had to prove Barbara's innocence.

Her move paid off. Since Silva was out of jail and we feared for Barbara's life, we agreed that day to drop the charges against her and to bring felony charges against him. Silva had been arrested on a misdemeanor violation of the order of protection, but the bail was very low and he was able to come up with enough money to get out. The tape gave us enough evidence to prosecute him for a felony violation of the order of protection. We needed to get Silva in jail before he could hurt Barbara again. We were concerned that once Silva found out that the charges against him were being elevated to a felony and that his claims against Barbara would be dropped, he would fly into a rage and do serious harm to Barbara, if not kill her. We instructed Barbara not to tell anyone what was going on so that Silva would not become even angrier before the next court date. We told Claudia that we would not drop the charges against Barbara until after the next court date when we filed the new charges against Silva and, hopefully, put him back in prison. Trusting us, Claudia instructed Barbara that it was okay to speak with me and we proceeded with the case as if Barbara was not a defendant anymore.

Barbara and I worked late that night preparing a new complaint so that I could arraign Silva on the felony charges on the next court date. The complaint was complicated by the numerous police reports that Barbara made which had not been followed up on because she had been arrested. The Discovery Channel also got wind of the change of circumstances and were taping us with abandon. Suddenly, I could not simply walk across the street with Barbara to go to court. We had to enter and exit the building five times so that we could be taped from different angles.

Because of the change in Barbara's situation and in the tenor of the case, we had to change the rules on the video crew, which they were not too happy about. When Barbara was a defendant, Claudia had the right to view and edit the tapes before the crew could use them. Barbara could also speak to the crew with little consequence. I was subject to a different set of rules. Once Barbara became a complainant, I instructed her that she was not to speak about her case in front of the cameras, at all. She was only allowed to speak with the crew about how she felt or what she had done that day, but not about the case or what she'd said to me about it. This directive was necessary because I was subject to a rule requiring that I turn over to the defense any written or recorded statement in my possession made by a witness that I intended to have testify at trial. This was also important because if either of us revealed the content of our conversations, the attorney/client privilege would be lost. When I was interviewed by the crew, I never said anything to them that was not public record. I am sure that it did not make for the most compelling footage.

The Discovery Channel also wanted to make Elisa an integral part of the case. Elisa would have had little or nothing to do with the case were it not for the documentary. Silva was being charged with the lowest level felony there is, an E felony. Elisa would not have had the time to personally oversee this case, having to supervise so many other cases within the bureau involving so many more serious charges. In this case, however, the Discovery Channel had us reenact things for the camera crew. They had us reenact the first meeting with Barbara by having her come into Elisa's office with me and Claudia (poor Eisenreich, who is really the hero of the story, was not even there). They also had us reenact Barbara's preparation for her Grand Jury testimony. Barbara, Elisa, and I sat in Elisa's office where Elisa instructed Barbara about what would happen in the Grand Jury. In reality, Elisa had no part in such routine preparations. The conversation happened in the privacy of my office with little fanfare.

When the case was next in court, I went alone and informed the judge of the new charges against Silva. I also told the court that based on our investigation and the evidence presented to us by the defense, we would be dropping the charges against Barbara. Silva and his attorney went berserk. Brianna, who was about four months pregnant at the time, started yelling and screaming from the audience. The judge was impressed enough to set $15,000 bail, much higher than we usually got for this level of crime and more than Silva could afford. I'm sure that Silva's inability to control himself in court did not help the judge's opinion of him. He started cursing me out. He tried telling the judge that Barbara had entrapped him by taping the conversation. He was dragged into the holding pens, kicking and screaming.

I made the grave error of walking out of the courtroom alone. Brianna followed me down the hall, cursing at me and calling me a bitch. She was crying and screaming and telling me that it was all Barbara's fault and that "she was a liar," and "why was I listening to her and not to Silva?" I said nothing to her and walked away as quickly as I could. Honestly, I felt terrible for Brianna. I have no doubt that she was as enamored with Silva as Barbara had been at first. I was sad to know that she was just going to be the next victim on his list and that if she stayed with him, the baby she was carrying would watch its mother suffer. I'm sure he was telling her all of the things that he had told Barbara when their relationship started and had her completely convinced that Barbara was making up the whole thing. She yelled after me, "Don't you understand that she's lying to you? She's making this all up because he left her for me! She's jealous!" Over the months that the case continued, Brianna came to court for every appearance except when she was in the hospital giving birth to her son. She cried and pleaded with us to let Silva go. She was sometimes conciliatory with me and other times so aggressive that she was almost arrested a couple of times. Often, when I was arguing to the court or putting in evidence, I would direct it at her. I kept hoping that she would figure out who she was dealing with at some point, but she didn't. I also kept trying to get the judges to allow me to play the tape, but they wouldn't. I thought that maybe if Brianna heard it, it would at least stick in the back of her mind, but I never had the chance.

Over the months after I indicted the case, Barbara and I were on a roller-coaster ride together. Generally, a case such as hers was routine enough that it would not have occupied much of my time. I had handled a number of similar cases before. However, Silva was relentless. There were threats and accusations flying left and right. Brianna started calling Barbara and showing up at Barbara's father's home. Barbara started bringing in tape after tape of Brianna cursing her out in Spanish and telling Barbara she was going to get her. It got so bad that Barbara had to file a police report against Brianna and threaten to have her arrested, pregnant or not. Barbara was getting pressure from her family to drop charges. She had shipped her daughter to Puerto Rico to live with her mother while the case went on because she was afraid her daughter would get hurt. Now that Silva was in jail, she wanted to get her daughter back, but couldn't afford to. To top it off, Barbara got pregnant again by another boyfriend and, although I could not have asked for a more cooperative witness, her pregnancy was, once again, high risk and she was often unable to come into court.

To top it off, the defense attorney, George Gottleib, was impossible, disorganized, and unfamiliar with the law. He'd come stumbling into court with his hair sticking up all over creation and papers flying everywhere. He felt it was appropriate to launch personal attacks against me in court, while I never thought it was appropriate to make a case personal. Gottleib was burying me in paperwork, so that I felt like all I ever did was answer motions in the Silva case. It was uncommon to see this in my office because most of the defendants we dealt with were on public assistance. Since publicly funded attorneys were not "retained," or paid by their clients, but rather appointed by the court and paid by the state, they had little time or inclination to write motion after motion. Most of what we got was boilerplate, fill-in-the-blank type stuff and our responses, likewise, literally consisted of filling in blanks on forms that were then typed up by someone in the secretarial pool.

Silva's attorney, on the other hand, seemed to have nothing better to do than to flood me with poorly written motions. Mostly, he sent me letters about things that could have been easily resolved with a phone call. Instead, we spent hours a day killing trees. Silva refused to plead guilty and, like his client, Gottleib was a screamer. Court appearance after court appearance I had to listen to the two of them screaming and whining back and forth about the same stuff over and over again. At the same time, the Discovery Channel wanted to interview Silva. Frankly, I wanted them to because, by the time the case went to trial, they would be finished with the editing process and I would be able to cross-examine him with whatever he said to the video crew. Ultimately, the crew did interview Silva in jail and, at that point, with the trial still a few months away, they informed me that they were wrapping things up and wouldn't be filming anymore.

A few months later, it was finally time to go to trial and the Discovery Channel was in its last phases of editing the documentary. We flew in Barbara's mother from Puerto Rico for the trial and I spent the days before trial preparing Barbara for her testimony. On the day we were to begin jury selection, I walked over to court with my *voir dire* and files prepared. As always when I prepared for trial, I had slept little the last couple of days, but my adrenaline kept me wired. I had my opening and summation outlined on index cards. My plan was to get Gottleib to stipulate to putting the tape of the phone call into evidence before I gave my opening statement. This meant that he would agree that it was in evidence without my having to go through a series of questions with Barbara to authenticate the tape and then move it in by asking the judge for permission to make it evidence. Since Silva had admitted in the Grand Jury that the tape was of him, there was really no reason for Gottleib not to stipulate to it. My plan was to start and finish my case with excerpts of the tape. I was going to open with Silva telling Barbara that he would kill her and that no one would ever find her. I thought that might stick in the jurors' minds when Silva claimed that Barbara had framed him into having the conversation and that he was totally innocent.

I was totally pumped up for the case and could not possibly have been more prepared so, of course, as soon as the court officer went to call for a jury, Silva decided that he wanted to plead guilty. Gottleib told the judge that if the judge gave Silva 1-1/2 to 3 years, Silva would plead guilty. The judge agreed, and now it was my turn to kick and scream. I felt strongly that if any E felony deserved the maximum sentence, it was this one. To top it off, by doing this, the judge would have all of the time running concurrent. When a person is charged with more than one crime on more than one occasion, the time can generally run either concurrently, or together, or consecutively, each successive sentence beginning when the preceding one had ended. If Silva was pleading to five counts of violating the order of protection on five different dates, for each count he could have received a minimum of probation to a maximum of two to four years. The judge could run that time concurrent, so that if he pled to each count he would receive two to four years of jail on each count, but the time runs together so he only does two to four years prison all-told. The judge could, alternatively, run the jail time consecutively, meaning ten to twenty years when you aggregated all the time for each charge. Judge Globerman offered Silva 1-1/2 to 3 concurrent and Silva pled guilty.

Prior to sentencing on a felony matter, each defendant is interviewed by a probation officer and a "pre-sentencing report" is generated. The report details a brief personal and arrest history of the defendant, any substance abuse history, and gives the defendant the opportunity to make a statement about his guilt and his motivation for pleading guilty. After much hollering on my part, the judge told Silva that the sentence depended on his pre-sentence report being favorable and that, if it was not, the judge would give Silva two to four years. I begged the judge to listen to the tape before he made the final decision but he refused, finally getting angry with me for being so argumentative.

I was not happy at all with the result, but at least the judge didn't give Silva straight probation. I went back to my office and let Barbara know what had happened. Barbara's reaction was mixed. Although she had been dreading testifying against Silva and was terrified of facing him in the courtroom, she had also gotten herself prepared to do so and was looking forward to it as a cathartic experience. She was not happy with the small amount of time that Silva was getting either but, like me, was just happy that the judge didn't give him straight probation. Also, since Silva had already been in jail about nine months when he pled guilty, I had to explain to Barbara that he would be credited for that time so, in reality, he would be out in less than a year. I told Barbara when the sentencing date was and encouraged her to come to court to make a victim impact statement. She agreed to do so even though the sentencing date was within weeks of her due date. I called the Discovery Channel, updated them and asked them to include in their report the fact that Silva had pled guilty. I was sure that, in his interview with them, he had denied everything and I wanted the public to know that just because he said he was innocent, did not mean that he was. They told me that they would "see if they could add it to the voice-over," but that it might be too late in the editing process. I was fuming. I knew that DA Robert Johnson had the right to view the tape before it aired. I went to Elisa and asked her to see if he would be willing to refuse his approval unless they added the plea information. I am not sure exactly what transpired at that point, but the guilty plea was added to a voice-over. At least the viewers would know that, although he said he was innocent on camera, Silva ultimately admitted that he was guilty in court.

On the sentencing date, Barbara, myself, Claudia, and Nora, the crime victim advocate who had become Barbara's good friend throughout the course of the case, all went to court. Claudia, like myself, was extremely upset about the plea. Barbara prepared a statement that she read to Silva. It was a beautiful statement and I hope that it helped give her some closure. She let Silva know that he had not won and that he hadn't kept her down. After Barbara spoke, it was my turn. I was reluctant to say much because I did not want to take away from the impact of Barbara's speech but I, once again, asked the judge to reconsider his sentence. I pointed out to the judge that in the pre-sentence report, Silva was once again denying his guilt and saying that he pled guilty only because he was concerned that he would get a stiffer sentence if the case went to trial. Once again, he said that everything was Barbara's fault. I told the judge that for this alone, Silva should not be allowed to take the plea. "Judge, he is someone who has shown again and again that he has no respect for the court or for women or for authority." I also pleaded with the judge again to listen to the tape. "Your honor, every time this case has been on, Brianna has been in court to support her husband. She has no idea who she is dealing with and she still goes home at night thinking this is all Barbara's fault. If you don't want to listen to it for yourself, at least let me play it for her so that we are not sitting here again in two years with her as the victim." Once again, the judge wouldn't allow me to play the tape. He questioned Silva about his denial of guilt and after Silva apologized and said it was his fault, the judge was satisfied and imposed the sentence he had promised Silva.

When the documentary aired, I was terribly disappointed. First, the story was cut in such a way that it appeared to be Elisa's case instead of mine. Her first response was to apologize to me and let me know that she didn't know that I would end up on the cutting room floor like that. Her second response was, "Fuckin' great. Now everyone is gonna' think I have nuthin' betta' to do than some f'in E felony. . . . Linda Fahsteen is gonna' laugh her ass off." I also totally lost my faith in journalistic objectivity. I was under the mistaken assumption that documentaries are supposed to be unbiased. Boy, was I wrong. Jesus Silva looked like an innocent victim while Barbara looked like some uneducated, skanky Bronx chick who'd framed her boyfriend out of revenge. They said little to nothing about the abuse inflicted on Barbara and they also did not play the tape. It bothered me tremendously that they seemed to make such an effort to shed a sympathetic light on Silva and made no effort to be unbiased. In the end, I came away from my experience with the show believing that there is no way to know what actually happens other than to live through the events oneself.

I thought that, at the very least, a crew making a documentary would want to be at the sentencing. I told them when it was and none of them showed up. The show had not yet aired and was still in the final stages of editing. Even if they decided not to say anything about the sentencing in the final production, at least they would have seen Silva admit his guilt first hand instead of hearing it from me. Maybe deadlines are more important than accuracy, or maybe they were afraid that actually hearing Silva admit his guilt would mean that they had to re-edit the entire thing. First, we killed the angle that the DA's office was wrong to prosecute Barbara. We also took away a sexy case where a woman is prosecuted for domestic violence against a man, which is rare, and made it just another battered woman's case. Their angle at that point was to leave it open as to who was really the innocent party; hearing Silva admit his guilt would kill that angle, too. Maybe it wasn't sexy enough to have simply aired a documentary about a battered woman getting justice or maybe they just couldn't be bothered with having to redo portions of the tape.

Silva went to prison on October 4, 2002. The New York State Department of Corrections has a public website where you can look up inmate information. It reveals that Silva was not released from custody until February 25, 2005. I can only guess that the reason that his sentence is longer than expected is because he violated his parole. Most likely, by contacting Barbara.

THERE WAS A second case featured on the Discovery Channel alongside mine. It was the *People of the State of New York v. Tabitha Walrond*. My friend from the Golden Dildo case, Robert Holdman, prosecuted Walrond for manslaughter in the starvation death of her infant son, Tyler. For several weeks, the case was the biggest in the country. The defense in the case claimed that Tabitha Walrond's baby failed to thrive because Tabitha was unable to produce adequate breast milk due to a breast reduction several years earlier. Failure to thrive lacks a precise definition, mostly because it describes a condition rather than a specific disease. Children who fail to thrive do not receive or are unable to utilize the calories needed to gain weight and grow as they should. But rarely is the failure to thrive so severe that it leads to death as it did in Tyler's case.

The defense also blamed the system for Tyler's death, claiming that he did not have health coverage and was, therefore, not taken for regular checkups. They claimed that because Walrond saw her baby every day, she did not notice that he was starving until it was too late. And, although many of us at the office believed that Tabitha intentionally starved her baby to death, she was not charged with intentional murder, but rather with reckless disregard for her child's well-being.

The press billed the case as the evil Bronx DA prosecuting an indigent teenager whose baby failed to thrive because she could not produce adequate breast milk. But anyone who sat through that case understood, by the end of it, that little Tyler Walrond did not fail to thrive. He was starved to death. Most people, however, did not sit through the case and their warped sense of what the case was really about was colored by how the press, and later the Discovery Channel documentary, slanted the reporting to suit their agendas. One woman from the National Organization for Women called the prosecution misogynistic.

The Tabitha Walrond case was a lesson to me about the assumptions that people, including myself, make with little information. If you run the name Tabitha Walrond on the Internet, you'll see hundreds of postings in support of this poor black woman from the ghetto who was punished just for being poor and black. But few of these people cared enough to come to the courtroom or to see the pictures of that little boy or to learn what the case was about. The press was willing to take a stance on the case as a wrongful prosecution but they were not willing to show the pictures because they were "too graphic and disturbing." Had any of the press cared to look at the pictures of Tyler Walrond, they would have seen an infant so dehydrated and wasted at death that he looked literally mummified—merely skin and bones.

While the defense tried the Walrond case in the press, the district attorney steadfastly refused to comment to the press prior to trial and reiterated time and time again that the case would be tried in the courtroom. And contrary to the picture that the defense painted for the press, the case against Tabitha Walrond was not about how much breast milk she could or could not produce. It was about her failure to take Tyler for help when it was apparent that he was starving to death.

There are legitimate cases of failure to thrive where a mother may not see that her child is not being properly nourished. With mothers who breastfeed, the inability to notice more than normal weight loss is possibley due to the constant closeness between the mother and child. Additionally, intake cannot be measured as with a bottle. Unfortunately, and rarely, additional weight loss is not observed and the child may suffer dehydration and brain damage or, in rare cases, even death. These extreme cases, though, occur within the first one to two weeks after birth. Not after two months. And, with rare exception, the mother will take the child in to be checked before the condition is life-threatening. Tyler, on the other hand, was two months old and had lost 40 percent of his body weight by the time he died. He was the height of a one-month-old because lack of nourishment stunted his growth. Dr. Milewski, the deputy chief medical examiner, testified at trial that Tyler's was the most severe case of infant starvation that she'd seen outside the Third World. Even the defense expert admitted that she'd never seen a baby this old die from failure to thrive.

Myself, everyone at the DA's office, and the rest of the country followed the Walrond case closely. Friends from all over the country called and asked me why we were prosecuting this case. It was reported on national news and there was a piece about it on *20/20*. It sometimes ate me alive that no matter how much the defense attorney would comment on the case, District Attorney Johnson refused to say anything more than that the case would be tried in a courtroom where it belonged. He refused to show the pictures of the child to the press or to allow Holdman to comment publicly on the case. Although I think Mr. Johnson was right to take this stance, as he did with every other case, it was very frustrating to me.

I went to battle over the case with my close friend, Julie, who, at the time, was working for the Manhattan borough president, C. Virginia Fields. Fields was a strong opponent of the case but never set foot in the courtroom to watch the trial and never saw the pictures. Julie and I met at Barnard College, an ultra-liberal, feminist women's college on the Upper West Side of Manhattan. I reminded her about our common roots and how this should give her more confidence that I would not support the case if it was really about what the defense claimed. We argued about the case because while she, like many other women around the country, felt strongly that the case targeted women, and specifically breastfeeding women, I felt strongly that most people had no idea what the case was really about. "There are causes worth taking up," I told her, "but this is not one of them." I told her that if her boss cared so much about the injustice of the case, then she should care enough to actually sit in the courtroom and learn a little more about it before rushing to judgment. "She'll find out that breastfeeding and women have nothing to do with the case at all."

One day, I was coming into my building and my doorman introduced me to Ronnie Eldridge, my local counselwoman. Ronnie had been outside The Bronx courthouse, with hundreds of others, campaigning daily against the prosecution. When my doorman introduced us, she confronted me about the case. I told her that maybe this was not the cause she wanted to take up. She, too, never set foot in the courtroom and never saw the pictures. She was too busy making a public showing outside. I suggested that if she wouldn't go to the trial to see for herself what the case was really about, I would happily bring the photos home for her to see. She declined, claiming that she didn't need to see any of those things to understand the case. Ignorance is bliss, I guess.

My sister-in-law was a member of La Leche League, an organization dedicated to education and encouragement about breastfeeding. She was kicked off of her La Leche breastfeeding e-mail thread for daring to suggest that this was a starvation case, not a failure to thrive case. Yet, all these women knew was what the press told them. Whenever anyone in the DA's office asked me why DVS was prosecuting the case, I suggested that they go see Holdman, talk to him a little about the case, look at the pictures, and decide for themselves if Tabitha Walrond failed that child or not. Without exception, everyone who did this ended up being strong advocates for the prosecution, and many of them were pregnant mothers. In fact, while the trial was standing-room only and many people were turned away from the courtroom because there were no seats for them in the gallery, a large group of pregnant women from the office made sure to arrive early enough each day to take a seat behind the prosecution table to show their support.

THE FIRST FEW days of the trial, through jury selection and openings, the press continued to take Walrond's side. The day the trial began, and before hearing a single bit of evidence in the case, the *New York Times* had an Op Ed against the prosecution. The judge continued to refuse to put a gag order on the defense, the press continued to jump to conclusions and to poison the public and possibly the jury, and the DA continued to refuse to comment. While the prosecution and the defense attorney agonized over their cases, Walrond agonized over her appearance. Showing no concern whatsoever for her fate, as the trial progressed and the attorneys became more haggard, Walrond, realizing there would be cameras outside the courtroom and sketch artists inside, made sure to get her hair and makeup done each day and to dress for the photographers. One day, I saw her posing for the sketch artists, chin on hand, and asking them to make her prettier. Every day when we broke for lunch or concluded for the day, she would rush out to the cameras like something out of a bad made-for-TV courtroom drama. When the jury was in the courtroom, she would put on an award-winning display of crying, eye-wiping and head-hanging but, as soon as the last juror exited, she would wipe her face and commence cracking jokes with her family. I didn't feel bad for her. I was disgusted. For her, it was not about her dead son or her responsibility but an opportunity for publicity. Her behavior was not different or more remorseful in the documentary.

Then, one day, the whole thing changed for the defense, for the prosecution, and for Walrond. The turning point came on the day the prosecution showed those photographs for the first time. Finally, the people who cared enough to actually see what was going on in the trial got it. They got that this case was about the fact that Walrond could not have missed the fact that this child was starving. And the reason they could not comprehend that fact before they saw the photographs is because they'd never seen a baby that looked like that, and it's something that one cannot picture without actually seeing it. Tyler didn't look like one of the starving babies on TV with the distended bellies and scrawny arms. He looked, as the prosecutor said in his summation, like a head with twigs. Every muscle in his little body was visible. You could see the shape of each bone and joint through his thin skin. The pictures were so terrible that even after all of their criticism of the case, all but two local news stations refused to show them. The other stations said that the photographs were "too graphic" for national television. As we were walking out of the courtroom that day, Holdman was finally vindicated when a member of the press came up to him, took his hand and said, "We owe you an apology. The press owes you an apology." And while they never actually apologized on national television, the reports changed significantly. When the jury came back with a verdict of guilty, the outcry about the indecency of the verdict was far quieter and not made by anyone who sat in that courtroom.

I write about this case even though it was not my own because, along with Barbara's case, it was pivotal to my whole understanding of how media can affect a case. I spent almost every day in the courtroom watching the case along with my chief, co-workers, and the media. Sometimes, I think certain people just need a cause even if they don't understand what the cause is about. So many people just believe whatever the media tells them and have no interest in getting to the truth. Or, the media has so jaded them that it's impossible to overcome their preconceived notions. But, in the end, I guess that all of us who understood and supported the case were there for the same reasons that people who protested the case were so outspoken: because we believed that a terrible injustice had been done to an innocent human being.

BY THE TIME I handled Barbara's case, under the scrutiny of the Discovery Channel crew, I must have handled well over 100 battered women's cases. I was much smarter and more realistic than I had been a few years earlier. I was certainly much more jaded. I heard all of the stories that battered women told. The patterns were clear. I thought I was beginning to understand the signs that an abuser gave off early in the relationship. I certainly thought that such a thing could never happen to me. I know I would never let someone hurt me. But I was also certain that I would not pick someone to date in the first place who was capable of abuse. I had a 100 percent certainty that I could smell a bad person a mile away and that a bad guy would not even get to a first date with me. I may be only five-foot-two but I am a force to be reckoned with when I need to be and I'm no pushover. On good days, I was called an honest and fair prosecutor. And on better days they called me a pit bull. But, as tough and smart as I may be, even I have to sometimes learn lessons the hard way. With all of my experience, even I could be fooled. . . .

13

COULD IT HAPPEN TO ME?

THEY SAY TO always trust your instincts. Not mine. My instincts are inevitably wrong about almost everything. Take my sense of direction, for instance. Once, I was driving from Connecticut to New York and did not realize I was going in the wrong direction until I hit Sturbridge, Massachusetts. My premonitions are always wrong too. When I was 15, I went on a teen tour across the United States. Somewhere around Chicago, I had a premonition that my grandfather had died. My inability to reach my parents over the next two hours sent me into a tizzy. I was sure that they were at the hospital at my dead grandfather's bedside. When I finally reached my Dad, I was shaking and sobbing into the phone. He told me, "Calm down, we were just at the movies."

My self-defense instincts couldn't be worse, either. The summer of my sixteenth birthday, I was studying drama at Yale. Walking home from the gym one afternoon, I was attacked by four girls. I told them that I was just coming home from the gym and did not have any money. They said, "That's okay. We just wanted to beat up a white girl." It was broad daylight. In silence, I watched at least 10 people walk or bike by a mere half block away as the back of my head was repeatedly pummeled to the point where I had a concussion. I was like a deer in the headlights. I could not call out for help. I couldn't run. I just stood there and took it. One man on a bicycle saw what was going on. He stopped briefly, said, "I bet you wish someone would help you," and then he pedaled away.

But when it comes to people, my instincts are unassailable. Once, I made the error of ignoring the voice in my head telling me to stay away from a guy I dated in high school, and it almost got me in big trouble. I was a junior and my brother set me up with Nachum, a guy he worked with at a local deli/restaurant. Nachum seemed nice enough. He was a couple of years older than me and very handsome, with thick dark hair and olive skin. He was also intelligent and far more worldly than I was, having been born and raised in Israel and having already completed his military service. Most important in my book, my brother liked him.

Our first two dates were double dates with my brother. Nachum was an absolute gentleman, holding the door open for me, pushing in my chair, holding my hand in the back seat of the car. At the end of each date, he kissed me on the cheek and didn't even try anything else. He seemed like the perfect gentleman, but something about him made me uncomfortable. I kept trying to talk myself out of it because I couldn't put my finger on what was bothering me. He'd done nothing to make me feel this way. In fact, he'd been a complete gentleman. Eventually, I talked myself into giving him one more chance, hoping that my discomfort would subside. I agreed to a third date.

Once again, we were going out with my brother. Nachum came over to our house and we all got in my brother's car. We headed a few towns over to pick up my brother's date. Nachum was in the front seat with my brother and they were joking around about people at work. When we got to the girl's house, my brother got out of the car and went to ring the doorbell. Nachum then climbed into the back seat with me. When my brother stepped into the house for a moment, Nachum leaned over and kissed me on the lips for the first time. There was nothing more to it. It was a brief peck on the lips, but it made me nauseous. I almost gagged. I was uncomfortable the rest of the night. At dinner, Nachum kept trying to take my hand under the table. I kept finding excuses to pull it away.

My parents were out for the evening, so after dinner my brother suggested that the four of us go back to our house and watch a movie. When we got to the house, Nachum and I went to the den where the television was. My brother winked to us that he was taking his date downstairs to "see his room" and that they would be right back. He said that we could start the movie without him. Nachum and I were alone for the first time and I didn't like it.

I was young, naïve, and inexperienced with men. I had been a chubby, insecure teenager who had not dated much. I lost a lot of weight around age 14 and boys had started to take interest, but the whole dating experience was new to me. Nachum's interest in me was flattering, but I really didn't want to be alone with him and I wasn't quite sure how to handle the situation. When Nachum leaned over to kiss me, I allowed it because I couldn't find a reason not to. He'd done nothing wrong to me. So I let him kiss me and then suggested that we watch the movie. Nachum ignored me, grabbing me and trying to kiss me again, sliding his hands from the small of my back forward. I grabbed Nachum's hands and told him to stop. I tried pushing him away but instead of stopping, he shoved me back on the sofa so that I was trapped under him. He forced his hands onto my breasts. I kept trying to grab his hands away and continued to tell him to stop, but he was much stronger than I was. He pinned my wrists. I told him that if he didn't stop I was going to scream for my brother. Nachum leaned forward until his nose was touching mine. He looked me right in the eyes and whispered, "And what the hell do you think he's doing downstairs." I struggled to get away and Nachum continued to pin me down. He took the collar of my white button-down shirt between his teeth and pulled so hard that several of the buttons popped off. That's when I started screaming.

My brother was up the stairs and in the room before Nachum even had time to get off of me. My brother was a bodybuilder and not small by any stretch of the imagination. He picked Nachum up and literally threw him out the door. After that night, we jokingly referred to Nachum as the "Nachtopus," due to the number of hands he seemed to have grown during "the incident," but I never found any of it particularly funny. And on that night, I promised myself that I would never ignore my instincts again.

It is not necessarily something that someone says or does that makes me uncomfortable. I either am comfortable or I am not. It's that simple. I trust that feeling with people I date, with the friends I make and, as an ADA, I trusted it with the witnesses I interviewed. That instinct has served me well for years. So strong was my belief that people give off vibes or clues about what they are really like that it was impossible for me to believe battered women who told me that they never saw it coming. Well, maybe it's more accurate to say that I believed the clues were there and these women chose to ignore them. I am not talking about women who allowed the violence to escalate after the first hit. I am talking about the clues that I believed one gets long before the first hit or even the first incident of verbal abuse. It's the part where you are just not treated well or made to feel good about yourself that I thought started the whole thing. I believed that battered women somehow found men who would beat them and that women who would never allow themselves to be battered would not be with a batterer in the first place. I believed that these people find each other and stay with each other for a reason—that it's a symbiotic relationship.

Most of the time, I was right about the clues. Often there was an ex-girlfriend or a wife telling the latest victim that the guy was abusive, but she would ignore the advice thinking that the ex was making it up because she was jealous, like in the case of Barbara and Brianna. Sometimes, the new girl believed the ex but thought her relationship would be different. Many times the clues were in how the batterer treated others long before the beating started. Especially how they treated their own mothers. In some of my cases, I never found out from the victim what the clues were but I was certain that they were there, nonetheless. This I believed with my whole heart until Tommy walked into my life.

IT WAS AUGUST of 1998 and I was sitting at my desk trying to tackle the pile of papers that seemed to just keep shifting from one corner of my desk to the other. It was one of those clear, sunny days that make it impossible to concentrate. My friend Asha and I had already made arrangements to eat our lunch outside on the steps of the Supreme Court building. We planned on picking up some food from the "cart lady" who sold homemade West Indian food just outside our office building, and then walking across the street to the courthouse. Just before I left for lunch, a head poked around my doorframe.

"You ride?" he asked, pointing to the motorcycle helmet sitting on top of my bookcase.

"Just learned," I said. He nodded. I grinned and went back to typing away on my laptop.

"You online?" he asked.

"Not at the moment, but I have Internet access here." He nodded. I grinned. He walked away. I couldn't stop thinking about him. He was so adorable. He was stocky with thick brown hair, lively brown eyes, and the cutest little button nose. He was wearing a dark blue short sleeve sweater with one thick white stripe across the chest. As short as our conversation had been, I managed to talk to Asha about him all through lunch. I knew that he was a cop and that he had a case with the girl in the office next to mine. Asha and I tried coming up with some excuse for me to ask her what his name was. I had never asked a guy out before, but I figured, "What the hell?" I thought I'd get his number and then try to muster up the courage to actually call him. He saved me the trouble. By the time I got back from lunch, there was a message on my machine from him. "Hi, uh . . . Sarena . . . this is Tommy. The, uhhh, motorcycle dude. I was wondering if you'd like to go riding some time." He proceeded to leave his beeper number and mumbled something about "call if you want to," and "if you don't want to, that's okay." I thought that the message was so cute and shy. I called Asha, all excited, and asked her how long I had to wait so it wouldn't look like I was too excited. "Screw being cool," she said, "call him now."

So I called Tommy right away. And he sounded so excited to hear from me. He said he'd been telling his partner all about me and he couldn't believe I actually called him. He told me that he got my name off the door placard and then called me through the main number at the office. We made plans to go out that night. I couldn't wait.

That night, Tommy and I went out with some friends of mine and we had a blast. He was sweet, affectionate, and incredibly funny. I laughed so hard with him that my stomach was sore the next day. He was just what I liked in a guy—tough on the outside, but with a heart of gold and a great sense of humor. I couldn't wait to see him again. We went out two more times and each date was better than the last. And then, boom, he stopped calling. He changed his pager number and I had no way to reach him except to call his precinct, which I was not about to do. I was totally baffled. I had no idea what went wrong. In fact, I thought things could not have been better. It stung my ego for a few days and then I pretty much forgot about it.

Fast-forward to about four months later. I was on my way to meet my friend, Peter, in Chelsea. We were going with a bunch of people to watch the Halloween parade in the village. I was dressed like Medusa in a faux snakeskin dress and black snakeskin boots. My hair was braided in corn-rows and I had attached green rubber snakes all over my head. I was wearing yellow cat-eye contact lenses with an elongated black pupil. Just as I was getting out of the subway at 23rd Street, my cell phone rang. It was Tommy. I was shocked to hear from him after all these months. He told me that he was on the train heading to the city to meet some friends and was wondering if he could see me later that night. I was angry, but let my curiosity get the best of me. I was interested in hearing his explanation for why he had disappeared on me that summer and then how he had the cojones to call me after all this time. We agreed to meet at Peter's apartment after the parade.

Tommy arrived around 9:00 and I greeted him coldly at the door. He gave me an awkward hug that I did not return and a kiss on the cheek that I turned away from. I was surprised by his appearance. When I had last seen him in August, his hair was close-cropped and he was a little bit preppy. Now, his hair was long and a bit unkempt. It also appeared as if he had not shaved in several days. Tommy had the Virgin Mary tattooed on his forearm. The artwork was not very good and he had jokingly referred to the tattoo as "Mary of Maudlin." He was generally embarrassed about it and made an effort to hide it under long-sleeved shirts. This time, it was displayed in all its buck-toothed glory. Even his clothing was slightly different, which, although still neat, was decidedly less preppy and more "street" than the last time I'd seen him. We had an awkward and stilted conversation during which he told me that he was awaiting a transfer to the Narcotics Division where he would work as an undercover police officer. This explained his appearance. It was part of his "transformation," as he described it. About half an hour after Tommy's arrival, some of the people at the party lit up joints. We took this as our exit cue. Tommy couldn't risk having "dirty urine" from inhaling the fumes.

We headed uptown to a local diner where I knew several of the employees. I wanted to be on my home turf. We were able to find a free booth. We sat down and ordered a couple of burgers. I told Tommy that it was explanation time. Tommy apologized, saying that he had moved to a new apartment and switched jobs since I had last seen him. He said that he was sorry that he had just disappeared like that. He also told me that he had been dating someone else when he and I met and that she had given him the ultimatum that they either move forward in their relationship or end it. He said that he "wanted to do the right thing," so he gave the relationship another try, but that he couldn't stop thinking about me. He said he had missed me, that things were not going well with the other girl, that he had ended the relationship, and that he wanted to start dating me again. I told Tommy that I might consider talking to him again, but not unless he had completely ended things with the other girl. He promised he had. I told him that maybe we could start by just being friends. At least until he totally burned his bridge with the ex and until I could get comfortable with him again.

In the middle of this serious conversation, Tommy started to crack up. "What?" I demanded, a little ticked off. "I'm sorry," he said. "It's just hard to have a serious conversation with someone wearing yellow, cats-eye contact lenses who has snakes tied to her head." I started laughing. I had totally forgotten about my get-up. He gave me his new cell phone and pager numbers and we began talking again.

I HAD THE best of intentions when I told Tommy that I could only be his friend. I thought he was kind and funny and perhaps had just made a judgment error. I found him to be incredibly gentle and attentive with me and I guess that I believed what he told me about leaving the other girl because I wanted to. I never questioned not having Tommy's home number. He was an undercover, which meant that he worked crazy hours, often sleeping at the precinct, or so he said. When he was home, "it was just to crash and he never answered the phone anyhow." Besides, we went out four or five nights a week, so how could he possibly still be with her? I was trying to keep the relationship casual and wanted things to progress slowly. Tommy, on the other hand, expressed clearly that he wanted something more serious. He sent multiple e-mails a day and called me often. It didn't bother me that I was never at his apartment. After all, he had a car and I didn't, so it was easier for him to get to me than for me to get to his place in Westchester. Also, he explained, he was temporarily renting a downstairs apartment at his parents' house and he was embarrassed to invite me over until he moved out of their place. We even went out one night with his sister and brother-in-law, so it wasn't like he was hiding our relationship. Somehow, I managed to ignore the fact that his weekends were rarely free. He worked a lot of overtime, he explained. There was an explanation for everything. It's embarrassing to admit now, but I guess I believed what I wanted to believe.

My parents never liked Tommy. I blamed it on his religion, his appearance, and his occupation. I accused my parents, my Dad especially, of not even giving Tommy a chance just because he was a cop. I blamed it on the fact that every time they saw Tommy he had a different hair color "for his cover." I blamed "Mary of Maudlin" and the Low Rider with the 1400 cc engine that my dad called a "donor-cycle." But I should have known better. My parents have never judged people based on their appearance alone. I had boyfriends over the years with some hair, no hair, blue hair. None of that ever mattered to them. My dad just kept saying that he didn't have a good feeling about the guy. He said, "Undercovers deceive people for a living, Sarena." But I didn't have a bad feeling about Tommy and I trusted my instincts. I didn't necessarily think that he was the person that I was going to spend the rest of my life with, but I liked him. So I ignored my parents, I ignored the absences and omissions, and I continued dating him.

IT WAS SOME time around April of 1999. Tommy had become an undercover around November of the prior year so that he could earn his detective shield, and he was already counting the days until it was over. In the NYPD, anyone who spends 18 months as an undercover automatically earns his "gold shield." Tommy was paying his dues in the hopes of transferring to the elite Crime Scene Unit.

We were spending a rare weekend together. We spent all Saturday fishing in the rain. That night we went to a local fish restaurant. It was BYOB, so we brought a nice bottle of red wine with us. Tommy liked it so much that he saved the cork. We laughed at ourselves for going to a fish restaurant after throwing an entire day's catch back in the lake. I spent Sunday afternoon teaching Tommy how to use a manual camera. He claimed it was to help him prepare for the photographs that he would have to take in the Crime Scene Unit to which he was hoping to eventually transfer. Tommy had seen the photographs that I had taken in college, mostly of my brother's bodybuilding competitions. He said that he liked them and asked me to show him how I did it. I taught him all of my "secrets" for taking photographs in low light. I like to use a super high-speed film and no flash. I liked the grainy quality of it. He practiced by taking snapshots of me.

The next day, Monday afternoon, I was sitting at my desk at work. Tommy was meeting me for lunch and had just called to tell me that he was leaving the precinct and was on his way over. My phone rang just after I hung up with Tommy. I picked up: "Bronx DA's office. This is ADA Straus."

The women on the other end said, "Hi, this is Kathy. Tommy's fiancée." "Fiancée?" I stammered. Suddenly I felt cold and, for some reason, I believed her. I spent the next 10 minutes or so listening in silence and not doubting a word she said. Kathy proceeded to tell me that she knew I didn't know what was going on because she'd read all of my e-mails. She explained how he'd been duping both of us over the last four or five months. She was a night nurse in a pediatric ER and worked 12-hour shifts. On the nights she was working, Tommy would spend the evenings with me. He spent his days off and most of his weekends with her. She told me that she and Tommy had been having problems, but that he was blaming her for them. She also said that the previous month, when Tommy told me he'd been in Florida visiting his cousins, he'd really been in Aruba getting engaged. Kathy said that she became suspicious over the weekend when he claimed to be going away on a fishing trip with the guys. "It was raining the whole weekend, so I figured, how could he be fishing? I kept paging him and calling his cell phone but both were turned off. When he got home, he told me that he didn't have a signal up at the fishing cabin."

Kathy waited for Tommy to go to sleep and then she went rummaging through the trunk of his car. She found the film, the wine cork and a picture of me as a child that Tommy had begged me for a copy of. He said he adored this one photo in particular and told me that he had put it in his locker at work. Kathy told me that Tommy called us by the same nickname and had asked for a picture of her as a child under the same ruse. Both of our photos were in the trunk. Hers, a picture of her in her ballerina costume. Mine, a picture of me in my Raggedy-Anne dress. After searching the trunk, she hacked into Tommy's America Online account and spent the rest of the day reading e-mails that he'd sent me. Apparently, he saved all of them.

She knew everything about me—my occupation, all my phone numbers, my e-mail address. She had read several of my poems. She even knew my niece's name and was just begging me to please tell her that it was not my child with Tommy when he walked into my office.

I've never had a poker face. As soon as he saw me he knew something was up. "What's wrong," he asked.

I held out the phone to him. "Say hi to Kathy."

Tommy grabbed the phone and slammed it down on the cradle. I'd never seen him angry before. I'd never even heard him so much as raise his voice. He stormed out of my office and I followed him. My phone was already ringing again behind me. I followed him all the way to the parking lot and jumped into the passenger's seat of his car before he could back out. His cell phone was ringing. His pager was vibrating. And when he didn't answer, mine started.

"You owe me an explanation!" I shouted at him.

"For what! You shouldn't have been talking to her."

"I didn't call her, she called me," I answered, already defending myself against something that I didn't do.

Tommy proceeded to twist everything around. He told me that Kathy knew how to lie to me because she'd read all the e-mails. He claimed that nothing she said was true and that I should have hung up on her—that she was jealous and was just trying to break the two of us up because she knew he was in love with me. Suddenly, it was my fault and her fault. But nothing was his fault. He admitted that he'd gotten engaged to her, but he said that it was "just to shut her up," and that it "didn't mean anything." I sat and listened to him give his lame explanations and excuses. I heard him out. And then I got out of the car and walked away. I never looked back, but just because I was ready to let go doesn't mean that he was.

As soon as I got back to my office, the phone was ringing. Kathy had already left me several messages. After trying to ignore the phone for an hour and missing calls from witnesses, I finally picked up. It was Kathy again. She told me that she'd like to "meet me for drinks and talk." She suggested plots that we could hatch together to get revenge. Clearly, she was a game player too. And while at first I felt sorry about what had happened to her, now I was just getting angry. I told Kathy that I didn't want to be in the middle of things and that if she had questions, she should ask Tommy. I told her that my life was not an episode of "Geraldo," that we were not meeting for cocktails, and that I wanted to be left alone. I told her never to call me again.

I screened my calls at home and kept my cell phone turned off, but I had to answer the phone at work. Neither Kathy nor Tommy were going away that easily.

About two days later, Kathy called me at the office again. Her voice was high-pitched and panicky. "Sarena, I know you don't want to talk to me but please, listen. Tommy just left my place. I was in the shower and he was banging and banging on the door. He put a hole in it with his fist. I finally came out and he took my diamond ring and then he threatened me with his gun. I think he's on his way to see you." Kathy sounded terrified and, for the first time, I got scared.

The phone rang just after I hung up with Kathy. It was him. He asked to come over to see me. I asked him where he was coming from and he said, "The precinct." I knew that he was lying.

I told him "Don't come here," but, a few minutes later, I looked out my window and saw him pulling up.

Since Tommy had a badge, he didn't need permission from security to enter the building. He came right up to my office. Asha, who is about 87 pounds soaking wet, was the only person at the office who knew what was going on. I called her and told her what was happening. She was waiting with me when Tommy walked in. She crossed her little arms over her chest and refused to leave when Tommy asked her to give us some time alone. I told Asha it was okay and I agreed to speak with him, but only in a public place. Asha shook her finger at him and, staring him down in a manner that was surprisingly intimidating, said, "If you so much as lay a hand on her . . ." She turned on her heels, clicking angrily away down the hallway.

We went downstairs to the food court. Tommy looked possessed. His jaw was working and I could see the sinew flexing. He stared at me without blinking. The look in his eyes was terrifying. I told him what Kathy had said. "I suggest that you leave me alone," I told him. "If she calls me and I hear anything that even remotely sounds like you might be hurting her, that will be the end of your career. Do you understand me?" He tried, once again, to tell me that she was just trying to play me, but I'd had enough. "Frankly, it no longer matters to me who is telling the truth. I just want both of you to leave me alone."

THERE ARE THREE phases to the cycle of violence known as battered woman's syndrome. The first is "the tension building phase." The second is "the acute battering incident," and the third is the "contrition phase." This final phase is where the batterer showers the victim with affection and promises never to do it again. The experts say that, at first, it is the apologies and remorse that keep the victim in the relationship. But later, what keeps her in the relationship is fear of leaving. The fear of leaving can be for many reasons. But the most dangerous reason that battered women do not leave their relationships is fear that leaving will make it worse. Sometimes, they even fear that if they leave the batterer will kill them.

In the 1960s, a man named Martin Seligman did research on learned helplessness. In his experiment, two groups of dogs were put in hammocks. One group of dogs were given shocks that they were able to stop. The other group of dogs were given shocks that they were unable to stop no matter what they did. Later, both groups of dogs were put in a room that was divided in half by a low barrier. One side of the room was electrified and the other was not. The dogs were then placed on the electrified side and shocked. The group of dogs that had been able to stop the shocks in the hammock jumped over the barrier, went to the other side of the room and escaped the shock. The group that was unable to stop the shocks in the hammock did nothing. They had learned their helplessness from the previous experiment. They just lay down and whined. Even though they could have escaped the shocks, they didn't try.

Learned helplessness has since been applied to a variety of human problems, mostly depression. But the principle has also been applied to battered women in abusive relationships. In their situations, repeated beatings, like electric shocks, seem inescapable. At first, the battered woman believes she can control the violence by changing her behavior—the "It's my fault" syndrome. She tries doing what the abuser wants or refraining from conduct that she thinks causes the violence. When this doesn't work over time, the woman begins to believe that she can do nothing to stop the violence. She doesn't see the freedom on the other side of the room. The repeated shocks of past abuse cause her to become passive and she can no longer see life any other way.

I would add to this theory of the syndrome that before the cycle of physical violence starts, there is a much more subtle cycle in which the abuser begins testing his limits. A batterer needs to slowly ramp up, to see how far he can actually go before he becomes physically violent. It is a subtle dance that begins with other types of maltreatment that are not so obvious. Deception, dishonesty and blame, for starters.

EVEN THOUGH I got out of my relationship with Tommy as soon as I found out that he was deceiving me, I had a feeling of helplessness because no matter how long I ignored Tommy, he would not go away. It felt like it would never end. Things seemed to be out of my control. I was scared. I was embarrassed that this was happening to me of all people, a domestic violence prosecutor, and I didn't want to tell anyone other than Asha. But the situation was bad enough that I felt that I had to tell my parents what was going on in case something happened to me. My father, who truly believed that Tommy was dangerous and that everything Kathy told me was true, made me stay home for a couple of weeks. My mother had my locks changed and left a picture of Tommy with my door-man along with strict instructions that no one, even if they recognized him and even if he flashed a badge, was to allow him up to my apartment. I had anxiety every time the phone rang. Then the nightmares started.

When I was awake, I was not that scared of Tommy. I didn't really believe that he would actually harm me. But in my sleep, I was terrified of him. He stabbed me, stalked me, and shot me night after night. For a few weeks, Kathy would call me obsessively, saying things like, "I know you saw him last night. Well, right before you saw him he was fucking me," and other assorted pleasantries. When I hung up on her, she simply left a scathing message on my machine. Tommy called me obsessively, too, and continued sending e-mails. When I left my instant messenger on overnight, I would wake up to pages and pages of one-sided monologue from him. He would write for hours—mostly things that he knew would make me laugh. One thing I will say for Tommy is that he was one funny bastard. But the way things were now, this frightened rather than amused me. When I would block his e-mail address, he would simply get a new one and instant-message me under a different name.

I consulted an expert on what was going on and was advised, as I had advised so many of my female victims before, not to answer Tommy no matter what. "He'll keep upping the ante until you contact him. He'll keep changing tactics—humor, anger, gifts. He might even tell you he's been hurt. Once you answer, he will know the price and he won't back off. Once he knows what it takes to get you to answer, he won't stop." She was right. Tommy tried every trick in the book to get me to answer him. I resisted and finally, eventually, the calls and messages became less and less frequent. And then, it was four whole months without hearing from him. Finally, I felt secure that it was over. But it wasn't.

One night, I had a dream that I was in a mall. On my way out of the mall, I saw Tommy standing by the doorway. He had a rust-colored stain over his heart. It was the first time I'd dreamed about him in a long time where I was not afraid. I was about to walk right by him but, when I was just out the door, I turned around and went back. I kissed him on the cheek, smiled, and walked away. The dream books all say that dreaming of a stain indicates a superficial and reversible mistake in your life and that the location of the stain is most important. I guess the dream was my way of saying goodbye to him and forgiving myself for allowing myself to have been in a relationship with him. It was a superficial and reversible mistake, and I was entitled to move on. I had the dream because I thought that it was over.

Just a couple weeks after the dream, there was another e-mail. The violent dreams came back with a vengeance. Tommy's hold over me was through the anxiety that I could never have the security of knowing it was totally over. He would sometimes wait four or five months before I would hear from him again. Every time I got comfortable that I would never hear from him again, he would resurface. I could not file a criminal complaint against him because the messages were not threatening in any way that I could prove in court or explain to the police. It was the persistence and oddness that was frightening.

The following spring I started dating someone else. He was supposed to meet me at my apartment but for some reason, had to cancel. I arrived home and was informed by my doorman that someone had dropped off a package for me. I offered to carry the package up to my apartment, but the doorman said that it was too large and heavy. He brought it up for me. It was a brand new electric bass guitar and amplifier with an "anonymous" note from Tommy. Tommy was a talented guitarist and when we were dating, he had promised to teach me to play. Now, over a year after I had last seen him and at least five months since the last contact, he sent me this bizarre and expensive gift? What frightened me most was that he'd delivered it personally.

I didn't know what to do. I felt like the dogs in the shock traps with no way to stop this. I talked to Asha. I talked to a lawyer. The gift interfered with my new relationship. I was concerned that another gift or Tommy himself might show up, so I told my new boyfriend the whole story. He didn't take it too well. He said that the last thing he needed was a confrontation with a psychotic cop. He was critical about my choices when I told him the whole story. "How could someone so smart be that stupid," he accused. I wondered that myself.

I received one final instant message from Tommy in January of 2001, almost two years after ending my relationship with him. The following is only a few lines of an instant message that went on for pages and pages. I time-stamped it and sent a copy to my attorney along with copies of numerous similar messages:

NYPDcopNarcDiv (1:16:08 AM): This is NYPDcopNarcDiv to Sarena, repeat, this is NYPDcopNarcDiv to Sarena . . . Ya got ya ears on? Over.........

NYPDcopNarcDiv (1:30:14 AM): Bronx Narco: "Bronx Narcotics to Central K." Central: "Go with your message Narco." Bronx Narco: " Central, I'm trying to reach Sarena, I have an emergency transmission. What are you showing on your screen?" Central: "Stand by narco. I'm checking." Bronx Narco: "!0-4. Standing by"

NYPDcopNarcDiv (1:35:08 AM): Central: "OK Narco, I'm showing Sarena on my buddy list at this time." Bronx Narco: "10-4 Central, I'm showing her on my buddy list as well. Can you verify if she's able to receive any transmissions at this time?" Central: "I do believe Sarena's up and running."

NYPDcopNarcDiv (1:40:27 AM): Central: "Narco, I'm going to try and raise Sarena. Central to Sarena, central to Sarena. You on the air?"

NYPDcopNarcDiv (1:44:35 AM): Central: No response Narco. I do believe that you being totally dissed at this time K."

NYPDcopNarcDiv (1:45:35 AM): Bronx Narco: "Central, I do believe that as well. What do you recommend I do now?"

NYPDcopNarcDiv (1:48:41 AM): Central: "Hmm. I'm thinking. Gimme a friggin minute. This could go on all night."

NYPDcopNarcDiv (1:50:15 AM): Central: "Did she get the bass?" Bronx Narco: "I don't know.

NYPDcopNarcDiv (2:04:43 AM): Bronx Narco: "Central, is it possible Sarena's away from the screen at time?"

NYPDcopNarcDiv (2:05:17 AM): Central: "I don't know."

NYPDcopNarcDiv (2:13:59 AM): Central: "Well, narco, it's after 2 AM, and it's obvious that you got a good ball-kickin' from Sarena this evening. Maybe you should call it a night?"

NYPDcopNarcDiv (2:15:24 AM): Bronx Narco: "Roger that Central. Roger that. My nuts is a-ache-n."

NYPDcopNarcDiv (2:16:15 AM): Central: "Good-night Narco"

NYPDcopNarcDiv (2:16:35 AM): Bronx Narco: "Good-night Central"

NYPDcopNarcDiv (2:17:03 AM): Grandpa Walton: "Good night John-Boy"

NYPDcopNarcDiv (2:17:25 AM): John-Boy: "Good-night Pawww."

NYPDcopNarcDiv (2:19:47 AM): FYI, The proceeding conversation was probably the most fun I've had alone in awhile. I'm easily amused . . . LOL Good night Sarena . . . Wherever you are. . . . ;-)

Over an hour after beginning, he'd finally logged off. Not a very threatening message unless it's from someone you've had no contact with for two years who may have threatened his fiancée with a gun. And it was bizarre. I got one more e-mail from him inquiring about the guitar and then a message where he whispered my name into the phone several times.

I did not know what to do. My training told me that I had to keep ignoring him and that he was upping the ante to force me to respond. But that guitar became an excuse for Tommy to constantly try to contact me to see if I'd received it. Finally, I decided that I had to be proactive in some way and see if that would end it. I had my lawyer send the guitar back to him with a letter saying that the next time he contacted me, it would be reported. I never heard from him again.

Where were the hints that this kind, sweet, affectionate person might be capable of violence? Did I miss danger warnings? I'm not sure. Maybe most of what Kathy said *was* lies, but in the end, did it really matter? I knew as soon as his duplicity came to light that Tommy had to be out of my life. Maybe the only thing that separates me from a battered woman, or even a dead one, is the fact that I didn't stick around to find out.

THE UPSIDE OF learned helplessness is that, at least for the dogs, there is a simple cure. While the dog that has learned helplessness is being shocked, someone simultaneously pushes or leads him to the other side. The dog learns that, in this new situation, he can escape the shock. After a few sessions of being pushed over the fence while receiving the shock, the dog once again behaves normally and goes to the other side on his own when shocked. At this point, the once-paralyzed dog's behavior can no longer be distinguished from that of a dog that has never had the experience of being helpless.

People are, of course, more complicated than dogs, but there is a similarity. With children or adults, the cure is to demonstrate that they can escape, even if you have to lead them through the process a few times. Martin Seligman's later experiments turned toward "learned optimism." He started to do happiness studies and found that one of the major factors in people's overall level of happiness in life is closeness to friends and family. It was my support network of friends and family that helped push me over the barrier and take a positive action to defend myself. They did not judge me or tell me "I told you so." But they held up my fists when I was tired of fighting and helped me go one more round. And like most bullies, in the end Tommy was really a coward. When the threat was turned on him, he ran away. I only wish that all fights could be won without anyone getting hurt. But, as I also learned at the DA's office, sometimes you can be as brave and fight as hard as anyone could wish you to, but things do not always work out so well.

14

JUST AN OLD MAN WHO DRINKS COFFEE AND WORKS FOR JESUS

"Suffer little children, and forbid them not to come unto Me."
—MATTHEW 19:14

"I'm just an old man who drinks coffee and works for Jesus."
—BROTHER CHRISTOPHER MURPHY

"JUST LIKE EVERY caring and concerned parent, Tanya Paulson wanted what was best for her children Peter and Shaniqua. She wanted them to feel loved. She wanted them to get a good education and she wanted them to be safe. And to that end, Tanya entrusted the care of her only daughter, Shaniqua, to a man who sits about fifteen feet from you. A teacher, a member of the clergy and, ultimately the person that she last expected would be the person who raped her daughter.

"Ironically, you're going to hear from Tanya that she worked for the board of education. She raised her two children, Peter and Shaniqua, here in The Bronx. She lives here in The Bronx with them and with her fiancé. And she made personal and monetary sacrifices in order to send her daughter, Shaniqua, to a school called Blessed Sacrament, which is the place she thought to be the best place for her child. So, in a world where we all know the dangers to our children—the robbers, the drug dealers, rapists, murderers—in a world where people would hurt our children, she unknowingly and with the best of intentions and with love in her heart, sent her child right into the arms of a man that would hurt her.

"Shaniqua is fifteen now and for three long years she kept this secret inside of her. You can imagine what that would do to somebody, and you're going to see what it did to her. It ate away at her and it practically destroyed her. It turned a bright, friendly, happy eleven-year-old, who did well in school, to a girl who was so depressed that she could hardly get out of bed. Who, between the time this happened to her and the time that she told somebody about it, gained almost 150 pounds. Who is so ashamed of herself that she doesn't even want to bathe some days or get undressed. Who went from being an excellent student who got awards to someone who was failing out of school.

"You're going to hear from an expert in this case and that expert is going to talk to you about this depression, about what that was a symptom of. But you don't need an expert to tell you what depression looks like. You don't need an expert to tell you that it's no coincidence that Shaniqua started showing all of these symptoms one day when she came home late from school in sixth grade.

"So what happened to Shaniqua Paulson? What happened to Tanya's happy little girl? Shaniqua was eleven years old when she started sixth grade at Blessed Sacrament School here in The Bronx. She had a bunch of teachers that year and one of her teachers was the defendant, a man named Christopher Murphy★ or, as she called him, Brother Chris. And you'll hear the students were not so fond of him. He yelled at them. He demeaned them. He called them names. He told them they were worthless, they were stupid. And yes, sometimes he would hit them. And his students were afraid of him. Shaniqua was afraid of him. But Tanya is going to tell you that she ran a tight ship at home. She's going to tell you she was a strict mother and she's going to tell you that

---

★ I have changed the defendant's name in this case. Although the case received wide press coverage and his name is readily available, I have made up an alias nonetheless. This is not out of respect for the defendant or because I do not believe he is guilty. I do believe he is guilty. It is out of respect for our legal system and the right of those who are acquitted whether I agree with that acquittal or not.

she respected the defendant. That she thought her child was getting a good education from him.

"So, in February of 1996, one week before Valentine's Day, Shaniqua was asked to do an honor. She was asked by her teacher to stay after school and help him grade some papers and she was excited about this. The bell rang. And Shaniqua went with the defendant to a room to help grade the papers with him.

"She walked into that room to put her stuff down and when she walked into that room, he locked the door behind her and that's when he stole her childhood. He threw that eleven-year-old girl down on a desk and he raped her.

"When he was finished raping her, her told her that if she told anybody, he would kill her. And he also told her something else. He told her that because of who she was and because of who he was, that no one would believe her. That he was "just an old man who drinks coffee and works for Jesus."

"By the time this trial is over, ladies and gentlemen, you're not going to wonder why this girl waited three years to tell anybody that this happened. You're going to wonder how on earth, how in the world, she ever got the courage to tell anybody.

"So for three long years she carried this secret inside of her and it almost destroyed her until someone came along who, for whatever reason, touched her in a way or reached out to her in a way that she was able to tell him what happened to her. Until, finally, she couldn't take it anymore and she confided in a trusted teacher.. A teacher nothing like *him*, a teacher who did what was right and who did what he could to help her.

"You're going to hear about how Shaniqua testified in the Grand Jury and the Grand Jury returned what's called an indictment. And what the Grand Jury found was that the defendant, Christopher Murphy, on or about February 9, 1996, in the county of The Bronx, being male, did engage in sexual intercourse with Shaniqua Paulson, a female, by forcible compulsion. And they found that the defendant, Christopher Murphy, on or about February 9, 1996, in the county of The Bronx, being eighteen years old or more, did engage in sexual intercourse with Shaniqua Paulson, to whom the defendant was not married, who was less than fourteen years old. And, finally, that the defendant, Christopher Murphy, on or about February 9, 1996, in the County of The Bronx, did knowingly act in a manner likely to be injurious to the physical, mental, or moral welfare of Shaniqua Paulson, a child less than eighteen years old.

"You're going to hear from that teacher who was someone not like the defendant. You're going to hear from Tanya Paulson. You're going to here from Shaniqua Paulson. You're going to hear from a couple of doctors and you're going to hear from the detective who performed the investigation and arrest in this case.

"Finally, at the end of this trial, you're going to hear from me one more time when I get up and ask you to convict the defendant on all charges. Thank you."

So, I BEGAN the case of the *People of the State of New York v. Christopher Murphy*. It was my albatross. I spoke before a courtroom that was standing room only for the next two weeks. All of the major New York papers reported on the case daily. I prepared for that case with every ounce of my ability and it consumed me for a year because everyone told me that I could not win it. I believed in Christopher Murphy's guilt and I wanted to prove, more than anything, that they were wrong. But they were right. And whether it is the law that failed Shaniqua or the system or the jury, I still do not know. But I do know, with every fiber of my being, that there was nothing else I could have done to be ready for that case. I also know that there were things that I knew about Christopher Murphy that the law did not allow me to tell the jury. And whether those laws are right or wrong, I still don't know.

To WRITE A poem about a case, I must first come to terms with it. I must understand for myself what transpired, how to cope with it. I never wrote a poem about the *People v. Christopher Murphy*.

It was spring of 1999 when Elisa called me into her office. I entered the room and saw six solemn faces staring at me. All the big guns— Elisa, Alvin, Astrid, Mike, Rosemary, and Bobby. The last time I was called into Elisa's office to face The Panel was when I was the brunt of a joke. When I got there, Elisa proceeded to announce to the room that she had a dream that I was having an affair with the former chief of the bureau. She then proceeded to fall out of her chair, laughing. I could tell by the expressions around the table that this was not such an occasion. "I need you to take a case," Elisa started. "It's not an easy one. You're not gonna' win."

"Okay," I said, "I've won the unwinnable before. You said that about my case with the guy who stabbed his son-in-law in self-defense, you said that about the woman who refused to testify after her boyfriend shot her in the head. What's different about this one?"

"The defendant is a Marist Brother and the victim is claiming he raped her three years ago. We have a cold case. Whatever physical evidence there may be can no longer be connected to him. He's automatically going to have respect in the community. You're dealing with a religious jury pool. You're fucked." Everyone around the table nodded in agreement. And so began my mission to prove them wrong.

Prosecutors all have cases, at one point or another, that they know they will lose but take on principle, nonetheless. They also all have those cases that they just can't handle. Then there are the cases that consume them, that become their mission in life. Brother Chris consumed me for the next year. It was the case that no one else wanted for personal reasons, for religious reasons, because of the amount of press it was going to receive even though it was "a loser." As I immersed myself in that case and got to know about Brother Chris and about his victim, Shaniqua, it became my mission in life to stop Brother Chris, to make sure that he would never harm another child again.

I failed in that mission.

Up until the Brother Chris case, I had the utmost faith in our criminal justice system. Sure, mistakes are made. Innocent people are convicted. But far more often than that, the guilty are freed. I believed, and still pretty much believe, that it's just about the best system there is. And, I believe in jurors. I believe that the majority of them take their jobs seriously and want to do what's right. I believe in the laws being strongly biased in favor of defendants, even at the risk of freeing the guilty, because I'd rather free the guilty than put the innocent away. I believe in my very marrow that I never convicted an innocent man or woman, and that is how I sleep at night. The system is designed to protect the innocent and not to incarcerate the guilty and I believe that is right.

Part of this bias in favor of defendants is that prosecutors are possessed of a wealth of information that never goes before a jury. While the laws in each state vary, the laws in New York are particularly pro-defendant. This means, more often than not, we could not introduce evidence of prior convictions or arrests to a jury, especially for similar crimes. The idea behind this is that you are not allowed to convict someone of a crime based on a defendant's "propensity" to commit that crime. In other words, say I was prosecuting a 70-year-old man for sexually abusing a child and he had been convicted of doing it twice before and arrested for it 10 times before. Unless I was able to get the evidence in under some legal exception, I could not tell the jury about the prior incidents. This leaves a jury thinking that this 70-year-old man is committing an act against a child for the first time at such a late age. For obvious reasons, this makes the case substantially more difficult to win because, rightfully so, the jury is thinking that if he has not done it before now, he probably didn't do it this time. I understand the rationale behind this rule: that just because someone did it before does not mean that they did it this time. But it's certainly hard to stomach when it means that someone you truly believe is guilty is going to walk or that their freedom means that more victims will inevitably suffer. This also means that prosecutors often walk into a courtroom with far more evidence of guilt in their file than will ever come before a jury.

Despite what we hear on the news about prosecutors withholding exculpatory evidence, I believe it's an incredibly rare circumstance. Although I know there are prosecutors out there who want a conviction at any cost, I personally did not know any of them. The people with whom I was close at the DA's office were of the finest moral character and, without exception, would go out of their way to make sure that they did not put an innocent man or woman in jail, especially for something as terrible as violating a child. Just like anything else, the problem seems much worse than it is because you don't hear about the everyday heroes breaking their backs to dot every "i" and cross every "t" to insure that innocent people don't go to jail. You only hear about the small percentage of bad eggs. It's like I used to say when people criticized the police department. Most of the cops I dealt with were fine, caring people who believed in their job. But if you have 40,000 of them and 1 percent are bad eggs, well that's 400 bad eggs and that many people can do a lot of damage. Like the other prosecutors I know, I held myself to this high standard.

UP UNTIL BROTHER Chris, I had only one acquittal on a felony and it was a case that I wanted to lose. The case involved an eight-year-old girl who accused her grandfather of sexually abusing her. The older sister, who was 17, actually complained on behalf of her sister after allegedly walking in while she was being fondled by granddad. The 17-year-old claimed that the grandfather sexually abused her as a child, too, but that she had never told anyone. She said that whenever he was around, she kept a close eye on her sister because she was afraid the grandfather would abuse her sister.

It is actually very common for outcries to occur this way. It's called "delayed disclosure." Many children will never disclose the fact that they were abused at all. Often, however, adults who were abused as children disclose because they are afraid that someone they love will be abused by their abuser. They find the courage to tell in order to protect someone else. In the case of this eight-year-old and her 17-year-old sister, there was a tremendous amount of hostility between the older child and her grandfather. The family claimed that it was because the grandfather was mean to the older girl and would tease her about her weight and appearance. They also said that he hated the girl because she was half Dominican and he openly disliked Dominicans. I was personally unsure whether that was the root of the hostility or it was because the grandfather had abused her. Nevertheless, the crimes that the 17-year-old said were committed against her had occurred when she was between 7 and 10 years old. It was too far in the past for me to prosecute. The family believed that the older girl put her sister up to lying about the abuse in order to get revenge on the grandfather. This is just about the number one defense in child abuse cases. It is also something family members will often say when they don't want to believe that an accusation is true. This argument was, therefore, not persuasive to me without more information.

What complicated the case and made me uncertain about the younger child's credibility were two things. First, she was inconsistent in her account of what happened. But it was difficult for me to tell if the child was changing details because she couldn't keep her story straight or because she was trying to tell me what she thought I wanted to hear. Second, several members of the family, including members that believed the child at first, were telling me that the child was recanting her story. They claimed that the child said that the older sister put her up to the lie and threatened to hit her if she told. Again, it was difficult for me to know if the family was just saying this to try to get the grandfather out of trouble or because it really happened.

In the end, I brought the child to my office five or six times to speak with her. She steadfastly stuck to her story whenever she was with me. I spoke with the older sister, trying to coerce her into telling me that she had put her sister up to this. She stuck to her story, as well. I had a detective speak with the older sister as I watched through a two-way mirror. The detective tried to scare her into coming clean by telling her she could go to jail for perjury if she was lying about this. She still told the same story. I also had an aunt, who the little girl allegedly recanted to, speak to the little girl while I watched through a two-way mirror and listened in through a monitor, but the child still maintained that she was abused.

In the end, although I thought that the likelihood was that the grandfather was guilty, I was just not certain beyond a reasonable doubt. And if I could not be sure beyond a reasonable doubt, the jury certainly could not be. I went to Elisa and petitioned to dismiss the case. I just didn't want to take the risk of going to trial if I was not sure. However, Elisa insisted that unless the child recanted to me, we could not drop the charges. Ultimately, the case went to trial and I put everything in front of the jury. I even called the aunt who the child had recanted to as a witness. I decided that the right thing to do, the just thing, was to let the jury know everything that I knew and leave the decision to them. The jury acquitted. I'm not quite sure how I would have handled it if the defendant was convicted. But at least I had a clear conscience that I told both the defense attorney and the jury every bit of exculpatory information that I had.

BROTHER CHRIS'S CASE was a totally different ballgame. I had a 100 percent belief in the victim. It was the first acquittal that really hurt. It was the first time that someone I prosecuted and who I truly believed was guilty walked away a free man. Before him, I had a three-year winning streak, something I consider quite an accomplishment in The Bronx.

But, I had known that, before the trial even started, whether I won or lost it, I was emotionally finished with this job. I couldn't take it any more. I think I knew all along, somewhere in the rational portion of my brain that took no part in the prosecution of Brother Chris, that I was going to lose this one. And I couldn't handle it. I have even tried since then to convince myself that maybe he really was innocent so I can stomach his being out there, or Shaniqua having to live with the verdict, but I can't convince myself of that, either.

"SHANIQUA WAS SUCH a happy child," Mrs. Paulson began. "Everyone just loved her. Everyone told me what a pleasant, polite child she was. She was always laughing. She always said 'please' and 'thank you.' I just didn't understand what happened to my child. She started to change. Her grades dropped. She stopped smiling. She went from an 'A' student to failing out of school. She gained over a hundred and fifty pounds in the last three years. I kept asking her 'What is wrong with you, Shaniqua.' She wouldn't get out of bed. She stopped playing with her friends. She wouldn't bathe or undress. Now it all makes sense. Why didn't she tell me, though? Why wouldn't she let me help her?" Tears streamed down Mrs. Paulson's face as she told me her story in Dr. Cahill's office at the Child Protection Center. It was my first meeting with Mrs. Paulson. We talked while the doctor examined Shaniqua's hymen with a colposcope in the room next door. A colposcope is an instrument used to examine the tissues of the vagina and cervix through a magnifying lens. During examinations for rape trauma, high-magnification slides would be taken of any injuries. We often used prints of these photographed injuries as evidence at trial. The doctor was taking the first step in gathering my evidence.

This conversation with Mrs. Paulson was my first clue that Shaniqua had really been raped. Without knowing it, Mrs. Paulson was describing symptoms to me. She was telling me about a girl who had experienced something terrible, so terrible that she could not cope with it.

I met Shaniqua shortly after her examination. Shaniqua was a beautiful young woman. At 14, she was already taller than me and morbidly obese but she had gorgeous, wide shiny eyes that disappeared when she smiled. She had high cheekbones and dark clear skin. She shyly shook my hand while looking down at the floor. This was a girl altogether different from what I usually dealt with in The Bronx. She had none of the brashness, overconfidence, inappropriate maturity, and sexuality that I had seen in the girls I had met. She was soft-spoken and very reserved. She dressed to cover herself, in big baggy clothing. Shaniqua came from a loving, hard-working family. She lived in a clean, orderly home. When her younger brother found out what had happened to her, he crawled into bed with her every night to hug her before they went to sleep. She came from a family with such love, and it was all destroyed in minutes.

I felt Shaniqua had been through enough that day. This was her first gynecological examination. And as if those are not bad enough to begin with, Shaniqua was mortified to have to be naked, to have photographs taken of her vagina. The examination showed that this 14-year-old girl had a healed tear to her hymen that was consistent with penetration sometime in the past. I decided to wait until the next day and start by talking to her in my office.

"My mom sent me to Blessed Sacrament because she wanted me to be safe," Shaniqua began the next morning. Ironically, Shaniqua's mother, Tanya, worked for the board of education. She wanted a better life for her children and she understood that, in the neighborhood where she lived, there were too many dangerous influences in the public schools and in the streets. Tanya was very strict with her children. She insisted on always knowing where they were and who they were with. She spent money that she didn't have to send her children to Catholic school so that they would have a chance at a better life. Few of the children who came into my office as the victims of crimes had such love and support in their family. Although it was heartbreaking to see them end up in such a terrible situation, it also gave me hope that they were going to pull through this ordeal together. I still cling to that hope.

When Shaniqua was in sixth grade, her teacher was Brother Christopher Murphy. None of the children liked him. He would yell at them and curse. He was violent with them. Shaniqua came into his class fearing him, having heard from a friend's sister that he once hit a kid. She personally witnessed him twist a child's arm until the child cried. Along with these facts, there were the typical rumors that children spread about teachers, including that he filled his coffee cup with whisky. But none of those rumors included tales of him sexually abusing students.

Shaniqua was a good student. She would occasionally be reprimanded for talking to other kids in class but, all in all, her behavior reports were excellent. Her third grade picture shows a chubby girl in a plaid uniform staring down at the ground with a shy grin on her face.

Shortly after I began my investigation in the case, I got a call from a retired detective who saw a report about the case in the *Daily News*. He told me that in the mid-eighties he had investigated Brother Chris, along with another brother and a priest, for alleged sexual abuse at Assumption Academy in The Bronx. Reverand Bernard Lester and Brother Timothy Bradley were indicted and acquitted for sexually abusing students. Brother Chris was never indicted in the case. This certainly got my interest.

I began to do research on Brother Chris about these prior accusations but met with little success. I ordered the Assumption Academy file from the archives so that I could look at the write-ups in that case, but no one could locate the folder. I finally met with some success when I sent a Freedom of Information request to the FBI. They sent back papers indicating that in the mid-eighties, Brother Chris had indeed been investigated by them for allegedly sexually abusing a male student while on a school trip to Canada. The boy alleged that Brother Chris had fondled him in the shower. The Canadian government refused to press charges and the US lacked jurisdiction to do so at the time, so, once again, Brother Chris went unpunished.

Throughout the course of his career with the church, Brother Chris was moved just about every two years. He taught all over the United States and in American Samoa. Since rumors abound that the church often deals with allegations of sexual abuse by simply moving the alleged perpetrator to a different school, I wondered if there had been complaints against Brother Chris in the past that had resulted in his being repeatedly moved.

Meanwhile, I worked with Shaniqua and Tanya on their memories of events surrounding the rape. Shaniqua was able to narrow the time frame down to shortly before Valentine's Day, during the month of February. While Tanya could not recall the specific day, she did remember a day that Shaniqua came home late from school.

Tanya remembered that day because Shaniqua was never late from school or anywhere else without calling to let her mother know. Normally, either Tanya would pick Shaniqua up from school or Shaniqua would go home with a friend. That day, Shaniqua was supposed to come home with her friend and should have arrived by 3:30 PM. By four, Tanya started to worry. She called the friend's house, but got no answer. She tried calling the school but no one picked up in the office. She kept sticking her head out the door to look at the bus stop down the street, but she did not see Shaniqua. Finally, at 4:30, Tanya picked up the phone to call the police and, at just that moment, Shaniqua walked in the door. Tanya recalled that Shaniqua's hair was a little messy and that she had a big hole in her tights. She remembered that her first question was not "Where were you," or "Why are you late," it was, "What happened to your tights?" Tanya thought she asked that because it was unlike Shaniqua to ruin her clothing. "She was a careful child."

Shaniqua told her mother that she had snagged the tights on one of the wooden desks at school and that they ripped. Shaniqua said that at that point she went into the bathroom. While she was in the bathroom, Shaniqua had seen that she was bleeding from her vagina. The blood was on her clothing. She took off her tights and her uniform, tied them in a plastic wastepaper bag and threw them out the bathroom window. She took a shower and went to sleep.

Tanya did not recall any of Shaniqua's uniforms being missing, but acknowledged that she had three or four of them and, that if one was badly worn and thrown out, she would not have remembered, as it was a common occurrence. She also did not recall if Shaniqua did or did not take a shower because it was not unusual for the child to shower after school, either. What she did recall is something that most mothers remember as a happy day.

"I remember the next day I went into the bathroom and I saw a bloody tissue in the wastepaper basket. Shaniqua and I are the only females in the house so I went into her room and asked her if she got her period. She told me, 'I guess so.' I was so excited. I remember that I hugged her and ran to call my sister. I told my sister, 'Shaniqua is a woman now!' I also remember that it was three or four months before she got her period again. I was a little worried, but when I told my sister, she said not to worry about it because sometimes girls are irregular at the beginning. When she started menstruating regularly a few months later, I thought nothing more of it."

This was my first big break in the case. Tanya's recollection was powerful corroboration of several elements of Shaniqua's allegations. First, it supported what Shaniqua had told me about coming home from school late after having been raped by Brother Chris. Second, the fact that Tanya observed that Shaniqua bled, but did not get her period until several months later, supported the fact that the bleeding had been a consequence of Shaniqua having been raped, rather than that she got her period. Finally, there was the hole in the stockings.

I never prepared my witnesses together. Sometimes, when I was giving instructional or background information, I would speak to several witnesses at once, but when it came to discussing the actual facts of the case, I separated people so that they could not compare notes or correct each other. If there were going to be any inconsistencies, I wanted to know about them well ahead of time. In Shaniqua's case, I did not even review general instructions with them in the same room. Tanya was very nervous and traumatized by Shaniqua's claim. While Shaniqua's reaction was to withdraw and become somewhat of a hermit, Tanya's response was the opposite. Tanya was extremely hyper. She lost about 20 pounds awaiting the trial and when she would come to my office, she would get horrendous verbal diarrhea. She had to keep herself constantly busy or she would get shaky. After the first two or three meetings, where I spent some time speaking with Tanya and daughter together, I began separating them, otherwise Shaniqua would just become silent and Tanya would do all of the talking. Both of them told me that, since the day that Shaniqua disclosed the rape, neither of them had spoken about what happened. Of course, they could have lied to me about it but, given Shaniqua's shyness about the case, I believed that it was true. Tanya also asked me if she should push Shaniqua to talk about what happened and I told her not to. "It's enough that she has to talk to me and to the police about it. Let her talk about it as much or as little as she wants."

This is not to say that they could not have compared stories on their own to come up with some kind of consistent testimony but there were enough inconsistencies that it seemed clear that they really did not discuss their testimony. Sometimes, the differences in people's testimony can be as helpful as the similarities. As long as they don't differ on crucial facts, variations in minor details can lend credibility to the testimony. It was when people were too consistent that I sometimes started to worry about their veracity.

Shaniqua described the rape to me in detail. She told me that when Brother Chris raped her, there was an after-school program going on in the cafeteria down the hall with about 50 or 60 five- and six-year-olds making the expected ruckus. Shaniqua walked into the room that Brother Chris indicated to her. He locked the door behind her and pushed her face-down on the desk. She explained to me that Brother Chris did not pull down her tights and underwear but rather ripped a large hole in her tights and pushed her underwear to the side. Brother Chris was not a tall man but he was very overweight, both at the time of the incident and at trial. Shaniqua, on the other hand, was much smaller, both in height and weight, at the time she was raped. She explained that he held her down with one arm but that his weight alone was enough to keep her pinned to the desk. She said that it was painful when he penetrated her but that she did not know if he ejaculated. When he was finished, he told her not to tell. "No one will believe you anyway. I'm just an old man who drinks coffee and works for Jesus."

As I said, I do not believe that Tanya knew any of these details before she watched Shaniqua testify at trial. She, could not understand how important it was that she remembered that hole. It was the first time that I had a glimmer of hope that I might win the case. Her testimony about seeing the hole in the tights on the day that Shaniqua was late coming home from school significantly bolstered Shaniqua's description of how the rape occurred.

I GOT ALONG extremely well with Shaniqua and Tanya. In fact, I came to know much of their extended family throughout the course of the trial, and I think that they liked and trusted me. I did, however, run into one bump in the road a few months before trial.

I had a case with an eight-year-old whose grandfather sexually abused her. Her nine-year-old aunt, who was the grandfather's daughter, was in the bed when it happened and denied seeing anything. The girls, who lived in the same building and were more like sisters than aunt and niece, stopped speaking to each other because of the allegations. In fact, the whole family was shattered. I believed the eight-year-old and was fairly sure that her aunt was being abused too and was protecting her father. Nevertheless, the child had no physical findings (the abuse was oral sex, so she wouldn't have, anyhow) and with the aunt testifying that she was in the bed and saw nothing, I had no chance at a conviction. When the defendant offered to plead guilty and take two years in jail, I jumped on it. Although I explained my reasoning to the family, they refused to accept that the punishment was so small and demanded that we go to trial. I refused and took what I thought was the best I could get under the circumstances. The family called DA Robert Johnson to complain about me. Once he heard the facts, he supported my decision and he and Elisa both spoke with the family again, explaining my rationale. But they were not appeased. At sentencing, the child made a speech about how much she hated me and how I had let her down. A month later, Tanya called and told me that she wanted a different ADA to handle her case. Apparently, Shaniqua and the eight-year-old went to the same group therapy and the eight-year-old had spoken about what happened to her on several occasions. Her anger was directed toward me. Tanya was now worried that I would give Brother Chris a plea that was more lenient than what they felt appropriate. I explained the situation to her and the reason for the plea. It seemed to appease her enough that she stayed with me.

It is hard to describe the terrible emotional burden that you take on as a DVS prosecutor. You put so much heart and effort into your cases. The feeling when a victim turns on you is one of betrayal and remorse. I was very hurt by the whole situation. I couldn't blame the family for being angry and frustrated, but it was painful that it was directed at me. I knew that I made the right decision, but I also wished I could have done more for them. I felt bad for Tanya because it must have been difficult for her to even call me and raise the issue. Although she and I had a wonderful relationship, I guess that if it had been my child in such a situation, this information would have concerned me too.

About a month after I left the DA's office, I got a call from Mary Clark-DiRusso, the assistant who had helped me with my very first DVS case with May. She informed me that right before the defendant with the nine-year-old daughter was due to be released from prison, the daughter came forward and admitted that the defendant had abused her and that she'd seen him abuse her niece, as well. She explained that she had denied the abuse earlier because the father had told her that if she disclosed the abuse to anyone, he would kill her mother. When she was faced with the reality that her father was about to get out of jail, she finally came forward. As a result of the daughter's allegations, the father pled guilty to a whole new set of crimes. He will spend another five years in jail and then be deported. The family told Mary that they felt bad about taking their anger out on me. After time, they understood my decision. They asked her to tell me that they were sorry. I was just happy to hear that they had peace in the family again and hopefully some closure to all of their pain.

FINALLY, AFTER OVER a year of doing everything that I could to prepare the case against Brother Chris, it was time for his trial. The case was assigned to Judge Martin Marcus. Judge Marcus had a reputation among ADAs for being tough but fair and extremely intelligent. I was happy about the selection, but knew that Judge Marcus would be a stickler on the law about what evidence of Brother Chris's prior bad acts I would be allowed to talk about at trial. With little case law to support me, I futilely argued that the prior allegations of sexual abuse by Brother Chris should be admissible. My motion was summarily—and quite properly—denied because the prior acts would prejudice the jury against Brother Chris and make it believe that, since he had been accused of similar crimes in the past, my charges against him were more likely to be true.

I also argued that evidence of Brother Chris's extensive use of corporal punishment should be allowed as evidence to be presented to the jury. Judge Marcus agreed to allow Shaniqua to testify about the use of corporal punishment, but only with respect to those events about which she had personal knowledge and only to the degree that those incidents affected her state of mind, both during and after the rape. I also sought permission to have Tanya's sister testify about the phone call where Tanya told her that Shaniqua got her period but the judge disallowed that testimony as "cumulative and bolstering."

Prior to and throughout the case, I continuously consulted with ADA Dan McCarthy, whose strategy on flight as eveidence of guilt I'd tried to follow on the Juanito case. McCarthy was a legend at the office and any time he that he was trying a case, the courtroom would be packed with

ADAs furiously taking notes on everything he said. Dan was amazing. Every time I went to see him, I wished I had a tape recorder. It was like every word that came out of his mouth was exactly what I wanted to express, but 10 times more eloquent. He was a mentor to me on this case and his guidance was invaluable to me throughout the trial.

Jury selection and opening statements were uneventful. The defense hired an expert to consult on the jury selection, which I had never seen done before in a criminal case in The Bronx. I could not tell what, if anything, this expert added to the process. I never had a case before where anyone had the resources for something as indulgent as a jury selection expert. Since the Vatican was paying for Brother Chris's defense, the resources at his disposal were almost unlimited and this was reflected in the level to which the defense attorney prepared for the case.

I recall little of the defense attorney's opening except that he made some kind of analogy about a kid who doesn't like broccoli so he lies and says that he ate it when he really threw it under the table to the dog. He likened that to a student who does not like her teacher falsely claiming that he raped her. I thought it was the most absurd comparison that I ever heard so, of course, I went back to it every opportunity I got, mumbling, "Broccoli?" under my breath all the time.

I called Tanya to the witness stand first. Normally I called victims to the witness stand first but in this case, and after much consultation with Dan, I decided that it would be better to let Tanya testify first and leave the jury a little hungry. Also, Tanya was not allowed to observe the trial until after she testified. Since Shaniqua wanted her mother in the room during her testimony, I had to put Tanya on first.

Tanya did neither well nor poorly. She was simply too upset and nervous to deal with the defense attorney's badgering. She did fine on direct examination but on cross, the defense attorney got her completely flustered by peppering her with questions about whether Shaniqua really was a good student or not. He went through every report card and comment the poor kid got from kindergarten on. I repeatedly objected, but the judge allowed it to go on for quite some time. The defense had the distinct advantage of having access to just about anything he wanted from the school. He had not even subpoenaed Shaniqua's school records, which was the appropriate method to obtain personal information about a witness at trial. Instead, the school had merely released Shaniqua's records to the defense upon his request. The defense then used those records to cross-examine Tanya for hours on background information that should have been of little issue. The Vatican was not playing fair, and while this behavior may have meant a civil case for the Paulsons, I could not do anything about it in my criminal case. Like any good attorney, the defense hardly mentioned the rape at all on cross-examination. He successfully took the jurors' minds off the important issues in the case and allowed them to focus on minutia.

Next, I called Shaniqua to the stand. When she first took the witness stand and laid eyes on her rapist, she broke into hysterical sobs. The judge quickly excused the jury and took a 10-minute break. I followed Shaniqua into the hallway, attempting to calm her down. In the meantime, Shaniqua's family was fighting with the defendant's family because the defendant's family kept trying to take their seats. They all ended up crushed together on the benches for the next couple of weeks with everyone refusing to yield an inch of space or move to another bench.

Once Shaniqua regained her composure, she testified well. She admitted that she hated Brother Chris even before the rape. She said that he was mean to the students. That he would yell at them and insult them in class. She testified that he told one girl, an 11-year-old, that she was a whore. She indicated that all of the students were afraid of him and that she once saw him bloody a kid's nose, and that she had also heard that he hit her friend's sister. She said that she did not tell anyone about the rape because she was afraid of him and because she did not think anyone would believe her.

Shaniqua explained that, when she finally did tell, she did so for several reasons. First, she couldn't stop thinking about it and the depression was getting to be too much for her. Also, since she was no longer at the school, she finally felt that it was safe to tell. Finally, and most importantly, her little cousin had just started at Blessed Sacrament. She was afraid that if she didn't say something, Brother Chris might harm her cousin.

On both direct and cross-examination, Shaniqua maintained an amazing level of composure. She never lost her temper. She spoke softly and answered questions directly, and she did not cry again until she was finished several hours later. I was very proud of her. But several things hap-

pened on cross-examination that were irreparably harmful to the case. The
defense attorney launched extremely damaging attacks, some justified and
others totally inappropriate. First, he confronted Shaniqua with a note that
she allegedly passed to a classmate during sixth grade talking about having sex with a boy at the school. Normally, in a rape case, evidence of a
victim's sexual conduct is not admissible. However, where, as in this case,
we were claiming that the defendant was the only possible source of vagi-
nal injury, the defense is allowed to demonstrate that there were other possible sources. I objected strenuously to the defense being allowed to
question Shaniqua on the note. I pointed out that it would have been
incredibly bizarre for the defendant to have kept the note all of these years
unless he knew he'd have to defend himself from Shaniqua's allegations
someday. But the judge allowed it, carefully instructing the defense that
he was going to be strictly limited in his questioning.

In order to introduce a piece of evidence at trial, the document must
first be authenticated. This means that someone has to testify to the accuracy and origin of the document. The defense attempted, without first
authenticating the note, to read it in front of the jury. I went berserk. I
jumped up and started screaming objections. The judge likewise chastised
the defense. He took us both into his robing room and, for the next 10 minutes, refereed our screaming match. Every time I tried to speak, the defense
cut me off. Finally, I looked at him and said, "Every time I talk you cut me
off. I allowed you to speak without interruption, now you allow me."

"Every time?" he said, "Every time?"

"Grow the fuck up," I retorted, storming out of the judge's chambers.

I won that round. When we went back out, the judge warned the
defense not to try a stunt like that again without first having the document identified. The defense showed the note to Shaniqua. She denied
recognizing it or writing it and, at that point, the defense could not get
it into evidence. But the jury was left wondering what was in the note,
and that was a bad thing.

I was not so successful in the next round of behind-the-scenes legal
fighting. The defense attorney's final attack on Shaniqua was devastating.
He handed her an autograph book that Brother Chris had all of the students in her class sign. Shaniqua recognized the book and recalled that
the week or so before finals, the defendant handed the book around the

class and demanded that each student sign it. The book was, of course, filled with praises since grades had not even come out yet. Some students had written that "he was a little tough, but they knew it was just because he cared," but what else were they going to say?

Shaniqua's entry was altogether different. In fact, it was bizarrely different from the sentiments of the rest of her class. It went beyond praising his teaching to outright love and adoration. She said, in her entry, that he was wonderful and kind and the "best teacher she ever had." The entry expressed affection toward the defendant that was outright inappropriate. Even had she not been raped, the entry would have been strange, to say the least. Shaniqua admitted that she had written the note, but tried to explain it by saying that he passed it around before they got their grades, so she had to write something nice. But the other students wrote something "nice." Shaniqua's entry almost made it seem like she had an infatuation with Brother Chris.

When Shaniqua's cross was finished, we broke for lunch. I went back to my office and I was very upset. As much as I loved talking to Elisa before a trial, I hated talking to her during one where things were not going well. She had also watched Shaniqua testify. She called me into her office during the lunch break and, instead of being a cheerleader, she gave me a blow-by-blow of how horribly things had gone. I was devastated. I knew well enough how bad it had been without her hammering the nails in the coffin.

I went back to my office and tried to reach Dan McCarthy to get his advice, but he was not in. A few moments later, Dr. Donald Lewittes walked in. For this case, I was once again using Dr. Anne Meltzer as an expert witness, the same doctor who testified for me in my first felony jury trail. However, I had also spoken to Dr. Lewittes who had testified about child sexual abuse accommodation syndrome on many of my bureau's cases in the past. He was interested in watching Shaniqua testify and was present for her direct and cross-examination. He had come to my office to give his opinion on the autograph book.

"I can't understand this," I told him. "How could she have written that?" Dr. Lewittes had an interesting take on the whole thing and, in a way, it made perfect sense. He replied, "Did you ever hear of Stockholm Syndrome?"

. . .

IN STOCKHOLM, SWEDEN in the summer of 1973, four hostages were taken captive during a botched bank robbery. The stand-off lasted for six days. Finally, when the hostages were about to be liberated, they inexplicably actively resisted rescue. Later on, the hostages helped to raise money for their captors' defense and refused to testify against their captors at trial. According to some reports, one or two of the hostages even became engaged to captors.

In 1974, heiress Patty Heart was kidnapped. By her account, she was held hostage for about two months, blindfolded in a closet and not even allowed to use the bathroom alone. Hearst detailed her captors isolating her and making her think she would never be rescued. She was physically and sexually abused and force fed positive propaganda about her captors and negative propaganda about her loved ones. In April of that same year, Hearst took up arms and joined her captors, the Symbionese Liberation Army or "SLA", in a bank robbery. Over the course of the next many months, the SLA sent out numerous tapes in which Patty denounced her capitalist upbringing and proclaimed her genuine support for the cause. The defense of brain washing (Stockholm Syndrome was a phrase not yet coined or understood) was a difficult one, hard to prove or to make people understand. In spite of her defense that she participated only under duress and representation by the famous attorney, F. Lee Baily, Patty was sentenced to seven years for armed robbery.

With these two highly publicized cases and several other examples that came to light, experts started noticing a common thread of strange behavior among certain former captives and looked for an explanation. The experts detected common circumstance among captives displaying this odd behavior. They felt they could not escape a certain situation, that they were isolated and would not be rescued. They were threatened with death. These hostages also all reported about the "kindness" of their captors. But the kindnesses were not something the average person would characterize as such. A small courtesy, such as allowing someone to go to the bathroom, seemed to the hostages to be an example of why the captors were actually good people.

It often takes as little as three or four days for this extreme psychological transformation to take place. The behavior is the result of a subconscious strategy of trying to keep the captor happy in order to stay alive. The hostage becomes obsessed with identifying the likes and dislikes of the captor and their politics. The result is a survival mechanism that results in the warping of the captives' psyches to such a degree that they start believing what they are telling their captors. They end up really feeling sympathy for their captors' circumstance and that their actions are justified. Often, they will even feel love for their captors.

As the syndrome has become better understood, it has been used to explain the behavior of members of religious cults, battered women, incest victims, prisoners of war, Holocaust victims and, most importantly to me in the case against Brother Chris, emotionally abused children.

Lewittes explained to me that virtually anyone can get Stockholm Syndrome if the following conditions are met. First, the person perceives that there is a threat to her survival and has the belief that her captor is willing to act on that threat. Second, the person perceives small kindnesses in the captor's treatment of her within a context of being terrorized. Third, the person is isolated from any perspective other than that of the captor's and, finally, the person believes that there is no escape.

On June 14, 1985, while flying from Athens to Rome, TWA flight 847 was hijacked. One of the passengers was an American navy diver. He was beaten, shot in the head and his body was dumped on the tarmac. Several of the passengers were held until June 30. After his release on June 30, one of the hostages from Flight 847 was quoted as saying; "They weren't bad people. They let me eat, they let me sleep, they gave me my life."

Stockholm Syndrome is a survival mechanism. The people who get it are not lunatics. They are fighting for their lives or for their sanity. Lewittes explained that he believed that Shaniqua was so irrevocably terrorized by the rape, and then by the fact that she had to live with her rapist on a day-to-day basis, that she indeed began to sympathize with him. "She had to find things to love about him in order to survive." Shaniqua needed to make Brother Chris happy so that he would not harm her again, and in order to do this she had to find things to like about him. Lewittes also conceded, however, that it would be an extremely hard sell for the jury. "People have perceptions about how others should act under given circumstances. If someone does not act the way people believe she should act, they often don't believe her." I was well aware of this from my previous experience with juries and I knew that this situation was an even more difficult one than I usually faced.

Dr. Meltzer agreed with Dr. Lewittes's hypothesis. She explained to the jury that, indeed, Shaniqua may have had Stockholm Syndrome and she walked them through the indicators. But I could not read the jurors' reactions. The law does not allow doctors to testify as to whether a victim is lying or telling the truth so, of course, the defense brought out that Dr. Meltzer had not examined Shaniqua. "No," she explained, "because I am not allowed to. But I can draw conclusions about someone's mental condition based upon their surrounding circumstances and whether their set of behaviors falls into a known pattern. What makes it an identifiable mental condition is not the uniqueness of their response but, rather, the similarity of response to others who have been through the same thing."

"And, of course, that's assuming that you are given information that is complete, truthful, and accurate. Correct?"

"Of course. I can tell you that if a certain set of facts are true, and if the individual responds in the way described, that it is or is not consistent with a pattern of behavior known as 'Stockholm Syndrome.' "

The rest of the trial was fairly uneventful. The defense spent a lot of time focusing on the room where Shaniqua claimed that the rape occurred, claiming that it was a bathroom and not a storage room at the time of the rape. Since Shaniqua thought she knew which room the rape occurred in but could not say with certainty, the argument was really moot. If, indeed, the room she thought the rape occurred in was a bathroom at the time, the jury knew that it could have been the room next door or across the hall. Like many schools, several of the rooms were identical and their functions changed from year to year, so there was little reason for Shaniqua to remember exactly which room the rape occurred in. The defense called about seven witnesses just to talk about the use of basement rooms at any given time. I thought it was pretty much a waste of time and did not even bother to cross-examine half of them. My case was made or broken long before any of them got on the stand.

THE JURY DID not even deliberate a day before acquitting the defendant on all charges. They explained to a newspaper reporter that, while they believed that something had happened to Shaniqua, they were just not certain beyond a reasonable doubt that the defendant did it. When no one else was around, the defense attorney told me that it was not that he thought that the defendant was not capable of rape. He just did not think that it was likely that he raped a girl. "If you told me that it was a boy," he confided to me, "I would have believed it."

Shaniqua was not in the courtroom for the verdict. She and her family agreed that it would be best for her to get whatever the news was from home. I went outside with her family and met with a hysterical and inconsolable Tanya. Her eyes were glassed over and she kept grabbing me and shaking me, saying, "They think my little girl is lying! They think my little girl is lying!" Her family kept trying to pull her off me and finally managed to get her in a car just when I was going to insist on calling an ambulance.

I had no idea how to react or what to do with myself. I guess I felt the same way that Tanya did. As the jurors filed out, observing what was going on, I wanted to run over and shake them and say, "Do you understand what you did! He's done it before! He'll do it again! Don't you see!" But I couldn't. Maybe some prosecutors would disagree with me. Some of them may have gone over and shoved it in their faces that this was not the first time some kid said that Brother Chris raped them. But they made their decision based on what the law allowed me to put in front of them. And as much as I did not like that decision, it was unfair to make them second-guess themselves based on things they were not allowed to know. And it would be unfair to the next defendant whose case they heard.

Gia Cavellini, a junior assistant who second-sat me on the case, squeezed my arm. "You want to go back or sit for a while?"

"Let's sit," I said. I could hardly talk and I was trying so hard not to cry but I was not ready to face my bureau and I was not ready to talk to Elisa about the case. I was also not ready for people to try to console me by telling me that we always knew that I'd lose the case, so I shouldn't feel so bad.

We went around behind the Supreme Court Building and sat on the marble staircase leading up to a columned portico. It was a sunny and warm summer day. Gia put her arm around my back and we just sat there for a while in silence before slowly making our way back to the office. When we got back, I closed my door and started looking for a new job.

Tanya called me two or three times in the following weeks just to tell me that she knew I had done my best and that they weren't angry with me, but I'm not so sure that was true. I think they were trying not to be angry with me but they had to be second-guessing everything that had happened. I know that I would have.

I saw Gia in November of 2002. It was just over a year since I had left the office and I was visiting people on my way to Game Four of the World Series. Gia told me that she had tried to reach me a few days earlier at the law firm I had been working at, but they told her I was not there anymore. "I'm so glad you happened by here." She smiled. "I saw Shaniqua the other day. She works at my supermarket at the checkout. She told me that her family is moving to New Jersey next month. I just wanted to tell you that she looks wonderful. She lost weight and she seems really happy." I left the office that day with a smile on my face and the weight of the world off my shoulders.

SHANIQUA, WHEREVER YOU are, I want you to know that I am still proud of you and you are still the bravest person that I know. I hope that you are proud of me, too.

15

BURNOUT

On his three-month birthday

Khalif's father cuddled him
and fed him a warm bottle of milk.
He felt the cold air on his face
as his father opened the window
felt his father kiss him on the forehead
than hold him gently out into space.

When you're three months old
it takes all your strength just to lift an arm
or cry for food
so imagine his freedom
as he sailed down fifteen floors.
Weightlessness and movement and air.
Too young to know fear
and eyes only able to focus enough to see
his father's loving face above him
and not the ground below him.
He thought he could fly.

And by the time he hit the ground
and his still un-closed skull
opened like a Day-Lily
it didn't matter any more
because by then he was soaring again.

I have to believe it was that way.

MY YOUNGEST VICTIMS were infants, but my youngest victim who could talk to me was a precocious little boy named Tyrese. He was one of the brightest, most articulate two-years-olds that I've met to date. Tyrese's case terrified me because it was an example of how the people that you trust the most can be the ones who hurt your children.

Tyrese lived with his grandparents and his mother, who was finishing her degree so that she could become a corrections officer. His family were wonderful, loving people. His grandparents had been drug addicts who overcame their addictions to become productive contributors to their community, including being active on their community board and with the board of education. The grandfather's childhood friend, "Uncle T," helped raise their daughter and he was loved like a member of the family.

A few months before his arrest, Uncle T had come to the grandparents asking for help. He, too, had gone through rehab and needed their support while he looked for a job, got back on his feet, and got out of the neighborhood that spawned his addiction. Seeing in him the possibilities of success that they had achieved, the grandparents took Uncle T in. They put a roof over his head, fed him, and got him to his rehab meetings. In exchange, all they asked was that he babysit Tyrese occasionally. None of them were concerned about him being alone with the child. They had known him since they were children themselves. He had helped raise their daughter and although the daughter recalled his drug usage during her childhood, she maintained that he never laid a hand on her in an inappropriate fashion.

On a normal afternoon the grandparents were running some errands and asked Uncle T to watch Tyrese. When they returned from their errands, Tyrese came running out to their car to greet them. He had his usual grin on his face and, as was typical, began running his mouth a mile a minute as soon as they pulled up. They asked him what he did that afternoon: "We had McDonalds. We watched TV. I took a bath. We took a nap. Uncle T put his wee wee in my butt. We got up. We. . . ."

"At first," the grandparents said, "we didn't pick up on it. Whoa, whoa, back up. What?"

"Uncle T put his wee wee in my butt."

They weren't sure whether to believe him. They couldn't believe it would be possible. They waited for Tyrese's mother to get home from school and they told her what Tyrese had said. She immediately rushed the boy to the hospital. Although the doctor reported that there were no physical findings, the hospital explained that Tyrese described Uncle T rubbing himself up against the child and ejaculating, but not actually penetrating him. Because he'd been bathed, there was, of course, no ejaculate recovered. "That's when we started to believe it," the grandparents said. "Because Uncle T told us he bathed the child, but he had never bathed the child before. We always did." Uncle T was arrested and Tyrese came to my office two days later.

Tyrese was one of the most charming children I'd met. He was too young to really understand what had happened but he described it to me without missing a beat. He sat on my lap in my office, coloring as we talked. About an hour into our interview, he swung his head around and told me, "You be my wife."

"Tyrese," I told him, "I just might wait for you."

When Uncle T was arrested, he gave a full confession to the cops. After speaking with Tyrese, I viewed the videotaped confession taken by the assistant DA who had been on duty the night of the arrest. Even by my skewed standards, it was one of the most bizarre statements that I'd ever seen. Uncle T began his statement by saying, "I had an affair with Tyrese. He was rubbing up against me while we took a nap. It wouldn't have happened if I wasn't so bored. If the government would just get me a job so I wouldn't be so bored, I know this won't happen again." Uncle T was almost jovial in his confession and seemed to have no concept that what he did was wrong or unusual.

I felt terrible for Tyrese's family, who were in court, without fail, every time the case was on the calendar. They kept wracking their brains trying to figure out where the clues were that Uncle T was a pedophile and how they could have prevented this. All I could tell them was that they had done nothing wrong.

At Tyrese's young age, even as bright and articulate as he was, he was not swearable. There was no other corroboration in the case other than the defendant's confession. And, since a defendant cannot be convicted using his statement alone and the testimony of an unswearable child must be corroborated, I had a bit of a conundrum. I argued to the judge that although the statements of both the child and the defendant had to be corroborated in order for me to prosecute the case, they corroborated each other and, therefore, I should be able to proceed with the prosecution. The judge disagreed with me and said that he would not allow the child to testify. This meant that I would not be able to prosecute the case and Uncle T, a guilty man by his own confession, would walk away unscathed. We had a Mexican standoff and, eventually, I approached my supervisors and asked them to consider "Article 78ing" the judge.

On rare occasions, when the prosecution believes that a judge is making a decision that is contrary to the law, the prosecutor may bring an Article 78 proceeding in the nature of a writ of prohibition, naming the judge as a respondent. A writ of prohibition is an order issued by a higher court commanding a lower court to cease from proceeding in some matter not within its jurisdiction. This drastic action was rarely taken and only if the judge was about to commit an egregious error. Not only was the measure severe and hard to win, but it would certainly not win me any friends among the judges.

I came to court on the next appearance date, prepared to tell the judge that if he did not reconsider his stance on allowing the prosecution to continue, I would bring an Article 78 proceeding against him. But as I walked into the courtroom, the defense attorney approached me with a reasonable plea offer. I took it and Uncle T pled guilty. It was the best thing for everyone. Tyrese would not have to testify and I was assured a conviction without further complication or animosity from the judiciary.

I wonder how Tyrese is doing. He'd be seven now. Does he remember any of what happened to him? More important, what will happen to him when he grows up and finds out what happened? It's a hard thing for a child to cope with. He has a loving mother and grandparents to help him to recover from this. I only hope that it will be enough.

MY YOUNGEST VICTIMS were babies, but my oldest defendant was a 77-year-old named Enrique Gomez. He was a feeble, small man with rheumy eyes and hunched over with arthritis. He was soft-spoken and looked preternaturally benign. Yet his was one of the most disturbing cases I handled.

It all started one day in a school playground. Gomez drove up to the playground in a van. During recess, he made lewd comments to a nine-year-old girl who immediately ran home and told her mother. The next day, during recess, the mother sat outside the playground looking for the van. Although she didn't see the van, she did see a car parked nearby with an old man in the driver's seat who fit the description that her daughter had given her. She approached the car without the man seeing her and observed him watching the kids and masturbating. She started scream-ing for help from the other adults standing nearby, who held the man until the police arrived.

In Gomez's wallet, the police found a stack of paper scraps with love notes written to someone named Veronique. The answers were in crayon. There were also two barely discernable Polaroids of a young girl stand-ing in a half-open doorway with her pants off. The police went to the defendant's home where he lived with his sister and she answered the door. They asked the sister if she knew a "Veronique," and the sister told them that Veronique was the six-year-old girl who lived upstairs. She added that the defendant spent a lot of time up there. According to the sister, he was a kind of "surrogate grandfather" to the child. The sister also informed the police that the defendant, years earlier, had abused one of his nieces, but the family "thought he was cured," and was not concerned about him being around the child. A search of the defendant's room turned up another 50 or so notes between Gomez and Veronique, two pairs of Veronique's panties and a heart-shaped crystal frame with her photo in it.

When Veronique's parents were first approached, they were at a loss to understand how the abuse could have happened. They swore that although the defendant was frequently in their apartment and was clearly fond of Veronique, he had never been left alone with her. It was not that they did not trust the old man; they liked him very much. They were just careful people and did not like leaving the child alone with anyone.

Veronique was a pretty child with long, straight brown hair. She was thin and on the smallish size, making her look younger than six. She was soft-spoken and very articulate. Veronique explained to me that there was a wall that cut halfway through the living room and separated the entrance hallway from the living area. She said that when her parents were in the kitchen, Gomez would put her back against the wall so that he was facing the kitchen and could see her parents in the kitchen, but they would not be able to see her behind the wall. Gomez would fondle the little girl behind the wall while he watched the kitchen, making sure her parents did not get up. If he saw any movement, he would step out from behind the wall and sit on the sofa, while Veronique fixed her clothing behind the wall. Veronique also explained that there was a door that led from the hallway into her bedroom. Although the door was soldered shut, Gomez would slip notes to her through the crack at the bottom of the door. She would write her response and slip the note back under the door. Those notes were the ones that we found in his wallet and apartment. The notes told Veronique that he loved her and that she should stop playing games with him or he would tell her parents what was "going on." He kept asking her to meet him at a hotel so that they could make love.

While Veronique did not always understand everything that Gomez wrote to her, she could read just fine and understood the basics. She understood his claims that she was "doing some bad" and she believed it. She also believed that Gomez could get her in trouble. Veronique's responses were, "Please don't tell my mommy. I do love you and I promise to meet you at the hotel." In later notes, Gomez chastised Veronique for not being at the hotel when she said she would. He wrote that she did not really love him and he was going to tell her parents. She told me that she never was really going to the hotel, but she was afraid that he would tell her parents that she was being "bad" if she didn't make him think she would.

Gomez may have been the most disturbed defendant I ever dealt with. While I'd heard other defendants claim that children would seduce them or use threats of getting them in trouble to keep them quiet, Gomez took the fantasy further than I'd ever seen—even more than Uncle T, whose claims of an affair were vague and disorganized. Gomez was trying to conduct a mature relationship with a six-year-old child, and seemed to believe the fantasy to the degree that he actually expected her to sneak out at night and meet him.

Gomez's attorney was a friend of mine and we spoke from the beginning about Gomez pleading guilty. My case was strong and it was not the kind of case that you want to take to trial. I was offering 15 years. Given all the evidence against Gomez and the prior conviction, the plea seemed more than reasonable to me. And, even though I was not offering the defendant the lowest number of years he could plead to for the charge, the judge refused to undercut me and indicated that he thought 15 years might have been too lenient. Gomez was asking for 10 years, reasoning that he was so old that if he stayed in that long, he would probably die in jail anyhow. On what turned out to be our final court appearance on the case, Gomez's lawyer was trying to talk him into taking the plea that I offered, reasoning that, if convicted at trial, he would only get more time than that. I overheard the defense attorney ask Gomez,

"What happened to you as a child that you abused this girl?"

"My mother abused me when I was a kid."

"And did that ruin your life?"

"More than you can imagine."

"Well, don't you understand that you just ruined this girl's life that same way?"

Gomez took the plea and, given his appearance, it was probably tantamount to a life sentence. In an odd way, I felt sorry for Gomez in ways that I felt sorry for few of my defendants. I didn't think he was necessarily a bad person so much as he was someone so profoundly damaged that he did not know how to love a child in a normal way and without there being a sexual component. It was the only way that he knew love as a child. I did not think that there was anything that could be done for Gomez except to put him in jail. No amount of rehabilitation or classes was going to prevent him from harming another child. I have no doubt that if he ever does see the light of day again, no matter how old he is, he will abuse a child again. He was tragic.

But Veronique and Tyrese's cases exemplify exactly what is so terrifying about these defendants. You don't know whom you can trust. Everyone believes that they would know if a person was abusing their child or they would know if someone is the type of person who would abuse a child—but they are wrong. You don't know. The boogieman really does exist, and he can be your neighbor or your uncle or your best friend. He is the person that you want to leave your child with and the person that your child wants to be with.

I had seen enough reality to last me a lifetime. I started to look for a job with a law firm.

A WEEK BEFORE I left the office, I was on my final homicide duty. I had already put in my resignation. The Mets were playing the Cardinals in their bid for the World Series. I sat at home, alone, watching the game and waiting for the pager to go off. At about 6:00 PM, I got a call from the four-four precinct about a shooting. They gave me the address. "Can't miss it . . . dude's right in the middle of the road." I drove to the crime scene. Both ends of the road were barricaded and a pushing crowd was gathered, straining against the saw-horses to try to see the body. I pulled my car up, beeping at the people to get out of the way. They responded slowly. When I finally reached the barricade, I self-importantly told the cop who was yelling at me "Can't ya' see the yellow tape?" that I was the Homicide Assistant. He lifted the tape so that I could pull the car through and apologized for yelling at me. "Been a long night already," he said with a wink.

A group of detectives and uniformed cops were futilely trying to block the crime scene from view by surrounding the body with cars. I say futilely because the body was right in the middle of a block full of residential apartments. While the people on the street could not see the body, the people in their apartments could. They were hanging out of the windows, whooping and hollering and enjoying the show. No amount of yelling by the cops was getting them back inside. While it appeared that everyone in the apartment buildings was looking out, all of the cops were looking in. They stood around the perimeter of the scene, looking in through ground floor apartment windows, trying to watch the game on people's living room televisions. I thought that it would have made an amazing photograph: all the people looking out and down from above, all of the cops looking in from below. The perimeter of the scene was dark and hazy. All of the car headlights pointed inward and shone on the body lying face down, alone, in the middle of the street.

As I waited for the medical examiner to finish his inspection of the body, I chose to join the cops, preferring the baseball game to staring at the bloody body lying on the asphalt. One couple in an apartment on the first floor was drinking beer on their sofa while their two small children, both less than 10, watched the medical examiner pick through the corpse's hair, looking for the bullet hole. The detective standing next to me saw the kids. "Aw jeeezus!" he muttered. "What is with these people?" He started whacking his hand on the windowsill. "Hey! Heeeey! What the hell is wrong wit' you two? Get those kids inside!" The couple looked at him, shrugged, and went back to drinking. "What the hell is wrong with people?" he muttered again, more to himself than to me. "And people wonder what's wrong with kids today. Boy, could I tell them a few stories." I nodded my agreement and then walked away from the cop and the children and toward the body.

I stood to the side watching the medical examiner do his work with methodical detachment. As the ME rooted around for the bullethole, the dead guy's scalp surreally moved around on his skull in response to the manipulations. It was impossible to believe that, just an hour earlier, this same young man was standing here in the middle of the street having an argument over a baseball game. It was hard to believe that whatever he said was worth killing him for. The ME announced that he could not find the exit wound. Not a surprise given the small caliber of the bullet or the fact that the same examiner, a week earlier, had declared a homicide a suicide after missing a stab wound in the back of the victim's head. I waited with the detectives for the ambulance to arrive and take away the body. Then, I rode back to the precinct with one of the uniform cops in the passenger's seat directing me.

Back at the precinct, I spent about another four hours interviewing witnesses who all saw nothing and heard nothing. I tried unsuccessfully to calm the victim's hysterical sister, who was able to provide no more information than the killer's race. My job was always as much social worker as lawyer and tonight, I was doing much more of the former than the latter. It was almost 1:00 in the morning when I finally got back home. I had missed a great game. The Mets were going to the World Series. It was going to be New York's first Subway Series since 1956. People beeped car horns joyously in the street and drunken revelers stumbled out of bars wearing baseball caps that declared their allegiance to one New York team or the other. I listened to no less than five intoxicated ramblings on my answering machine from my friends. "Where aaaar-rrreeee you! We're having so much fun!! SUBWAY SERIES BAAAAYYYYBBBBEEEE!!!"

I watched recaps of the game for a while, superstitiously avoiding getting ready for bed. It seemed like every time I was on beeper duty, the beeper would go off as soon as I snuggled into bed. Finally, by around 3:00, I couldn't keep my eyes open any longer. I got into bed with the beeper, a pad, and a pen next to the bed. The clothing I'd worn earlier that day was readily accessible in case I had to get dressed and go back out. I was actually feeling more confident than usual that I was in the clear because I'd had my body for the night and, after all, I'd never had two in one night.

Well, I tempted fate and, of course, my luck ran out. No sooner did I shut the light when the pager went off. "We got a body. Co-op City."

I groaned. Co-op City was just about as far from me as The Bronx could possibly get and totally unfamiliar territory. Once again, the detective on the scene did not have a cell phone so the desk sergeant, who had no information other than the location and that there was "one under" or an arrest, gave me directions. Within 45 minutes, I was on my way. Again.

It took me another 45 or so minutes to get to Co-op City and then I got lost in a totally desolate and dark cranny of the North-East Bronx. I called the precinct and explained where I was. "You're not that far." The desk sergeant gave me directions and five minutes later, I was lost again. I was in a very rundown and not-so-safe-looking neighborhood. There was not another soul in sight. "Wait right there," he told me, "and I will send an RMP out to escort you. It will be about five minutes."

"Are you fucking kidding me?" I retorted. "I 'aint sittin' here in The Bronx, alone, at four in the morning. How 'bout I keep driving and you talk me through this." The sergeant agreed with me that maybe being a sitting duck was not the best idea. He stayed on the line with me, giving me directions, until I was looking at Co-op City and then, annoyed, hung up. I drove around a loop of identical buildings, numbered in no particular order that I could decipher, at least three times. There was no one around to ask directions from—not that I would have stopped to ask anyhow—so I had to keep calling the sergeant until I finally saw the squad cars and yellow tape.

The sight that greeted me when I arrived at the scene was something I had never seen before. The two female cops who were the first to respond to the scene were totally shell-shocked. They stood leaning as much against each other as against their squad car. There was none of the typical cop banter. In fact, there was no speaking at all. The crime scene was also silent as, well, as a grave. One detective just stood there, hanging his head. No one had explained over the phone what had happened and I was baffled by the behavior of the cops. The detective's partner was taking notes near the crime scene and I walked over to him to find out what was going on. As he started to explain, he lifted the crime scene tape, allowing the two of us to pass under. He cautioned me to watch my step as he led me, solemnly, to the crime scene—a small plot of grass in the front of the building. I scanned the dimly lit patch of grass for a body, but did not see anything.

As my eyes adjusted to the dim light, I spotted a tiny object in the middle of the patch of grass. I walked toward what appeared to be a bit of trash or discarded clothing. I wondered if they had already taken the body away because I couldn't have been completely missing it like this. But, as I moved closer, I realized that I wasn't missing the body at all. The small pile on the grass was a tiny baby lying on his back. He would have looked like he was just dozing peacefully on the lawn were in not for the fact that the back of his head was completely gone. I turned away and stared at the ground for a few moments before looking up at the detective. We started to walk back out and he abruptly yanked me sideways just as I was about to step in a small, perfectly round, puddle.

"The baby was dropped from the fifteenth floor. He landed here," the detective said, indicating the puddle which I now realized was the infant's brain matter, "and then he bounced up in the air and landed on his back over there." He pointed about three or four feet away where the infant lay.

I asked what had happened. "You're best off speaking to the first officer," the detective said, walking me toward the two female cops.

I was introduced to the uniformed females whom I had seen when I first arrived. They were both attractive young women who looked to be in their mid-twenties. I guessed that they did not have too much time on the job. Both were slightly red-eyed, which could have been exhaustion or crying. I was not sure which, nor was I inclined to ask. I assumed that, like me, they would be reluctant to display too much emotion in front of their male counterparts. Being a female cop was hard enough without people thinking that you were soft. A petite redhead with her hair pulled into a tight ponytail at the nape of her neck started explaining what had happened. The three of us walked back over to the squad car as she told me their names, ranks, and shield numbers for my notes. They both leaned their backs against the car with their arms crossed over their bulky Kevlar-covered frames.

"We were working the twelve [midnight] to eight shift and doing routine patrol when we received a radio run of a woman whose boyfriend was in her apartment in violation of a full order of protection. We arrived at the location and took the elevator up to the fifteenth floor. The female caller answered the door. She seemed pretty calm and she wasn't beat up in any way, although she looked like she'd been crying. She told us that her boyfriend had been beating her and that she got a full order of protection about a month ago to keep him out. She said that she'd seen him a couple of times anyhow. They had a baby together and she let him come up and see the baby a few times. She had agreed to let him come over earlier that night to see the baby, but when he started acting up and yelling at her, she told him to leave or she'd call the cops. She told him that he couldn't see the baby anymore. She told us that he had cooperated and left, but had let himself in again a couple hours later with her key, which she claims she didn't see him take when he left. She said she told him she was going to call the cops and that he was acting a little crazy and saying that he just wanted to feed the baby and say goodnight. She picked up the phone and called 911. When we got to the apartment, she said that the defendant was in the bedroom with the baby, feeding him. We were about to go into the bedroom when he walked out. He seemed totally calm and he had the bottle in his hand. I asked him where the baby was and he told me the kid was sleeping on the bed. I stayed outside with him while my partner here went in to get the baby. She was in there a few seconds and I could hear her rustling around and she came out and said that the baby wasn't on the bed.

Me, my partner, and the mother all ran into the bedroom and the mother
was screaming, 'Where's the baby? Where's the baby?' We were all looking
in the closets and under the bed and that's when I noticed that the window was open. I ran to the window and looked down and that's when I
saw him. The defendant was standing in the doorway and I looked at him
and said, 'Did you throw the baby out the window?' He looked at me and
said, 'If I couldn't have him, no one can.' He told us that he was feeding the
baby when he heard us come in and that's when he threw the kid out the
window. If only we'd come right into the bedroom . . ."

She hung her head. Her partner had not looked up the entire time she
spoke. She didn't cry and her voice didn't crack, but I could tell she was
struggling. I knew there was nothing they could have done to stop the
guy, but I also understood that feeling that you are somehow responsible or wondering what else you could have done. "Okay," I told her, "let's
get back to the precinct and get you guys some coffee and then we'll go
over the details." I walked over and reviewed some facts with the detective assigned to the case. He informed me that the defendant was already
back at the precinct house. I called the DA's office and told them to send
over the video crew in case the defendant wanted to make a statement
and we all headed away from the crime scene and the tiny victim.

I stopped by a 7–Eleven outside the precinct and picked up a bunch
of large coffees. I made a habit, whenever possible, of bringing a few cups
of coffee with me wherever I responded on beeper duty. As I said, by the
time the ADA arrived at the scene or the station house, the cops had often
been working for hours, were exhausted, and were irritated by our
interference. The coffee was a simple, nice thing to do, which often broke
the ice and made the rest of the night a little easier. That night, the coffee was so popular that I gave away the cup that I was hoping to keep
for myself. I sat at a desk in the squad room waiting for the video crew
to arrive and for the detectives to finish debriefing the defendant. The
detective came out of the interview room anxiously inquiring when my
crew would arrive, as the defendant was willing to make a statement to
me. He wanted to get it done before the guy changed his mind. I called
the desk again to find out where the video crew was, but as I expected,
was told that they were "on their way." Finally, at about 5:00 AM, the video
technician arrived. He set up the camera in a back office with a chair next

to the defendant for the detective to sit in and another chair under the camera for me. He set up a clock and the microphone and within 15 minutes we were ready to roll.

The detective brought in the defendant, whom I was seeing for the first time. He hung his head and refused to make eye contact with me. He was in his early twenties, tall and handsome. He looked upset and exhausted. When he sat down, I introduced myself and asked him to hang tight a second while we got the camera rolling. I did not say anything until I got the go-ahead from the video tech, as I did not want the defendant to later be able to claim there was any conversation between us off camera. When the tech gave me the thumbs up that the camera was rolling, I began:

"The time is now 5:20 AM. We are seated in the detective squad interview room of the forty-fifth precinct. I am ADA Sarena Straus. Also present with me are a videotape technician and a detective. Is you're name Derek Slade, sir?"

"Yes."

"And do you speak and understand English?"

"Yes."

"I am going to read you a series of warnings commonly know as Miranda warnings. I am going to ask that you listen to each question carefully and respond by answering 'Yes' or 'No.' Do you understand?"

"Yes."

"Okay, you have a right to remain silent. Do you understand?"

"Yes."

"Anything you say can be used against you in a court of law. Do you understand?"

"Yes."

"You have the right to consult an attorney before speaking to the police or to me. Do you understand."

"I want an attorney."

I looked up. I looked at the clock: "The time is now 5:23 AM. This concludes our interview."

I abruptly got up from my seat. The video tech unplugged the camera. The detective took the defendant out of the room and was gone no more than a minute when he came running back into the room telling me that the defendant had changed his mind and wanted to make a statement.

"It's too late, detective. He lawyered up. I can't take his statement."

The detective and I went back and forth, arguing about the admissibility of statements after a defendant lawyers up. I was certain that, regardless of whether the defendant changed his mind—and there was really no time for the cops to have even coerced him— any statement I took after his request for an attorney would not be admissible. Nevertheless, the detective convinced me that it was worth a try. The worst that could happen is that the statement would be suppressed as taken in violation of the defendant's Miranda rights. We would be no worse off than we were right now. I agreed and the tech begrudgingly set the camera up again.

"The detective has informed me that you changed your mind and that you wish to now make a statement. Is this true?"

"Yes."

"Were you threatened or coerced in any way to change your mind?"

"No."

"Were any promises made to you of any kind in exchange for you changing your mind?"

"No."

"Okay. I am going to go through your rights again just to make sure that you understand them. Please listen carefully to each right and respond with 'Yes' or 'No.' "

I read the defendant his rights again. He responded to each one and I took his statement. He confirmed what the mother and the cop had said regarding his violation of the order of protection. He also confirmed the cops' fear that it was their presence that made him decide to throw the baby out the window, but not in such a way that I thought he could later claim that the murder was not premeditated. The defendant explained to me that he realized his girlfriend was going to stop him from seeing his son when she threw him out of the apartment earlier that night. He left for a couple of hours and mulled over the idea of never seeing his son again. He was soft-spoken and calm in his description of his deliberations and his decision. Before returning to his girlfriend's apartment, he decided to take his child's life rather than never see the boy again. He explained to me that he went back to say goodbye, that he gave his son a bottle and told him that he loved him and then, upon hearing the cops enter the apartment, threw him out the window. He repeated what he had told the cops: "If I couldn't see him, no one could."

By the time I was finished, it was already 8:00 AM. My debriefing was at 9:00, so I headed straight for the office and got my paperwork in order. I was physically and emotionally exhausted. The case was assigned to one of my supervisors and I kept trying to get her attention to talk to her about the case and about the issues with the statement. She would not even give me the time of day. I finally said to her, "Ya' know, I'm out of here at the end of this week. I did go to the scene and take the statement. You might want to know what I know before I'm out of here and it's too late."

"Uch," she rolled her eyes at me, "I really don't have time for this, Sarena." I was infuriated. I was frustrated. I didn't trust her with the case, but I didn't have a choice because I was leaving the office. And I couldn't get that image out of my head. I guess I wanted to talk to her about it. I felt like it was her obligation to understand how terrible it was. And if it didn't matter what I saw or heard or how I felt about it, then why did I have to go see it in the first place? That day, I didn't just feel ready to go; I felt like I was leaving a few weeks too late.

On Tuesday, April 24, 2001, The Bronx DA reported the following on their web site:

BRONX FATHER PLEADS GUILTY TO MURDER IN THE DEATH OF HIS THREE-MONTH-OLD SON

Bronx District Attorney Robert T. Johnson announced today that a 30-year-old Bronx man has been convicted of murder in the death of his 3-month-old son.

Derek Slade, of 2420 Hunter Avenue, pled guilty to Murder in the 2nd Degree "under circumstances evincing a depraved indifference to human life" in the death of his son Kharel Slade. Acting State Supreme Court Justice Ira R. Globerman set sentencing for May 15, 2001, in Part 37.
Under the terms of the plea agreement Slade will be sentenced to a term of 15 years to life imprisonment. Assistant District Attorney Astrid Borg-

stedt of the Domestic Violence Unit, who objected strenuously, recommended that Slade be sentenced to a term in excess of 22 years to life imprisonment.

The murder occurred on October 17, 2000, when [Kharel Slade's mother] awoke to find her estranged husband Derek Slade in her apartment in the bedroom with their infant son Kharel, sometime after 2:00 AM in violation of a Family Court Order of Protection. While [Kharel Slade's mother] awaited the arrival of the police the defendant threw the baby out the 15th story bedroom window to his death.

As Slade was being arrested for violating the court order the defendant was asked the whereabouts of his son to which he replied, "the baby was on the bed." After a frantic search, the child was discovered outside on the ground. The medical examiner ruled the child's death to be the result of extrusion of the brain due to blunt impact to the head.

"Extrusion of the brain due to blunt impact of the head." No one should ever have to see that.

The Job Interview

You ask me why I want this job
and tell me there is "no right or wrong answer,"
that I should "just be honest."
But I am limited to niceties
like "I am ready to broaden my knowledge base,"
and "the position I am in has become too cookie-cutter."
I'm supposed to tell you "I have a lot of trial experience
which will translate well in the civil field,"
and things about "My Learning Curve."

Just yesterday,
I interviewed seven-year-old Angela
who stroked her mother's head and soberly reminded me:
"We shouldn't talk about this,
it makes my mommy cry," and then
last week I interviewed a boy at the precinct
who stabbed his girlfriend eighteen times
gouged out her left eye and decapitated her

in front of her six-year-old autistic brother.
He told me that jealousy
would be a crazy reason to kill someone.
I saw the six-year-old out of the corner of my eye
Dixie Cup of orange juice that a cop gave him
shaking in his hand.

Honestly? I want this job because it's mundane.
I want to sit behind a desk and do research
about "Piercing the Corporate Veil,"
"Enforceability of Verbal Contracts," and
"Rent Abatement."

I mean really . . .
would you hire me because
I'm just tired of looking at dead ten-year-olds?

FRIDAY, OCTOBER 20, 2000, was my last day as an assistant district attorney in The Bronx. I left with equal doses of optimism and remorse. I loved this job—the work and my colleagues. I was good at it. I was leaving the comfortable and the familiar for unknown territory. Leaving criminal law for civil. My cases were my babies and I was afraid to let them go. Would someone else give them the love and attention that I did? But it was past time to move on. I handed in my security pass that, for five years, got me through the turnstile and into the office building. I packed up the last few things from my office—diplomas, drawings from the children I had worked with over the years, a photo of my Grandma in a big straw hat, two snow-globes that one of my victims gave me as a gift. I took a last look at my view of the parking lot in the Concourse Plaza Mall. I looked at the picture ID that officially identified me as an assistant district attorney. The girl smiling in the picture was 5-1/2 years younger than me. I smiled back at her, realizing that all of her expectations and more had been met by her first job as an attorney.

But losing my title was like losing a piece of my soul. I was always so proud to talk about my job when people asked what I did for a living. Being an ADA in The Bronx was interesting and exciting. Now, I was just another lawyer. I no longer wore the red cape of a superhero, fighting against crime and for justice. When I handed in that ID card, I had second thoughts and misgivings. Even as I write this book, I still think about turning around and running back to the office that I was so proud to work in for five years. Until the last few months of my work there, I woke up excited to go to work every day. Not many lawyers will tell you that they love their job. But I loved my job at The Bronx District Attorney's office.

There is also, of course, that element of sexiness to the job. When I would tell people I was an ADA in The Bronx, they couldn't believe it. And when I told them what unit I worked for and the types of cases I handled, they expressed such admiration for my strength.

So, if I loved this job so much, why did I leave? Sometimes I'm not sure it was the right choice and other days, when I think back on the trauma I dealt with, I know I did the right thing. I know that I couldn't handle the kids anymore, but at the same time, couldn't see myself doing anything else while I stayed at the office. I needed to channel my desire to help children in another way.

The hardest part about being in DVS was not being allowed to care. I knew, even as I did my best to get to know kids and to befriend them, that when the case ended, so would my relationship with them. We were taught that it was best for the children to let them go when the case was over because, ultimately, we would just be part of the history of a bad experience they had. It was not easy to sever ties when a case finished, to never know what happened to these kids. I didn't just prosecute the cases. I cared about the people involved. I want to know if they are okay. If they've been able to put it behind them. Has it even changed their lives for the better or made them stronger?

Shortly after I left the office, my sister-in-law, Molly, gave me a book called *The Gift of Fear*. The author, Gavin de Becker, bravely goes into some of the facts of his own traumatic childhood, an unfortunately typical story of spousal violence and its affect on him as a child. In one part of the book, he talks about a lecture he gave to prison inmates where he shared his history with them. He recounts how one of the inmates asked him how come their childhood's were almost exactly the same yet "I'm here and you are there?"

De Becker talks about the little things that can make the difference for a child. How one person who believes in you and sees the glimmer in your eyes can change the whole path of a child's life. He talks about the one person in his life who made him see the possibilities and see his own worth.

I wondered this about my father. What in his childhood enabled him to not repeat the pattern of abuse? I wonder to this day if, maybe, I made that difference in the life of even one child. Will any of them, as they grow up, remember that I believed them? That I thought they were the bravest individuals I would ever encounter?

I didn't keep a journal while I was at the DA's office. I did not know that I would have so many demons to exorcise and that so many of the people who touched my life when I was a prosecutor would continue to invade my dreams. I did not know that someday I would write a book. But, while all of the victims and their families haunt me occasionally, there are, of course, certain ones that visit me more than others. I speculate about how they will do out there in the world.

What are the long-term consequences, especially to my youngest victims? Claudia was only eight months old when she was brought to my office. Her abuse was discovered by a nurse in the hospital. Claudia's mother had just given birth to another baby and brought the newborn in for an examination. Claudia was in her stroller. When the nurse peered into the crib to look at Claudia, all she could see were the baby's eyes and nose. The baby was otherwise completely covered, even though it was warm. The nurse noticed a sore on the baby's nose and when she went to pull the covers away to examine it, the mother snatched the stroller away. The nurse tried to explain that she just wanted to check the baby's nose, but Claudia's mother kept pulling her away. Finally, the nurse got suspicious. She snatched the baby from the stroller and ran into a room with her, locking the door behind her. Little Claudia was screaming and when the nurse pulled the blanket away to examine her, she saw that Claudia was covered with bruises and sores.

Claudia was malnourished. At eight months old, she was only the size of a three-month-old. She had 12 active fractures over her body and several that were already healed. The back of her head was completely flat because she was left lying on her back all day. No one held her. When one of the doctors from Montefiore Child Protection Center discussed Claudia's case with me, she started to cry. It was the only time in five years that I ever saw one of these dedicated physicians driven to tears. The doctor told me that the first few days she was in the hospital, anytime someone would come near Claudia, the baby would cringe. "Imagine," the doctor said, "at only eight months, to already know fear."

But, babies are resilient and in a matter of just two days, Claudia was smiling at some of the nurses that she recognized and reaching for them. She could not be held for several weeks without great pain due to all of her broken bones, but she gained weight rapidly and it seemed like she would recover developmentally. I am sure that Claudia will be placed in a good home. But the long-term effects of her abuse are difficult to project. The doctors predicted that at least one of her legs would be misshapen. She could have other developmental problems from the bone injuries and malnourishment. It has been proven that neglected infants, even if the neglect is earlier than they can remember, can have lifelong attachment disorders. Claudia would be about seven by now. I wonder where and how she is.

PEOPLE OFTEN ASK me what you look for to know if your child is being abused. After five years, I am further from the answer than I ever was. Listen to them. Watch for age-inappropriate behavior. Talk to them. Tell them that it's okay to talk to you. My brother's children are now seven, three, and one, and my sister-in-law is reluctant to leave them with babysitters. I can't blame her. I tell her to put in a hidden camera. Watch videos of the babysitter with the children for a few visits until you are comfortable. If it was my child, that's what I would do.

I STARTED WRITING this book during Christmas of 2001, two months after I left the office. It started as an effort to jot down memories of my cases while I still had them, and it evolved into something else. As I write this book, I try once again to find my purpose in life and a worthy goal. This book is my first step. I figured that letting the world know what I did and how important it was is a good start. Letting people know that these terrible things are happening far more than they care to believe, but that there are a few brave souls out there willing to dedicate their lives to stopping them can be my next step in fighting the war and helping to make the abuse stop.

So why did I leave DVS if I loved it so much? I guess I just couldn't take it any more. I couldn't take dealing with the trauma anymore. I could not stop internalizing it. But at the same time, I couldn't see myself in a different bureau. I felt that if I went to another bureau, I would not feel as complete and would continue to hunger for the cases in DVS. I still do. When I started my new job at the law firm, I kept telling people that the work was interesting, but that I missed caring about what I did. I missed "having a heart for it." I miss making a difference.

My husband gave me a quote from Marcus Aurelius and told me to tape it to the back of my cellphone. He said that when I am feeling weak or overwhelmed, I should read the quote and that it will remind me of my strength. I have memorized that quote and it has remained taped to the back of my phone ever since. "You must be like a promontory of the sea against which though the waves beat continuously, yet it both itself stands, and about it are those swelling waves stilled and quieted." I tried to be such a force in the tempest that is The Bronx, and I continue to try to be that force now.

My Grandma is the matriarch of my family and, for all of us, has been at one time or another both the promontory that we clung to for safety or the very beating waves that we steeled ourselves against. She has no remaining enemies in the world but herself. Jews make their confession every year on Yom Kippur, the day of atonement. It is tradition among some Jews to beat a fist against their heart, with each sin they confess: "I have lied. I have cheated. I have stolen. . . ." I think that no one beats her own heart with the ferocity of my grandmother. But the most important element of forgiveness in the Jewish religion, and the one people seem to forget the most, is that it is not God who you are asking for forgiveness. That is too easy. In order to atone, you go to the people that you have wronged and you ask them for forgiveness. To not ask them to forgive you is to not make atonement. And to refuse to forgive if asked is, in and of itself, a sin. I do not know if my grandmother ever asked my father for forgiveness, but I think that day on the beach, she was asking me. She was giving me information that would allow me to hate her, but I don't. She also gave me information that allowed me to be constructive. To bring good from bad. I feel sad for my Grandma and for my father because they cannot go back and redo the past, but if we have all gone forward and taken this information and done something good with it, then the cycle of violence is broken.

Several months ago my Uncle Stephen, my father's younger brother, was diagnosed with brain cancer. Even as I write this, he fights for his life. My uncle is a scientist, a researcher at the National Institutes of Health in Washington, DC, where he has dedicated his life to looking for ways to save people or to make their lives better. When I think of a "good man," I think of my uncle. He is a quiet, serious man who is gentle and loving. He is patient and, even while he is fighting for his life, always has time to listen to others and to genuinely want to help them. At a family gathering last year, my uncle sat down next to my grandmother and told her, "Mom, it's time to forgive yourself. We all forgive you."

I TRIED TO do a great job as an assistant district attorney. If I was great, it was because I loved the job. I cared about my cases and the lives that I affected each day. I left the office with about an 80 percent conviction rate in a borough were there are convictions on fewer than 50 percent of the cases. But that is not how I measure my success. I measure my success by my ability to sleep at night. By my ability to look back at all of those cases that I prosecuted and believe that I did my best to do justice. The job is nothing like the television shows. It is not always so clear who the good guys are and who the bad guys are. Jail is not always the punishment that fits the crime. And, unlike television, you don't win them all. There is a reason that I did not choose to write this book only about the cases where I was the clear-cut victor against a clear-cut guilty party. That is not the reality of the situation. And sometimes reality is far more interesting and bizarre than fiction.

ONE NIGHT, I dreamed that I was walking along the boardwalk at an amusement park on the beach. I was holding my niece Aurora's hand. Suddenly, I lost my grip and she slipped into a crack on the side of the walkway and became trapped. I reached for her from every angle that I could, but try as I might, I could not free her. I awoke with tears streaming down my face.

I pray with all my heart that I saved even one of the children of The Bronx who crossed my path from slipping between the cracks. That even one person who reads this book will reach out to some child and save him. That someone will reach out and stop the hand of a parent on its way to hitting a child and damaging both of them irrevocably. This I pray with all of my heart.